Dear Reader:

The book you are a [ ] from the St. Martin's Tru[ ] *New York Times* calls "the leader in true crime!" Each month, we offer you a fascinating account of the latest, most sensational crime that has captured the national attention. St. Martin's is the publisher of Tina Dirmann's VANISHED AT SEA, the story of a former child actor who posed as a yacht buyer in order to lure an older couple out to sea, then robbed them and threw them overboard to their deaths. John Glatt's riveting and horrifying SECRETS IN THE CELLAR shines a light on the man who shocked the world when it was revealed that he had kept his daughter locked in his hidden basement for 24 years. In the Edgar-nominated WRITTEN IN BLOOD, Diane Fanning looks at Michael Petersen, a Marine-turned-novelist found guilty of beating his wife to death and pushing her down the stairs of their home—only to reveal another similar death from his past. In the book you now hold, COLD AS ICE, veteran author Carlton Smith details the strange, nationally known saga of Drew Peterson.

St. Martin's True Crime Library gives you the stories behind the headlines. Our authors take you right to the scene of the crime and into the minds of the most notorious murderers to show you what really makes them tick. St. Martin's True Crime Library paperbacks are better than the most terrifying thriller, because it's all true! The next time you want a crackling good read, make sure it's got the St. Martin's True Crime Library logo on the spine—you'll be up all night!

Charles E. Spicer, Jr.
Executive Editor, St. Martin's True Crime Library

OTHER TRUE CRIME TITLES FROM

CARLTON SMITH

COLD AS ICE

Carlton Smith

St. Martin's Paperbacks

COLD AS ICE

Copyright © 2010 by Carlton Smith.

Cover photograph of Drew Peterson by Richard Drew. Photograph of rings by Tetra Images.

For information address St. Martin's Press, 175 Fifth Avenue, New York, NY 10010.

EAN: 978-0-312-38884-3

Printed in the United States of America

St. Martin's Paperbacks edition/September 2010

St. Martin's Paperbacks are published by St. Martin's Press, 175 Fifth Avenue, New York, NY 10010.

10 9 8 7 6 5 4 3 2 1

CONTENTS

He knows how to manipulate the system, and his next step is to take my children away. Or Kill me instead.

I would really like to know why this man wasn't charged with unlawful entry, and attempt on my life. I am willing to take any test you want me to take to prove my innocents of charges against me, and also any lie detector test, on my statement that I filed against him. I really feel Drew is a loose cannon, he out on the streets of Bolingbrook patrolling, and just taking the law into his own hands. I haven't received help from the police here in Bolingbrook, and asking for your help now. Before it's to late. I really hope by filing this charge it might stop him from trying to hurt us.

—Kathleen Marie Savio Peterson,
November 14, 2002

The Circus: 2007

There is a perfectly rational excuse for the newspersons' seeming callousness: stories change with each retelling. Even a person really trying for the most faithful recital of events is almost invariably susceptible to slight modifications, certain little embellishments, with each recital. Accuracy of a story is in direct relation to how soon after the event it is recorded, and how frequently the story has been retold.
—Walter Cronkite, *A Reporter's Life* (1996)

1.
"Did You Murder Your Wife?"

So there they were, phalanxes of camera wielders, light techs, earphoned sound mavens, harried producers and their teenage sandwich holders, along with their fronts, the beautiful people perfectly coifed and clad, with makeup and microphones and pre-scripted nosy questions usually compiled by their cigarette-smoking behind-the-scenes producers who thought they knew what sold, but whose own visages were too real or too old to make the photographic cut. The rolling carnival came from broadcasters, cable networks, radio stations, bloggers, and even a few newspapers.

The media gaggle overran the short cul-de-sac and choked it off from normal suburban life. There were no tricycles or skateboards on this particular day—the neighborhood kids were outside the media perimeter, ogling in the background as the event unfolded.

Sometime in the afternoon, while the light was still good, the man of the hour finally emerged from his two-story house, looked around, and grinned. He held up a video camera and panned the scene, recording the media mob recording him. The crowd of so-called "content providers" went wild with hilarity.

The amateur reeled off a few quips, grinning. The reporters were gratified. It didn't much matter to them what the man with the camera actually said, only that they had the image of *him* taking pictures of *them*, the picture itself telling the whole story. "Did you get it?" a producer would demand of the cameraperson. The amateur with the video camera smiled and went back inside his house. He had what he wanted: visual proof positive that the electronic media marauders had invaded his privacy, had invaded his life, had destroyed his suburban neighborhood, which made it almost impossible for him to get a fair trial, if it ever came to that. It was the dark side of being under the spotlight, of being In the News.

As it happened, a little before Halloween in 2007, a report came to the attention of someone who was likely a twenty-something producer for a cable network headquartered in New York, Washington or Atlanta, scanning local news feeds from around the country. He or she probably recognized the "elements," as they're called in the news racket: a young mother, very attractive, vanished mysteriously. Cue the spider webs, the jack-o-lanterns, the costumes, the candy, the kids. Is this a story for the mythical national village, or what?

The vanisher was twenty-three-year-old Stacy Peterson, mother of Anthony, then four, and daughter Lacy, then almost three, as well as stepmother to two older children of her husband, Drew Peterson, a small-town cop in the suburb of Bolingbrook, a former bean field some miles southwest of Chicago, Illinois. Stacy was cute, white, easy on the eyes: definitely a qualifier, as far as the national media calculated its ratings demographics. And of course there were the little kids—*where's Mommy*?

Once the first cable network's researchers understood that Drew Peterson had been the husband of another woman who had been found dead in a bathtub more than three years earlier, in which the circumstances of death were in dispute, the starting gun fired.

By the time the entire saga had saturated the nation over the next two years, as many as six hundred people had become potential, if peripheral, witnesses, and the responsible authorities were left to separate the grains of truth from the chaff of media-driven gossip. It was a classic example of how a small story, without many facts, becomes a big story almost overnight, driven by modern media speculation.

Welcome to the unhappy new world of Drew Peterson, retired small-town cop, suspect in two, maybe even three or four murders.

Blue Lightning

2.
Stacy

By most accounts, the trouble began in September 2001. That was when Drew Peterson, the supervising night patrol sergeant of the Bolingbrook Police Department, the watch commander, first began flirting with Stacy Peterson, a seventeen-year-old clerk at the SpringHill Hotel in that small town, perhaps forty miles west-southwest of Chicago, Illinois. He was forty-seven, already thrice married, the father of four boys, and pretty well known as The Festering Problem of the local police.

Peterson had once been a member of the Metropolitan Area Narcotics Squad, also known as MANS, a dope-buying, door-kicking, multijurisdictional police contingent operating around Chicago's periphery, supervised by the Illinois State Police. MANS was the ultimate rush for a small-town cop, adrenaline well beyond writing traffic tickets and busting teenage neckers.

Then one day in 1985, he'd gone too far and was bounced from MANS, and almost fired from the Bolingbrook department. In fact, he'd actually been indicted for allegedly selling out to a big-time dope dealer. He'd been able to claw his way back, though, successfully refuting the corruption allegations. But his ceiling from then on was limited—he was just a uniformed patrol sergeant in a small town who worked the night shift, and he would never go anywhere else, professionally speaking. He was tainted.

Still, Peterson liked working the night shift—the Boling-brook departmental suits rarely bothered him. The town was his realm once the sun set. He knew who was who, what was up, and what was going down.

At seventeen, Stacy Cales was an attractive girl about to become a woman, in some ways much older than her years. By many accounts she was a flirt—she enjoyed being the center of attention of the slightly older boys who gathered around her. Peterson admittedly began trying to get her into the sack almost as soon as he met her, despite their thirty-year age difference. The fact that he was married, a father of four boys, meant nothing.

Stacy was petite—a little over five feet, and weighing just over a hundred pounds. Peterson was almost six feet in height, and pushing 180 pounds by the summer of 2001. Perhaps more impressive, he had the power that the callow youths buzzing around Stacy could never have, and he had command of the town's night-patrol force to make it stick. As a man among boys, someone with a gun and a badge, Peterson could be scary. The youths around Stacy slunk off, and left the field clear for the man with the authority.

Stacy had grown up a child of turmoil. Her mother, Christine Marie Toutges, had at seventeen become pregnant by a man named Ron Kokas, and in November of 1975, had given birth to a near namesake, Christina, also known as Tina. A little over three years later, Christine "Christie" Toutges married Anthony Cales in Las Vegas, Nevada. Three months after that, Christie again gave birth, this time to a son, Yelton. Another daughter, Jessica, followed two years later.

Based on published accounts, the Cales-Toutges marriage was filled with difficulties. At one point in 1983, while living in Downers Grove, Illinois, Christie Cales accused Anthony of threatening her with a gun, and asked for an order of protection. Then in December of that same year, a house fire in Downers Grove claimed the life of baby Jessica. Stacy was born a month later, on January 20, 1984. Another sister, Cassandra, followed the next year, and a fourth sister, Lacy, came the year after that. Then baby Lacy died, apparently of Sudden Infant Death Syndrome. At various times during this period, Christie was reportedly hospitalized for alcoholism and depression and arrested on several occasions, charged with shoplifting liquor.

In 1990, Anthony Cales filed for divorce from Christie, and was soon awarded custody of all three surviving Cales children, Yelton, Stacy, and Cassandra, while stepdaughter Tina Kokas was placed in foster care. Four years later, Anthony moved to Fort Myers, Florida, there marrying a woman named Linda Olson. Over the next few years, the family moved to various places in the South before returning to Illinois in 1997. By then, according to one account, Anthony and Linda Cales had separated. And according to another account Stacy later provided to a neighbor, Anthony Cales at this point left the three surviving Cales children to fend, at least temporarily, for themselves.

At some point around the same time, he provided Tina—now twenty-two, and living with her fiancé, Todd Ernest—with a handwritten document giving Tina guardianship over Stacy:

> Due to financial and housing complications at this time, I, Anthony Cales, give my step-daughter, Christina Kokas, temporary guardianship of my daughter Stacy Ann Cales.
>
> This guardianship to enable Christina Kokas to enroll Stacy Cales in school, and sign for medical attention, should it become necessary.
>
> This agreement to cease at such a time as I, Anthony Cales, see fit to end it and return Stacy Cales to my sole custody.

Cassandra was eventually lodged with another family, while Yelton was on his own, being over eighteen.

Then, three months later, in March of 1998, the Cales children's natural mother, Christie Toutges Cales, vanished. The story, as reported much later by the *Chicago Sun-Times* newspaper, was that Christie, living then in Blue Island,

Illinois, a suburb just south of Chicago, took her Bible and her purse and began walking to church, or possibly a friend's house. She never got there, and remains a missing person to this day, and, all factors considered, is most likely the victim of a random murderer, still unidentified.

The following August, in 1998, Tina and her fiancé Todd formally agreed to a guardianship order approved by the Will County Circuit Court, appending the handwritten declaration of Anthony to the application for formal legal guardianship. Then, a little over a year after that, something happened. It wasn't clear what, though—juvenile court records in Illinois are not publicly accessible. But the outcome emerged in June 2000, when Todd Ernest filed a legal motion with the same court "to have my name removed from the guardianship of Stacy A. Cales, since she no longer resides in my home." It appears that Todd and Tina were separating, and that Stacy had gotten into some sort of trouble at about the same time. Stacy was placed in a group home, but there is also evidence that she had been placed on juvenile probation, because three months later, in September 2000, a Will County probation officer, one Clarence Westbrook, served her with legal papers transferring her guardianship to another young man, James Maves, who identified himself as a "family friend." The fact that a probation officer had to sign the custody papers, rather than Tina (who had not legally abandoned custody, as her apparently estranged bridegroom Todd had) suggests that Stacy had been made a ward of the court.

Stacy's background, at least as related to this murky episode, would later suggest different possible interpretations as to the cause or causes of her disappearance in 2007—as would the opaque nature of the later Peterson family finances, which were associated with several possible money-laundering machines, including a rather notorious bar.

Peterson's lawyer Joel Brodsky would later say he had been unaware of Stacy's seeming juvenile trouble in 2000, and suggested that Peterson also had never known of it. Given Peterson's access to official police records at the time he first began wooing the teenaged girl, this assertion seems hard to credit. Later, there would be suggestions that Peterson had met Stacy even before her job at the SpringHill Hotel—that after leaving the household of her half-sister, Tina Kokas, Stacy had lived on the street, at least for a while, perhaps before entering the group home. The possible nexus between Stacy on the street and Peterson as the supervising night sergeant raises the possibility that Peterson's first encounter with the then-teenage Stacy might have occurred *before* Peterson later admitted. This might well have been a crime; in the spring of 2000, when Stacy was "no longer living" in the home of Todd Ernest and Tina Kokas, she would have been, at sixteen, underage in terms of legal sexual relations.

In any event, a year after getting a new guardian in September of 2000—James Maves—Stacy Cales supposedly met Drew Peterson for the first time at the SpringHill Hotel.

Within a matter of weeks, Peterson had Stacy in the basement of his family home in Bolingbrook, former farmland turned into a bedroom suburb southwest of Chicago, in the early morning hours, while his wife Kathleen and two young sons slept blissfully unaware, upstairs. Within a few months, Peterson had used his influence to obtain a job for Stacy with the Bolingbrook village clerk.

Well, Peterson had always been a randy dog—he admitted that, years later, when the mess came to full boil.

Whatever was going on with Peterson and his third wife, Kathleen Savio Peterson, at the time of Peterson's claimed first encounter with Stacy Cales wasn't clear, although once the thirty-six-year-old Kathleen realized what was going on in the basement while she and her boys slept above, it soon became a blood feud, and it was money that was eventually at stake.

She'd been tipped off by an anonymous note, which may have been penned by another Bolingbrook cop with an incentive to get Peterson in trouble. The Petersons had around a million dollars in community property. This was a rather large estate for a small-town cop with two previous ex-wives and two adult as well as two dependent children, but as Peterson later explained, he'd always had outside jobs and income—among them, a printing business in DuPage County, part-time work as a cable-television installer, a wedding photography business, and—rather oddly—a chimney-sweeping business.

"I've always had five or six jobs," Peterson later told reporters, in addition to his police work. He later claimed to at one time have had more than a hundred people working for him in his various outside-the-police-department businesses.

The anonymous letter to Peterson's third wife Kathleen—Kitty to her family—surfaced years later, after Peterson became the villain *du jour* of the cable mavens in 2007–08:

> This letter is being sent to you for your benefit. At this point and time you are probably well aware that your husband is having an affair. The girl's name (and she is just that, a girl) is Stacy Yelton, born [birth date provided, but was in error], resides at [and then an address in Bolingbrook].
>
> You may already have all of this information but if not, you will need it to prevent any further embarrassment and disgrace to you and your family. This affair has been going on for several months and several people have been aware of this situation. Because of her age (17) and the fact that she is an employee of the Village and because of Drew's age and his occupation, he holds a position of authority over her. Drew could be charged criminally for his intimate involvement with this minor.
>
> Village officials (mayor, trustees and everyone at the police department) have complete knowledge of this situation. It has been an ongoing joke within the department. The issue has been discussed and has been decided to conceal his behavior to protect the village and Drew. Because of his political alliance with [Bolingbrook politicians], they are protecting themselves from the embarrassment and the liability. The real victims

(being you and your family) should be the ones being protected from the embarrassment.

This is not the first time in the past year that Drew's immoral and unethical behavior has been concealed. This past summer Drew allowed the beating of an arrestee who was handcuffed and defenseless. The past fall Drew was suspected to have planted narcotics (cocaine) on two separate drug raids to obtain a substantial arrest to overshadow his recent behavior, and now his illegal intimate relationship with a minor.

Drew has been willing to sacrifice his integrity for his personal gain, with total disregard that his actions will embarrass and disrespect his wife and children. BEWARE whom you talk to within the village administration, and within the police department . . .

If there was more to this letter, it seems to have been lost. But its errors (the wrong birth date for Stacy, the wrong last name, "Yelton," which was Stacy's brother's first name, not Cales), seem to suggest that the writer wasn't all that familiar with Stacy, but knew her only through her connection to her older brother Yelton. On the other hand, the letter writer seemed to have some familiarity with the law regarding authority figures such as police officers and sexual relationships with dependent minors, as well as to an event that the general public wouldn't have known about, the alleged beating of a handcuffed suspect in connection with an arrest. All in all, it seems very likely that the letter to Kitty had come from a disgruntled Bolingbrook cop intent on causing trouble for Peterson and his allies in the Village government, supposedly including the mayor of the Village of Bolingbrook. According to some reports, this was the first time that Kitty realized that her husband had been sleeping with a seventeen-year-old girl.

Once Kitty read the letter, a bad moon was on the rise.

Some of the outside Peterson income came from a saloon in nearby Kane County, in the town of Montgomery, called Suds

Pub, which he'd first acquired with his second ex-wife, Victoria, but had somehow later managed to wrest away from her after their 1992 divorce and became its sole owner.

After marrying Kitty later in 1992, Peterson had installed her as the boss of the saloon. It didn't work out, though—according to Peterson, Kitty was a no-nonsense employer, unlike Victoria. He later claimed that he'd always seen the saloon as more of a clubhouse for his drinking buddies than a tightly accounted-for business. So, too, maybe there were eventual disputes about the books, where the money was coming from and where it was going. In any event, more than a decade later, when Kitty found out about seventeen-year-old Stacy's basement dalliance with her husband, she wanted her half of the assets—not only the house with the filthy basement in Bolingbrook, but half of the lucrative saloon as well.

This might well have been a problem, at least for someone. If the saloon was being used as a washing machine for illicit profits, as the later Peterson divorce files seem to suggest—cash businesses are great for this, and the putative owners aren't always the main beneficiaries—Kitty would have had a huge potential hammer over her ex-husband's head, one way or another, whether as principal, agent, or even informant for the IRS. Audits of liquor license holders in the state of Illinois are conducted under the aegis of the state government, the Illinois Liquor Control Commission. As it happened, the ILCC's records on Suds Pub were remarkably thin—the agency was later incapable of even telling who actually owned the place, apart from the licensee, and the dates when ownership was transferred from one party to another, let alone how much booze went out and how much cash came in.

The state of Illinois, of course, was once the stomping ground of the bootleggers Al Capone, Frank Nitti, Deanie O'Bannion, Hymie Weiss, and "Bugs" Moran—as well as the locale of the notorious, booze-inspired St. Valentine's Day Massacre in Chicago in 1929, in which Capone essentially wiped out Moran's gang in a hail of machine-gun fire.

In later years, the state became the venue of the latter-day "Outfit" of Sam Giancana, Johnny Roselli, Tony Spilotro (made lurid by Joe Pesci's roman-a-clef portrayal in the movie *Casino*), and Anthony "Tony Batters" Accardo, known for his skill with Louisville Sluggers on the bodies and skulls of his victims. In short, the state has always been a New Frontier for organized crime. The point is, the booze racket in Illinois is hardly pristine.

Under such circumstances, the Internal Revenue Service, Al Capone's own nemesis, is always waiting for someone to drop a dime, and usually for a cut of the action. Thus, what Kitty knew, and when she might have known it, and what she might have said, or threatened to say, might well be a motive in her eventual death, and not even one related to her ex-husband's doglike nature. Or even connected to him, at least directly—if Suds Pub was a cash-washing machine, there were others besides Peterson who might have wished to keep Kitty quiet. If that were the case, Peterson might have all the reasons in the world to keep his own lips zipped, even if he didn't do it himself.

Then there's also the fact that, before marrying Drew, Kitty had a job with a Chicago-area vending machine company. Vending machines have always been, like car washes or any other cash-intensive business, especially bars, a traditional mechanism for washing organized crime money. The prospects of potential money laundering—by whomever and wherever—only opens up new areas of reasonable doubt as to who killed Kitty, if in fact she was actually murdered. Illinois is a rough state, and the Chicago area, including Joliet, is in the roughest part of it.

Still, it's quite clear from the voluminous 2002–04 divorce record of *Peterson vs. Peterson* that Kitty was at the very least humiliated by her husband's cavalier dismissal of his marital vows and his basement infatuation with the sylphlike teenage Stacy. Assessing the divorce file, she clearly wanted him to pay up for the humiliation she felt, and wasn't about to let Peterson slip away without significant penance, as he had from his first two marriages. She was a fighter, and she would go the distance—until she wound up dead in a bathtub in the very same house with the odious basement, in early 2004. By then, Peterson had married his teenaged mistress, a child had been born, and Peterson and his third ex-wife were about to go toe-to-toe in a lengthy legal dispute over the disposition of their considerable joint assets.

But once Kitty was found dead in the bathtub—drowned, according to the autopsy—the contentious property settlement was moot: Peterson got everything. That was about the same time someone realized that Kitty was covered by a million-dollar life insurance policy. And once *that* asset was in the pot, along with the house and other assets, the whole stew began to emanate toxic vapors.

Three years later, around Halloween in 2007, the mixture exploded. The ensuing facts weren't exactly history—instead, mostly melodrama. But history is for the ages, while melodrama is our flat-screen fate, these days. Our tendency to make small events into large ones, our inability to distinguish between the mundane and the important, will forever tell our descendants about the true values of our culture.

3.

A Boy Named Drew

Any postmortem attempt to sort out the national media mess that the Peterson imbroglio became, with all its talking cable heads, followed by the eager crumb-eating bloggers, probably should begin with Drew Walter Peterson, clearly the central figure, if not the proximate cause of the whole thing. His compulsive failure to keep his pecker in his pants was the trigger of everything that happened, and it ultimately put him in jail. He readily admitted his randiness, his doglike nature—in fact, he wore it as a badge of distinction, and it drove the national news media wild with glee. If they knew nothing else, they knew that sex sells, especially alleged illicit sex.

What other forty-seven-year-old man would seduce a seventeen-year-old, and in his own family basement, no less? But then, why would anyone from Bangor to Boise normally care? Because the putative villain was someone with a badge and a gun, or so the subtext of the national media echoed. The talking heads soon suggested Peterson was a serial sex abuser who used his municipally granted lawman's badge to bend the supposedly naïve, innocent Stacy to his Mephistophelean will. So from the outset, the age disparity between the old roué cop and the onetime teenager was at the core of the national dialogue, with its frosting of prurient interest.

No one looked at the back stories, those involving Kitty,

or Drew, or Suds Pub, or even Stacy. And these back stories were all far more nuanced than the media could sort through, at least the way their advertising demographers had pitched the tale from its inception and the way the harried producers were apt to cast it. Too much unsavory detail about Stacy would blow up the jack-o-lanterns, the fake spiderwebs, the kids' candy, and ruin the media illusion.

Peterson was the oldest son of a Chicago area utility executive, and by all accounts was raised in a middle- to upper-middle-class home outside of Chicago. According to the statements he made later to those trying to tell his story, he saw himself as the class cutup, the wit, the wag, the practical joker, the guy who might pop up from the cake in a bikini at the graduation dinner just for the outrage, if not the laughs.

Peterson had always been glib, mouthy, a natural show-off, the performer, the wanna-be-famous, and this was something that fell out of the bottom of the national news frenzy that ensued after Stacy's disappearance—the true nature of his personality. For the content providers, it had little or nothing to do with the facts of the case, and all to do with the way things looked, which was mostly about how Peterson acted, once the lenses were focused on him.

Peterson didn't seem to be obviously, malevolently violent, and certainly not a homicidal maniac. No one described him as "a loner," the usual description disseminated in the news for a murderous psychopath, however actually untrue in reality. There was no red glare in his eyes, or saliva dripping from his lips, or neighborhood tales of inappropriate, intimate flashing exposure. Instead, he looked like the sort of guy who might cook hot dogs for the neighborhood block party on the Fourth of July.

For one thing, he had a sense of droll humor, and it certainly wasn't that of Norman Bates. The reality of Drew Peterson, as it would turn out, was a lot more complicated than Hitchcock's *Psycho*.

* * *

Born January 5, 1954, Peterson had a younger sister and brother. Raised as a Roman Catholic, he learned early on to identify cant and hypocrisy, the wellspring of ironic humor, and certainly got the jokes from *Saturday Night Live*'s inimitable Father Sarducci of the same era. He thought of himself as the class clown, always the one sent to the principal's office. He wore his reprimands as medals. He was bright, but in the era of the late 1960s and early 1970s, being countercultural was cool—we all saw it on *Laugh In*, *The Smothers Brothers*, then *Saturday Night Live*. Jane Curtain, Loraine Newman, and Gilda Radner, John Belushi as the Greek Samurai Chicago cheeseburger cooker, Chevy Chase as the pratfalling President Ford, all were staples in the life of the young Drew Peterson.

When Gilda Radner as Roseanne Roseannadanna asked, "What's all this talk about endangered feces?" it brought tears of laughter to a generation. Not only did Peterson get it, he wanted to *be* it—the star of the show. You had to laugh; it was how you knew you were alive in an era of deep disillusionment and cynicism about authority, post-Vietnam. And so he did.

After he graduated from Willowbrook High School in Romeoville, Illinois, in 1972, Peterson spent two years attending a community college, studying criminal justice, then joined the United States Army, and after training as a military policeman, found himself an enlisted soldier in the 516th Military Police Company. According to Peterson's own later account, this was an elite unit stationed at Fort Myer, in Arlington, Virginia, which provided area security to presidents Ford and Carter. He later regaled others with various tales of hijinks while in the unit—quick-draw pistol contests with other MPs, a co-ed couple of soldiers caught locked in a car severely out of uniform—all calculated to present himself as a fun-loving, wild-and-crazy guy, as the Steve Martin character on *Saturday Night Live* once portrayed. Peterson also married his high school sweetheart, Carol Hamilton, in 1974. Carol, seventeen at the time of the marriage, finished her last year of high school in Virginia.

By early 1977, Peterson was out of the army and looking for a job. He found one with the Bolingbrook Police Department that same year. Former military police officers had the inside track for hiring in police departments all across the country. After all, they had been very well trained, for free, by Uncle Sam.

4.
MANS and Wives

One of the most arresting aspects of the tale of Drew Peterson is the fact that at least his first wife, Carol, when interviewed in later years by the news media, never suggested that Drew Peterson had had any sort of propensity for violence, and certainly not murder.

This was in marked contrast to later claims by Kitty, who asserted, almost from the time she'd discovered that Stacy was fooling around with her husband in the family basement, that Drew Peterson was a violent, potentially homicidal exspouse. When asked by Diane Sawyer on *Good Morning America* if Peterson had ever evidenced any violent or controlling behavior toward her, the former Carol Hamilton denied this—as far as she could tell, she said, they'd had a very normal relationship, at least until she realized that Peterson was running around on her.

And even then, there was no violence. But once Carol found out that her husband was unfaithful, that was that. She seemed to harbor no fear of her ex-husband. She later married a high school friend of both of them, and maintained relatively cordial relations with her ex-husband in the years to follow.

Based on some accounts, it appears that Peterson's life from 1978 to 1980 substantially mirrored the existence of many other young suburban cops, all across the country—not enough time for family and not nearly enough money.

Carol gave birth to two sons, Eric in 1978, and Stephen the following year. Peterson soon was detailed to the Metropolitan Anti-Narcotics Squad (MANS), with all that entailed: nightlife, surveillance, disguises, penetration of dope dealers' rings, and drinking off the tension in local bars. Being young and reckless, as a lot of young cops are, he reveled in the assignment.

In an era after *Serpico*, then *Starksy and Hutch*, or a little later, *Miami Vice*, being a member of MANS was big-time *huevos*, at least for a small-town cop. MANS people wore beards, long hair and wide belts, packed big guns, and got a rush from crashing through dope dealers' doors on post-buy busts. There was a lot of risk, a lot of relief, and a lot of fooling around. The machismo was more toxic because the MANS people were second-tier. Chicago PD and DEA were higher on the cop pecking order, and consequently, the MANS people were rather less regulated by the higher-ups; they were the B-Team, and naturally wanted to show they were better than the A-Team. So it made the MANS people more reckless, more willing to bend the rules, more desperate to show they were Tubbs and Crockett. Peterson had been there, done that, in two stretches, for almost five years.

To buttress his tales of the wild life of the undercover drug cop, Peterson later produced old snapshots of the MANS crew—all of them bearded, grinning and some brandishing weapons, like some sort of psychedelic vision of the bandits from *The Treasure of the Sierra Madre*, only with "stinking badges." It is representative of an era known to every cop and dope dealer in America—cops posing as hairy crooks.

The life of any cop's wife is never an easy one, and especially for one married to someone leading two lives, by day a police officer, by night a drug-buying pseudo-hippie liable to have his head shot off by some desperate, coked-out nutcase. By 1980, after only six years, but with two toddlers, the marriage of Carol and Drew had reached its nadir. The odd hours, the role-playing, the tension—along with the needful as well as un-needful lies—had eroded whatever innocent bliss each had brought into the marriage back in 1974. As

Peterson later said, each was finished with the other. Rumors of Peterson's skirt-chasing after hours had left Carol cold. Peterson sued for divorce, and Carol readily agreed. She kept custody of the two boys, Eric and Stephen. For the next two years, Peterson lived the life of a bachelor narc.

For some undercovers, the excitement of leading a double life can be so intoxicating as to be addictive; life in a split world, adrenalized as it is all the time, can drive an ordinary person into a sort of schizoid frenzy. That's exactly why police departments across the country try to rotate cops out of such squads—too much time in the fast lane can ruin them forever, at least as effective cops. But it's always a balance—the longer a cop is undercover, the more he or she knows about the darker milieu, and the more productive he or she becomes; eventually, they know who all the bad guys are, and inevitably, some begin to make compromises.

Some, in fact, cross over—as Neil Young once put it in another context, out of the blue, into the black. The temptations of pocketing seized cash, short-weighting the actual amount of drugs taken, pocketing illicit firearms, looting the evidence locker, or making side deals for the protection of dealers in return for information, have been the bane of police departments across the country, ever since Richard Nixon's declaration of the "war on drugs" some forty-odd years ago. There is hardly a police department in America that hasn't had some sort of scandal driven by one or more of these corruptions, going back more than a generation, just as police departments faced similar moral failures back in the era of Prohibition.

With so much lucre available for the taking, with the bad guys raking in the dough, a policeman's pay can seem like a pittance, just as it did back in the 1930s. Getting even by ripping off the dealers and profiting by doing so can sometimes seem like real justice. Sometimes, undercover cops even feel it's their due—what the rest of us owe them for doing a dirty job for little pay, with little thanks.

In these circumstances, psychological or material or both, pulling an undercover drug cop back to reality is a matter of timing, an art, and not every police administrator gets it. For Peterson, that time came in the early 1980s, when Peterson was rotated back to uniformed patrol. The beard came off, along with the long hair, the wide belt, and the pressure. Peterson soon had a case of the bends, rising back to the surface so fast. Being a uniformed patrol cop was *so* boring.

Just after being rotated out, however, Peterson had married again, this time Victoria Rutkiewicz, a twenty-three-year-old divorcee with an eight-year-old daughter, Lisa. This marriage was to last until June 1991, approximately nine years. In an interview with Fox News' Greta Van Susteren—after Stacy's disappearance in November of 2007—Lisa asserted that Peterson, over the nine years he had been her stepfather, had abused her and had habitually intimidated her mother.

"I was hit with a belt for many years," Lisa told Van Susteren. She described Peterson as very controlling of her mother, constantly monitoring her movements. Eventually her mother left the marriage because of Peterson's infidelities, Lisa said. Later, her story would go further—not only had Peterson beaten her with a belt, she would say by 2009, he had also sexually abused her. Peterson's lawyers were outraged, and threatened to sue to shut her up, given that these incendiary allegations were being raised prior to Peterson's trial on murder charges. Not only were the charges untrue, they said, they were calculated to make money for his former stepdaughter from Peterson's by-then media-driven notoriety.

Actually, the court records from the 1991–92 divorce case with Victoria tell a slightly different story. According to these records, it was Peterson as the plaintiff who sued Victoria, not the other way around. Peterson had an attorney, one Edward D. Kusta; Victoria went unrepresented, and in fact the divorce was uncontested. By this point, Peterson and Victoria had accumulated some substantial assets, including three pieces of real estate and the saloon in nearby Montgomery, Suds Pub, along with a hundred shares of stock in something called Blue Lightning Incorporated, formerly known as The River Corporation. Blue Lightning became the corporate edifice for Suds Pub, which would later become such a bone of contention between Kitty Savio Peterson and her husband. Just how Peterson and Victoria managed to acquire this gigantic cash-flow asset on a patrolman's salary wasn't clear.

In a property settlement agreement dated January 21, 1992, Peterson was awarded a residence in Bolingbrook, and half the stock in Blue Lightning Inc. Victoria got real estate in Montgomery, and the other half of the Blue Lightning stock. A third piece of real estate in Bolingbrook, the former family residence, was to be sold, with $15,000 at close of sale going to Victoria. Peterson kept his 1988 Ford truck and a ski boat, while Victoria got the 1990 Pontiac and 1985 Camaro, which was probably driven by the then-seventeen-year-old Lisa.

Advantage: on paper, slightly in favor of Victoria.

Well before this divorce, however, by 1985 Peterson had cajoled his way back to MANS. And it was at this point that the plots surrounding Peterson first began to thicken, with subsequent possible consequences for the mysterious disappearance of Stacy Peterson, twenty-two years later, and even for the drowning death of Kitty Peterson, a little more than two and a half years before that. Sometimes, in homicide investigations, it's not as much what you did as who you know.

5.

The Dope Deal

According to various versions of the story Peterson later told, Peterson's troubles with the Illinois State Police began with a drug bust he and MANS made of a man named Anthony Rock in 1980, about the time Peterson was splitting from his first wife, Carol.

According to reporter Joseph Hosey of the *Herald-News*, a suburban Chicago newspaper that heavily covered the Peterson case from its outset, "Bindy" Rock was a rather notorious underworld figure in Joliet in the 1970s and 1980s. He had once been convicted of the murder of a Joliet policeman, William Loscheider, who had been a member of a police team staking out a Joliet liquor warehouse in 1970. The cops apparently had word from a snitch that a heist was about to go down. When Bindy allegedly attempted to burgle the place, Loscheider was fatally shot by another police officer who thought he was one of the burglars trying to get away. Or so the story went.

Rock was eventually convicted of a felony murder in Loscheider's death—that's what happens when someone gets killed in the course of a felony *you* commit, even if it wasn't directly your fault. After a series of appeals, Rock's conviction was upheld, but his sentence was reduced to time served. By November 1980, ten years later, Rock was back on the street. Peterson claimed that he nailed Rock that same autumn by inducing him to buy ten thousand hits of amphetamine, while posing undercover as a dealer. That case was overturned on appeal, and Rock was set free once more.

By 1985, Peterson later told Hosey, when he returned to the MANS unit, he was determined to get Bindy once and for all. He had the idea that Bindy had a number of local politicians on his payroll, including people in the Will County State's Attorney's office. He concocted a plan to convince Rock that he was a dirty cop, and to further this aim, he enlisted the help of one Gerry O'Neill, who also happened to be Victoria's brother, and therefore Peterson's brother-in-law. As it happened, Gerry O'Neill was a member of a Chicago-area motorcycle gang, Hell's Henchmen, at least according to Hosey. Peterson later told Hosey that bringing Gerry O'Neill along for the meet with Rock would help establish his own bona fides as a bent cop, proof he was in cahoots with bikers like Hell's Henchmen, and therefore ready to betray his badge.

Peterson and O'Neill met with Rock in late April of 1985. Rock was cautious—he suspected a setup by Peterson, although Peterson was intent on convincing him he was indeed a crook. Peterson told Hosey years later that Rock was right—he *was* trying to set him up, by pretending to be a bent cop.

"Peterson said he proposed a business arrangement with Rock in which he would buy cocaine from him in exchange for twenty percent of the front and ten percent of what was sold afterward," Hosey recounted, in a 2008 book he wrote after the initial stage of the Peterson case, *Fatal Vows*. "In his official report after the meeting with Rock, Peterson said he agreed, but told Rock he would look for a better connection elsewhere once he was started."

It's unclear who initially proposed what to whom, at least in the way Hosey framed his sentence. Was it Peterson proposing to buy cocaine from Rock, or was Peterson proposing that Rock buy cocaine from him? And who was going to get "started"—Rock or Peterson?

After hearing this version of old narco war stories from Peterson, though, Hosey tracked down Rock. "Rock told me

Peterson approached him with a plan in which Peterson would supply Rock from cocaine ripped off from his drug raids," expecting a cut of the action, Hosey wrote in *Fatal Vows*. Hosey said Rock told him he'd turned Peterson down—but that he still believed Peterson was genuinely dirty, not just trying to set him up. Hosey didn't report Rock's reasons for turning down the supposed proposition from Peterson, but he didn't really have to: "Bindy" had already been burned once by Peterson, and even if he thought Peterson *was* a crooked cop, he had no reason to trust him.

But then, if Peterson was actually on the take, why did he file an official police report of the conversation on May 3, 1985? One possibility is that he might have worried that Rock would rat him out—tell another police officer that Peterson was dirty—and that filing an official report was one way for Peterson to protect himself from the consequences of his own illicit proposition. And of course, his brother-in-law, Gerry O'Neill, might get caught someday in an unrelated pinch, and deliver Peterson as a crook to get out from under his own trouble. Sometime after this, according to Hosey, O'Neill was shot to death in Cook County by parties unknown.

It appears that Peterson whipped up this would-be sting or dope deal (however one views it) without the knowledge or sanction of the higher-ups in MANS, or his own department. When the Bolingbrook police chief got wind of this, he tried to fire Peterson. He asked the village board of commissioners to find Peterson guilty of disobedience, conducting an unauthorized investigation, misconduct, and failure to report a bribe offer. By then, too, Peterson had been indicted by a county grand jury for misconduct and failure to report a bribe attempt. Peterson was in a world of trouble by the end of 1985.

But three months later, the criminal charges were dropped, when a special prosecutor assigned to the case determined that the "he-said, he-said" nature of the charges made them impossible to prove—Rock was hardly a credible witness, given his previous criminal history. Gerry O'Neill's own credibility was in doubt, given his connections to the bikers. Then Peterson sued to get his job back, and won. Peterson retaliated by suing the prosecutor who had indicted him, the chief, the Village of Bolingbrook, and the board of commissioners, claiming improper dismissal and harassment, and further claiming that the prosecutor himself had been taking money from Rock. Eventually a judge threw Peterson's lawsuit out, but Peterson had made his point—if you bit him, he'd bite back.

Peterson went back to work for the Bolingbrook cops, although he would never again work as an undercover, even though it was his natural métier—he was a born actor, a more gifted dissembler than most narcs, as well as a congenital ham, which might well be three ways of describing the same thing. He would later claim that the Illinois State Police were out to get him from this moment forward, although if that were so, they missed their opportunity by initially failing to charge Peterson with murder in the death of Kitty Peterson almost twenty years later, in 2004. So it would seem that Peterson's claims of persecution by the Illinois State Police ring a bit hollow. It wasn't until late October of 2007, when Peterson's fourth wife, Stacy, disappeared, that the state police began to investigate Peterson in earnest, as we shall see.

Another, slightly different version of the Peterson-Rock imbroglio was recounted in another early book on the Peterson case, this one titled *Drew Peterson Exposed*, by Canadian Derek Armstrong, who claimed to be a novelist as well as a private investigator.

"I wanted this perp," Peterson told Armstrong, meaning Bindy Rock. "The state was after the guy. The feds were after the guy. I got the guy."

And: "This guy implicated a state's attorney for taking kickbacks," Peterson told Armstrong in May 2008. "Well, I wrote that in my report. . . . my director [of MANS] got me fired, I ended up getting criminally indicted for 'official misconduct' and 'failure to report an offer of a bribe' and nine counts of bullshit. And they fired me from the police department with no evidence I did anything wrong." Except, of course, for his failure to tell his supervisors what he was up to, usually a hard-and-fast requirement for undercover work, for obvious reasons.

It was only when he'd attempted to expose the corruption in the Will County state's attorney's office, Peterson later complained, that he'd been indicted in the Rock fiasco. By the time he'd been cleared and reinstated, Peterson said, he was broke. At that point, in Peterson's version of the events, he'd gotten involved in local politics, running a slate of candidates to wipe out the Will County and Bolingbrook old guard, which he saw as rife with corruption. Peterson's faction lost— narrowly, according to Peterson.

But after this, things became more bleak—Peterson claimed to have lost his house to foreclosure, and eventually, his marriage to Victoria.

"Marriage over, just like that," Derek Armstrong summarized. "House gone."

Well, actually, not "just like that." Once again, the facts appear to be at variance with the legend. The Will County deed records seem to show that it was Peterson and his first wife, Carol, who were foreclosed, not Peterson and Victoria, and not on the property Peterson lived in with his second wife, on Seminole Lane in Bolingbrook, but a rental property that Peterson, Carol, and another couple jointly owned. This occurred in 1986, according to real estate records in Will County, and it wasn't until five years after that, in 1991, that the Peterson-Victoria marriage came apart, as the divorce court records show.

By then, Peterson and Victoria had accumulated some substantial assets, as indicated above in their 1992 divorce settlement. And then, at some point after that, Peterson got Victoria out of her half of the Montgomery saloon— according to Armstrong, who seemingly got most of his information from Peterson himself—with a payment to Victoria of $100,000 for her half-share of Suds Pub.

"They stayed partners for a long while," Armstrong wrote

in *Drew Peterson Exposed*, "although in the end Peterson bought out Victoria for $100,000 and ran the business as a sole proprietorship after that. Again, with true entrepreneurial spirit, he drove the bar to resounding success. Fulltime cop, fulltime bar owner, now single again, playing the field."

The way Armstrong thus characterized him, Peterson seemingly had a big red P on his chest—SuperP, able to work two full-time jobs at a single bound, bar owner and cop, and chase more women in his spare hours. True entrepreneurial spirit, indeed.

Just how Peterson accumulated this money from 1986, when he seemed to be broke, or at least foreclosed upon, to perhaps a half a decade later, when he erased Victoria from her half-ownership of the lucrative saloon, wasn't made clear by either Armstrong or Hosey. However, Kane County real estate records give some hints, along with corporate records from the State of Illinois.

Based on the latter, it appears that Suds Pub, at 1250 South Broadway Road in Montgomery, Illinois, was incorporated as a business on March 5, 1987, with John C. Charest of Montgomery as president, and David Peskin of Aurora, Illinois, as the registered agent. Blue Lightning Incorporated was formed on May 13, 1991, with Drew Peterson as president, and later real estate records show that Blue Lightning's primary asset was the same property as Charest's Suds Pub. Thus it seems possible that, contrary to Armstrong's account (again, only from Peterson), Peterson didn't actually take over the pub until mid-1991, just before separating from Victoria in June of the same year. This appears to contradict Armstrong's assertion that Peterson and Victoria had owned the saloon throughout most of their marriage from 1982 to 1991.

So, something seems to be missing from this story, at least as Peterson told it to Armstrong—for instance, just how Peterson acquired the saloon, and when.

The fact was, the formation of Blue Lightning Incorporated came just less than a month before Peterson separated from Victoria (which is not to say they hadn't managed it for Charest previously). From the Kane County real estate records, it is clear that Blue Lightning Incorporated became the owner and operator of Suds Pub at some point between May 1991 and January 1992, when Peterson and Victoria reached their property settlement agreement, giving each marital partner a half-interest in Blue Lightning Inc., by then the new owner of Suds Pub.

Still, there's a caveat to all this: The 1992 divorce record of Victoria and Drew Peterson appears to show that Blue Lightning Inc. was a successor corporation to The River Corporation, whatever that was. Illinois corporation records seem to show that there was no such entity, at least registered in Illinois. Still, it's possible that The River Corporation, if it ever existed, might have been a lessee of Suds Pub from Charest et al. during the 1980s, and even before, and if so, Peterson and Victoria could well have run the saloon before actually buying it in June of 1991. The trouble is, the records aren't clear, and the state of Illinois' regulatory machinery wasn't paying very much attention.

As noted, the origin of the money Peterson (and seemingly, Victoria, given her half-interest as of early 1992) used to acquire the pub from Charest in June of 1991 also isn't clear. Charest's Suds Pub corporation ceased to exist—"involuntary dissolution," as the Illinois Secretary of State termed it—by July 1, 1992, although Peterson maintained the name of the saloon.

Putting these facts together in retrospect, it seems at least a possibility that Victoria was standing in as a nominee for her brother, Gerry, the supposed Hell's Henchmen biker, whom Peterson used as his "cover" while dickering with Bindy Rock back in 1985, although there's nothing more than speculation to support that thesis. But Gerry O'Neill's connection with the bikers, along with his relationship with Peterson, raises the possibility that at least some of the money for the purchase of the pub might have come from Hell's Henchmen. In other words, Drew Peterson might have become a bagman for a biker gang, using the Montgomery saloon as a washing machine for dirty money, in return for a piece of the action.

Hosey did not make it clear as to when Victoria's brother, Gerry, the "Hell's Henchman," was murdered in Cook County. Armstrong never mentioned *that* sad detail at all.

But records from the Cook County Medical Examiner, as well as the Chicago Police Department, show that Gerry was gunned down—"multiple gunshot wounds," as the medical examiner's records put it—on January 10, 1994, on South Calumet Avenue, on Chicago's far south side, just north of the Calumet River from Calumet City. This was once widely known as Cook County's wild side, home of speakeasies in the Prohibition Era, a safehouse for Al Capone in the late 1920s and early 1930s, and in the 1950s to 1970s, the location of more bars and strip joints per square foot than any other city in the country east of Las Vegas—"Sin City," some called it, at least in those days. Gerry O'Neill was forty-four years old when he was murdered there, almost nine years after accompanying his brother-in-law, Peterson, to the abortive meeting with Bindy Rock. The killing was two years after Peterson's split of the stock in the saloon with Gerry's sister, Victoria, and one year before Peterson apparently gave $100,000 to Victoria to move her out of Suds Pub.

Whether there are connections between any of these murky doings—with the alleged big-time dope dealer, Bindy Rock, Peterson's claims of official corruption, the 1994 gunshot death of Gerry O'Neill, or Peterson's apparently sudden reversal of fortune from broke to bonanza, from 1986 to 1992—isn't clear.

Nevertheless, they loom like shadows over all the events that were to ensue—from Kitty Peterson's cryptic death in a bathtub in early 2004 to the mysterious disappearance of Stacy Peterson on October 28, 2007. It was the backstory, as they say in Hollywood, one that the likes of Greta van Susteren and Geraldo Rivera either missed or ignored, in their demographically driven focus on Halloween candles and cobwebs. The rogue elements at work in the tale—bikers, possible dirty money, an unsolved murder of a connected brother-in-law, drugs, alleged police corruption, politics, wheels-within-wheels—all might easily make the disappearance of Stacy Peterson much more complicated and even unpalatable, demographics-wise, than the run-of-the-mill missing wife/suspect husband story it was initially portrayed to be, young mother of two or not.

In other words, once the candles inside jack-o-lanterns are blown out, it can be an ill wind, all around the family hearth. And it can also be very dark, and even very cold.

6.
Kitty

The Will County District Court records of the divorce of Drew and Victoria Peterson show that the couple last lived together as man and wife on June 10, 1991, less than a month after Peterson incorporated Blue Lightning. Peterson sued Victoria; he was the plaintiff in the divorce, she the defendant, just as with his first wife, Carol. Peterson and Victoria reached their marital property settlement in January of the following year, 1992—the one, as noted above, giving Victoria half the stock in Blue Lightning, as well as interests in other real estate in Bolingbrook and Montgomery.

Five months later, on May 3, 1992, Peterson married his third wife, Kathleen Marie Savio. Their first son, Thomas, was born on January 5—Peterson's own birthday!—1993, a little over seven months after that. A month later, on February 23, 1993, Drew Peterson borrowed $305,000 on a five-year mortgage from The Merchants National Bank of Aurora, Illinois, secured by the real estate and improvements of Blue Lightning, doing business as Suds Pub. The document recorded in Kane County did not specify the interest rate, or the amount of monthly payments for the bar. However, based on the term of the loan and the likely interest rate, the payments on paper should have been around $5,500 a month, unless there was a balloon payment that would have required a renegotiation of the original loan, which would have lowered the monthly payment rather substantially, but leaving the retirement of the debt to the future. For some reason, the loan document did not include Kathleen's signature.

Two years after that, on August 1, 1995, Peterson borrowed another $100,000 from the same bank, and the following year renegotiated this loan, extending its due date from August 1, 1996, to August 1, 1997. Both of these records *did* include Kathleen's signature as a co-signer, which seems to show that by then she was an equal partner in the pub, and that Victoria was out. The initial $100,000 new loan seems not to have been recorded by Kane County, and the extension, like the original mortgage, does not specify an interest rate or monthly payment figure, but it seems fairly likely that the total leveraged mortgage paid out by the Petersons to own the bar, including the additional loan and the extension—on paper—had to be around $4,000 a month, in addition to operating expenses: buying the booze, paying the help, the property taxes, the insurance, the utilities, the license fees, the taxes, the maintenance; in other words, rounding up all the usual small business suspects. Altogether, Peterson's outlay was probably close to $8,000 or so a month, maybe more, assuming the bulk of the original mortgage of $305,000 was deferred for later renegotiation.

Based on later records (by 2002 the mortgage on the saloon was down to $195,000), it appears that the Peterson pub paid its lenders off at a rate of about $50,000 a year, counting principal and interest.

Just how much the saloon actually grossed in this period is another mystery—it appears that the Illinois Liquor Control Commission in those days wasn't doing audits to match booze going out and dollars coming in. It's possible that the loan of 1995 was the source of the money Peterson used to buy his second wife, Victoria, out of Suds Pub, since the $100,000 figure matches that reported by Armstrong after his interviews with Peterson in 2008. By then, of course, Gerry O'Neill was dead. Just why Peterson would buy his second ex-wife out of a business that wasn't incorporated until only a month before he split with her in 1991 is yet another mystery. So was what she brought to the business,

other than the future ghost of her brother. This financial ma-
neuvering seems to suggest that there might be much more
going on with the subsequent death of Kathleen "Kitty"
Peterson, and the disappearance of Stacy Cales Peterson,
than initially met the eye.

If one believes the accounts of both Hosey and Armstrong,
Kitty/Kathleen Savio was more than a match in sheer willpower for her peripatetic, quick-to-unzipper cop/saloon-
keeper husband.

By their accounts, as well as those of others, Kathleen
Savio was a jewel of a woman—beautiful, even voluptuous,
at least as Peterson saw her. And she was very smart, probably quicker in some ways than her new husband. But on the
other hand, she was maybe not as knowledgeable of the
ruder ways of the world as her chameleonlike bridegroom,
who, long before meeting her, knew how to reflect the image
anyone wanted to see in him; after all, he'd been professionally trained as a liar by the state of Illinois' experts in undercover operations as a narcotics officer. Certainly she was
asleep when her husband adopted a seventeen-year-old parent-
less waif as his basement sex partner a decade later.

But once she woke up, Kathleen would become Drew
Peterson's worst nightmare. Unlike Carol or Victoria, she
would fight him to the end, however bitter. By early 2002,
as the ten-year marriage reached its nadir, Kathleen hated
her husband—in her mind, he had humiliated her, shamed
her before their children, her family and friends, and had even
assaulted her. If he had hurt her badly, she could certainly
return the disfavor, and with compound interest.

According to Peterson's account to Derek Armstrong, he
met Kathleen Savio "on a blind date," but provided no details as to where or when, or who, if anyone, facilitated the
introduction. This was around the same time that the pub,
according to Armstrong, had become somewhat notorious
in Montgomery for its "Green Felt Club," in which inebriated,
consensual sex was supposedly performed on the saloon's

pool tables. This, for what it's worth, was Armstrong's account in *Drew Peterson Exposed*, and given the provenance of most of Armstrong's relevant reporting, this information appears to have come from Peterson himself. Again according to Armstrong, the police chief in Montgomery was not a big fan of the watering hole, which he viewed as a character-sump run by the bad-boy cop from the Village of Bolingbrook, across the Kane/Will County line, because the saloon seemed to be an ongoing law-enforcement problem for his own town, about twenty miles west of Bolingbrook. And indeed, based on some contemporaneous reports in local newspapers, or from Montgomery municipal records, the Montgomery pub was a raucous establishment, with multiple alleged liquor-law violations, and by at least one account, open drug dealing. On one occasion, in fact, a convicted felon was arrested for being in possession of a handgun, which he'd fired in the saloon's men's room.

> A 26-year-old Aurora man was being held in lieu of $50,000 bail at the Kane County Jail, two days after being arrested on suspicion of discharging a handgun in a tavern restroom, police said. . . . [name omitted here] was charged with unlawful use of a weapon by a felon, not having a firearms owner's identification card, reckless discharge and theft by possession. He was arrested early Saturday at Suds Pub, 1250 S. Broadway Ave., after police were called to investigate a report of a man with a gun. . . .

Or so reported the *Chicago Tribune* on March 11, 1997. So the pub operated by Blue Lightning seemed to be a magnet of sorts for outlaws, or at least drunken suburban rowdies.

Whether Kathleen knew exactly what she was getting into with Peterson when she met him remains a matter of conjecture. About five feet four, around 120 pounds when Peterson first met her, Kitty was a spectacular beauty. Born June 25,

1963—nine years younger than Peterson—she was dark-haired and vivacious, certainly a live wire who from the start played well against Peterson's own insouciant irreverence. At the same time, she was, by most accounts, a rather volatile personality, certainly not the kind to sit at home and knit doilies. Kitty was smart, aggressive, and willing to crack the domestic whip over her husband. Peterson eventually came to see her as a shrew, and as much as he hated this controlling aspect of her personality, he still admired her willpower, even after she was dead.

Much later, when all the turbulence was in the air after fourth wife Stacy's mysterious disappearance, Peterson would suggest to Armstrong that Kitty was "bipolar," which probably owed more to Peterson's desire to portray his third wife as emotionally precipitate for purposes of exculpating himself from her demise, rather than by any informed assessment. After all, Peterson hardly had a degree in neuropsychiatry, but did have the cop jargon that allowed him to dismiss someone's complaints about him: every cop knows how to discount a beef by questioning the mental competence of the complainant, even if they have to use labels they aren't qualified to use, such as "bipolar."

Armstrong quoted Peterson: "I had the hots for her from the very beginning," Peterson told Armstrong, while brandishing her photograph in Armstrong's face. "No one, including myself, could stand up against Kathleen. When her temper got up, you stayed clear. When she swung, you ducked." The Kathleen he knew, Peterson said, was adventurous, bold, and in control, "the boss of the family unit," as Armstrong paraphrased. Perhaps significantly, Peterson would later use almost the same language to describe his fourth wife, Stacy.

By the time he encountered Kitty, Peterson was thirty-seven, and already the father of two teenage sons with his first wife, Carol, not to mention his stepdaughter, Lisa, who later would claim he had beaten her with a belt (and worse) while married to Victoria. When he met Kitty, it was 1991 or 1992. This was five or six years after the abortive dope deal with Bindy Rock and all the ensuing unpleasantness, and about the time he was splitting ownership of the lucrative if rowdy pub with Victoria, two years before Victoria's brother Gerry was gunned down just over the river from Calumet City.

By this point, Peterson's public persona had mostly formed—one part his own innate irreverent nature, another part his reaction to the way people reacted to him. The bad boy of the suburban cops had survived—barely—the prospect of being canned, prosecuted, possibly even jailed. He'd fought back, thrown aspersions in the other direction, and despite his difficulties with the Kane County authorities over the tavern he'd borrowed more than $400,000 to operate, he seemed to have settled into the beginning of his middle years. Still, Peterson kept his peculiar personality, so much like the droll undercover narc he once had been, and so different from the cops who wore uniforms and badges on their chests for all to see. Peterson reveled in flashing his disconcerting blend of self-deprecation, bawdy humor, a wry hint of ironic arrogance, affected insensitivity, all overlaying a depth of native shrewdness as to what people were really like. He liked to shock people with his seeming outrageousness, stinging you with the after-realization that he always knew something you did not, or so, at least, he wanted you to think.

On the surface, Peterson seemed to have a marked lack of sensitivity to others' feelings, an apparent indifference to the effects of his own shocking behavior, often expressed in crude, frequently sexist terms. It was only afterward that one might realize that Peterson's coarseness was an act, intended perhaps to shove you off-balance, in order to give him an edge. Yes, this crudity was cop-speak, but usually confined to locker rooms and bars, confined to the initiated and the perps, not inflicted on the general public. But at the same time, one got a glimmer of the Peterson underpsyche— the notion that this sort of talk, however offensive, however crude, was calculated to conceal someone who would never, ever lose control of himself, while putting others on the defensive by deliberately embarrassing them with his own coarseness. It was as if Peterson was scripted, that he'd written all his lines years before, and was now using them to manipulate others.

In a way, it often seemed that Peterson was still undercover, as if he'd never come back to the surface from his years as a narc. In some ways, perhaps, to Peterson, life was just some sort of game.

A little less than two years later, Kathleen again gave birth to a son, Kristopher, born on August 8, 1994. At least according to Armstrong—again parroting Peterson—Kathleen at this point was somewhat estranged from her own family. Peterson had soon formed the impression that they disapproved of him. From the Savio family perspective, their new in-law hardly had a sterling record as a husband, judging from his two previous marriages, and how he had abandoned his first two wives and two sons. But Peterson, to Armstrong, put this antipathy down to his occupation.

"They were instantly against the idea of their daughter marrying a policeman," Peterson told Armstrong. "They seemed to think all cops were cheaters. 'Policemen are dishonest.' They were always looking at me out of the corner of their eye. In ten years of marriage, they never warmed up to me."

This was an easy out on Peterson's part—the use of external prejudice to explain or excuse the incompatibility, when it could have just as easily been something about Peterson himself, not his badge. Finding things like occupation, or race or gender, to justify someone's much more personal objection is a slacker's way to avoid taking responsibility for one's own behavior. Sometimes, maybe even often, it isn't *who* you are or what you look like, but how you behave that people find objectionable, and hiding behind stereotypes to avoid this reality is one way to escape responsibility for one's own conduct. Whatever the reason—the Savio family didn't like Drew Peterson, and when Kitty eventually went to war with him, they were solidly in her corner. And when she turned up dead, they knew in their hearts who to blame.

Kitty had two sisters, Susan and Anna Marie, and brothers, Henry and Nick. In the confusing aftermath of Kitty's death in 2004, all would turn against their former brother-in-law, Peterson, and come to believe that he had murdered their sister in order to avert an onerous divorce settlement. Their antipathy might have been because Peterson was a cop, but more likely it had to do with Peterson the man, not the officer. For the Savios, Peterson had no integrity—he was a liar, a cheat and a fraud, and, worst of all, was arrogant to boot.

As Exhibit A for the Savios, there was the incident of April 28, 1993, less than a year after the marriage. Thomas was four months old. The tale is told by Hosey: "According to a Hinsdale Hospital emergency department report dated April 28, 1993, Kathleen Peterson was treated after she was 'involved in an altercation [with her] husband . . . was hit in [the] head' with a 'blunt object.'" Apparently the blunt object was "a dining room table." With all due respect to the credibility of the hospital's report—Hosey didn't say where he'd gotten it, but it seems probable Kitty's siblings provided it, years later—it doesn't seem very likely that Peterson hit his pregnant wife with "a dining room table." One can hardly imagine Peterson raising an entire table by one leg, waving it around, and then whacking his wife. More likely is a scenario in which Peterson might have shoved Kitty, causing her to hit her head on a table. In other words, it wasn't the table that hit Kitty, but Kitty, propelled by Peterson, who hit the table.

In any event, according to Hosey, Kitty was treated for nausea and dizziness. Hosey said the hospital's report noted that the police were notified. Later, the Bolingbrook police came to the Peterson house and tried to soothe his temper, according to Hosey, again apparently relying on information from the Savio family. But no formal report was ever filed, and no legal action was taken. Derek Armstrong, in his book, made no mention of this incident at all.

Still, Armstrong, acting as Peterson's amanuensis, whether willing or not, provided Peterson's side of the war with his third wife. According to Peterson, Kitty was simply too bossy, and maybe a bit mentally unstable. And later, she simply embarrassed him in front of the other Bolingbrook cops.

The problem, Peterson told Armstrong, began in the raucous pub, but eventually came home to roost.

"Peterson had just bought out the bar from Victoria," Armstrong reported, "and Kathy asked to manage it." If it's true that Peterson cashed out his second wife's interest in Suds Pub in August or so of 1995, that would mean that Thomas would have been a little over two years old, and Kristopher about one. Just why Kitty would have wanted to run a bar crammed with drunken rowdies, including the antics of the supposed "Green Felt Club," wasn't entirely clear.

Peterson's version to Armstrong was that she asked for the job, intent on proving her management skills. In any event, at least according to Peterson via Armstrong, the move was a disaster.

"You have to understand," Peterson told Armstrong, years later, "we were a close-knit family, my crew at the bar. I could leave them to do their own thing and trust them to do it. It was a fun place. Kathleen—Kathy—wanted to change all that. To make it a real business." Peterson speculated that after giving birth to Kristopher, realizing she was now the mother of two small boys, Kitty wanted to take control of the family finances, and saw the saloon as the best way to make sure of the financial future.

"She was all about the bottom line," Peterson told Armstrong. In Peterson's version to Armstrong, Kitty became too strict with the saloon's employees, including her own nephew. Of course, this might have had to do with the Montgomery police chief's unhappiness with the establishment, which could put its all-important liquor license at risk. In fact, the records show that the license was suspended on at least one occasion. But Armstrong didn't report that part.

Peterson tried to convince Armstrong that his third wife had mental problems, and that he'd tried to help her: "You don't get rid of somebody if they're sick," he said. But in the end, that's exactly what happened—damsel unrescued or at least unsuccored. By late 2001 he'd eventually retreated to the warmer embraces of the teenage Stacy Cales.

Whatever the difficulties between Peterson and Kitty, whether mental or monetary, by December of 1999, the couple decided to buy a new house. This was in a relatively new tract in Bolingbrook. On December 15 of that year, they agreed to acquire a very nice, brick-fronted dwelling at 392 Pheasant Chase Drive, agreeing to pay $277,000 for the property. The Petersons took out a $180,000 mortgage from Fleet Financial Services, which suggests that they were able to make a down payment of just less than $100,000.

The fairly large, two-story dwelling with a basement was in a nice part of Bolingbrook, just west of Weber Avenue, which was seen by many as the dividing line between the more unsavory neighborhoods of the suburb to the east, and the better areas to the west. Most of the houses west of Weber tended to be white, middle-class, relatively new in construction—an Illinois version of Orange County, California, perhaps, where old-line farm families, faced with the burdens of death and taxes, cashed in by turning their former cornfields into housing tracts. One of them, in fact, was the Charest family.

Just how Peterson managed to accumulate the cash to afford what appears to be a $100,000 down payment is another mystery, given that he seemed to be strapped for money in 1986, and was saddled with child support payments for Eric and Stephen, his by-now college-age sons from his first marriage.

Later, Peterson would claim to both Hosey and Armstrong that he'd always been "a worker." It was how he explained how enough money came in to pay the mortgages of the pub, the house in Bolingbrook, his toys—motorcycles, eventually an ultralight aircraft, a ski boat, a camper, a swimming pool, not to mention child support for four sons, as well as plenty of goodies for the fourth family he would eventually start with Stacy Cales. And there is no doubt that Peterson took in a lot of cash over the years, and in the absence of substantial federal and state tax liens, one must assume that all of it was properly accounted for.

But, as noted, bars, freelance photography, and even chimney sweeping are all cash businesses, as is, sometimes, the printing business—where what one takes in (less, perhaps, a handling fee) isn't always the same as what one pays out. It all depends on who keeps the books, or even how many sets of books there actually are.

7.
In the Basement

Later, the exact moment that the forty-seven-year-old Peterson first encountered seventeen-year-old Stacy Cales, would be unclear. Peterson had his version of the story. In this version, he'd been on night patrol with another Bolingbrook officer, who was enamored of one of the night clerks at the SpringHill Suites Hotel just off Route 55, the major southwest/northeast route into Chicago from the Joliet area. While his partner pitched his woo to the clerk, Peterson struck up an acquaintance with her own workmate, the barely nubile teenager Stacy. In his version, Peterson said they began dating in the fall of 2001, after the September 11 terrorist attacks, when Stacy was seventeen.

However, in the summer of 2000, Stacy had been living in a group home, and, if the Will County court records from that year mean anything, might also have been on some form of juvenile probation. She'd apparently left her half-sister Tina's house in the spring of 2000, according to the court records. Just what Stacy was up to in the year and a half from the spring of 2000 to September 2001 wasn't entirely clear, although it does seem possible that Stacy reunited with her half-sister a month or so later in 2000. Then, three months later, in September of 2000, Stacy had become the ward of James Maves, the Cales "family friend," who legally took over her guardianship from Tina, according to the court records.

But Stacy's activities in the summer of 2000 are hard to trace. Whether she first met Peterson after leaving Tina's house in the spring of 2000, or while in the group home that summer, or after being made the ward of James Maves in September of 2000 when she was 16—or, as Peterson insisted, a year later, in September of 2001, when she was 17—is known only to Peterson at this point.

In the absence of more definitive evidence, such as Bolingbrook police field interrogation reports, the backbone of patrol intelligence in any police department, it's always possible that Peterson might well have first contacted Stacy on the street in Bolingbrook as a patrol officer in the summer of 2000.

How she wound up in a group home for underaged girls, even if for a few months, is likewise obscure.

Peterson later told Armstrong that Stacy's ambition when he first met her was to be a dancer, which is possibly suggestive as to the milieu or at least atmosphere in which they might have first encountered one another. Or, as Armstrong reported it, Stacy had told Peterson very early on, "I want to be a stripper." But Peterson swore he would save her from that fate. "I'll take you away from all that," he reportedly told Stacy.

But the tale grows even more murky, once one hears from other sources. Sharon Bychowski, who would soon become the next-door neighbor of Stacy and Peterson (and eventually Drew Peterson's *bete noire*), formed the impression from Stacy herself that she'd first met Peterson "on the street" in Bolingbrook. Bychowski would later claim that Stacy told her half-sister Tina Kokas that she was having a sexual relationship with a policeman, Drew Peterson. Since Stacy was born in January 1984, and she apparently first left Tina's house in April or so of 2000, this suggests that she might possibly have been just over sixteen when she first met Peterson. (Tina was separating from Todd Ernest, and her own life was in a state of flux by April 2000, which was apparently one reason for Stacy's departure from the initial guardianship.)

Because the age of consent for sexual relations in Illinois is seventeen, if Stacy were sixteen, it's possible that Peterson jumped the statutory gun by more than a year. According to Bychowski, Stacy told her that Tina disapproved of Peterson—Tina thought he was a sexual predator.

Of course, it's also possible that Bychowski might have mashed together dates. Tina could have been referring to Peterson's admitted relationship with Stacy *after* September of 2001, or even after they married in late October of 2003, not one that had occurred in 2000. But as Tina is now deceased, and Stacy is missing, the only person who knows for sure is Peterson himself—after all, at the time, no one was taking detailed notes.

At some point after meeting Stacy, though, Peterson pulled strings at the Bolingbrook village office and got Stacy a part-time job. The village clerk, Carol Penning, recalled Peterson, the Bolingbrook cop she had known for some years, introducing her to Stacy, and asking if the village might have part-time work for the teenager. Penning later said she'd had no idea that Peterson had a personal relationship with the teenager at the time. Records seem to indicate that Stacy worked for Penning's office from early November 2001 to mid-December of the same year.

At some point after meeting Stacy, again according to Bychowski, Peterson began having sexual relations with her in the basement of the house at 392 Pheasant Chase Drive, while Kitty and the boys, then nine and eight, were asleep upstairs.

Hosey got this from Bychowski: According to his account in *Fatal Vows*, Stacy, after Kitty's death in 2004, had pointed out the house at 392 Pheasant Chase Drive where Peterson had previously lived with Kitty and the boys, and Stacy had told Bychowski that she and Peterson would have sex in the basement before Peterson divorced Kitty in 2002.

"So, wait," Bychowski told Hosey she'd asked Stacy, "he was bringing you here to the *house*?" Stacy said that was so: "Yes, we would go into the basement, and I would leave in the morning before Kathleen got up." Bychowski next suggested Peterson's line to Stacy while seducing her: He had told her that he and Kitty were no longer sleeping together, and only staying married for the sake of the boys, right?

"How did you know that?" Stacy asked Bychowski, at least in Bychowski's version of the story to Hosey. *That's what they all say,* Bychowski told Hosey she remembered thinking, and then telling Stacy exactly that.

In Bychowski's eyes, Stacy was naïve, and would always be that way, up until the day she vanished five years later. Still, at the time, Bychowski couldn't get over the gall of Peterson—seducing a teenaged girl in the basement of the house he shared with his wife and children, who were asleep upstairs, seemed the epitome of hubris on Peterson's part.

At some point after their basement trysts, Bychowski said Stacy told her, Peterson arranged for her to occupy an apartment in Bolingbrook, apparently rent-free: The apartment owner wanted police officers to live there, to keep crime suppressed in the complex, and offered units for free if police agreed to occupy them. (This may have been about the time that Peterson arranged for Stacy to take the part-time job with the village.) And around the same time, according to both Hosey and Armstrong, Peterson bought Stacy a Pontiac Grand Prix.

As for the trysts in the basement with a teenager, Peterson readily admitted his transgression, at least according to Hosey in *Fatal Vows*: "Just as when he was questioned about his alleged extramarital affairs while married to wives one and two," Hosey wrote, "Peterson freely admitted that he and Stacy would have sex in the basement while his unwitting third wife and boys slept upstairs."

Just when Kitty tumbled to the relationship her husband was conducting with Stacy Cales isn't entirely clear, but it probably was during the fall or winter of 2001–02. At some point in that period, according to Hosey, Kitty received the anonymous note telling her what was up. It appears that this might have been when Peterson arranged for the rent-free apartment for Stacy. From this point forward, Drew and Kitty were on a collision course, and by the time of the final impact, years later, the destruction would be awesome, and possibly even fatal.

By early 2002, it was fairly clear that Peterson was ready to terminate his marriage with Kitty. (Just why she hadn't initiated the legal proceedings herself isn't entirely clear, although it's possible that, as a Catholic, Kitty didn't believe in divorce; although also nominally Catholic, Peterson obviously did.) On March 4, 2002, Peterson obtained a loan of $220,000 from La Salle Bank to purchase another house at 6 Pheasant Chase Court, a small cul-de-sac off Pheasant Chase Drive about a quarter-mile or so away from the house he had lived in with Kitty and their two sons for the previous three years—the place with the basement. Stacy, at least, soon moved in to the new house at 6 Pheasant Chase Court.

This drove Kitty wild. It was bad enough that her husband had been having sex with a teenager in their family basement, but to see him buy another nice house in their own neighborhood a short distance away for his teenaged girlfriend, and to live there with her—that was really rubbing her face in it. To Kitty it was an awful insult. On March 11, 2002, Kitty asked for an order of protection against her estranged husband, claiming physical abuse, harassment, and stalking by Peterson. Kitty claimed that Peterson had telephoned her and threatened to come to the house at 392 Pheasant Chase Drive to "deal with" her. Her husband wanted her dead, Kitty claimed, and "if he has to, he will burn the house down just to shut me up." She claimed that Peterson had beaten her on various occasions during their marriage, and had generally terrorized her. At one point, she said, Peterson had broken through a deadbolt lock to get at her. Peterson's access to firearms, as a police officer, made her afraid for her life, she said.

Two days later, on March 13, 2002, Peterson filed for divorce—his third in just over two decades.

Peterson claimed that "the respondent," i.e., Kitty, had exhibited "extreme and emotional cruelty" to him by 1) "refusing to show plaintiff any attention or affection;"

2) "refusing to live or co-habitate with plaintiff;" 3) "refusing to speak to plaintiff regarding family matters, and remaining silent for great periods of time;" and 4) "maintaining an incompatible temperament, in that she maintained outward manifestations of insensitivity on those occasions when the plaintiff was in need of counseling and aid, reassurance or guidance, finally abandoning marital duties and the relationship."

In other words, Kitty had refused to sleep with Peterson anymore, and in fact, wouldn't even talk to him. Peterson asked for custody of the two boys, Thomas and Kris, and to rub salt in the gushing wound, he wanted Kitty to pay *him* child support, as well as temporary alimony, as if she had the wherewithal. For all practical purposes, Kitty was broke.

The house at 6 Pheasant Chase Court cleared final escrow that April, and that was when the war between Kitty and her estranged husband escalated even further.

8.

Peterson vs. Peterson

Kitty quickly reacted to her husband's divorce suit with her own countersuit against Peterson: She found a lawyer who filed an emergency petition asking for temporary sole custody of the boys, exclusive possession of the house at 392 Pheasant Chase Drive, and a restraining order against her estranged husband. She also wanted Peterson to fork over $550 every two weeks for the immediate future, at least until the court could get a grip on the family's actual financial status. Kitty agreed not to file any claim against the new house that Peterson had just bought at 6 Pheasant Chase Court, and Peterson agreed to "provide a written accounting of funds used for purchase down payment of said residence."

It was therefore clear that Kitty believed that her husband had hidden assets—money she didn't know about, but believed she, as his legal wife, was entitled to share. Perhaps significantly, Kitty's lawyer also convinced the judge "to notify Kathleen Peterson of any potential closing of Suds Pub within 14 days." From this, it appears that Kitty believed that her husband was deriving a substantial if possibly undeclared income from the saloon, and was concerned that he would try to conceal any future money from that source by "closing" the establishment, or at least declaring it closed, while finding someone to run it as a nominee. It also seems likely that Kitty believed Drew had used the pub as a means of making the down payment on the "love nest" at 6 Pheasant Chase Court, although years later, there would be no official records to support that supposition, only arguments from Kitty's lawyers.

Within the next month, tempers between Kitty and Peterson would flare up on several occasions. Despite the court order on March 22 enjoining each from "physical abuse, harassing, interfering with personal liberty and/or stalking the other party," the couple endured several nasty collisions. One occurred in early May, when Kitty claimed that Peterson had seized the family's Mercury Mountaineer, a $25,000 SUV that she had been using to take the boys to school.

A week later, Kitty's first lawyer, Brian Grady of Elmhurst, Illinois, asked the Will County court to find Peterson in contempt: Kitty claimed that Peterson had taken two days to remove his clothes and other personal effects from the house at 392 Pheasant Chase Drive, and in doing so, had damaged her own property. Kitty had thrown him out, but Peterson wanted more things from the house, Grady said. As for the SUV, Kitty claimed that she had taken the boys to communion practice at a neighborhood church, only to discover that the car had been swiped after she and the boys emerged.

Peterson had called her, Kitty swore in her complaint; "I have the car," she said he'd told her on the telephone. "Let me in the house."

Peterson wanted to get back into 392 Pheasant Chase Drive in order to pick up his waterbed, Kitty alleged. Unless he got the waterbed, she said he'd told her, she'd never see the Mountaineer again. Kitty called the Bolingbrook Police to help her reclaim the car. Peterson, under pressure, eventually relented, and Kitty got the car back.

This brouhaha occurred only two days after another court proceeding, in which Kitty was granted temporary custody of the children, exclusive if temporary possession of the house at 392 Pheasant Chase Drive, as well as alimony and child support, once more on a temporary basis. But there was more, according to the judge's order:

1) Neither party shall discuss in front of the minor
children any issues relating to this divorce, nor involve
the minors in any conflict arising from this divorce.
2) Kathleen Peterson has paid the 2001 joint federal
and state tax burden equaling approximately $11,000,
without prejudice to herself, and subject to further al-
location by the court.

It seemed as though Kitty had raided the $20,000 stashed
in their joint investment accounts to pay their taxes, which
included taxes on money over and above Drew's withholding
as a payrolled employee for the Bolingbrook police. Which
of course raised new questions: Where was the extra money
coming from, and why were the taxes unpaid?

An independent appraiser was appointed by the court to
ascertain the value of the house at 392 Pheasant Chase Drive.
And: "Both parties are enjoined from concealing, [or] destroy-
ing any personal property of the other." The court granted
Peterson five and a half hours of visitation with the boys on
Tuesday and Thursday evenings, as well as every other weekend, from 5 p.m. Friday to 7 p.m. Sunday—a fairly generous
visitation schedule, as such things went.

And there was Finding 4C: "At no time shall either party
have any unrelated person of [the] opposite sex present when
the children are present overnight."

By this point, after almost six months of conflict between
Peterson and Kitty, the Bolingbrook cops were well aware
of all the trouble that their problem officer had with his volatile third wife, as well as his besottedness with the nubile
Stacy. But as far as Kitty was concerned, the local cops were
always covering for Peterson—he was one of their own, and
he seemed to be well plugged in to the local political power
structure after so many years. The truth was, though, the local
cops were wondering what the hell was going on with their
older colleague, the former man from MANS. Domestic disputes were a staple in any suburban community, but it was
embarrassing to have to regularly treat one of their own as

one of the combatants, especially when it involved a teenage girl and a near-fifty-year-old cop, along with a mother of two pre-teenage boys.

Over the next eighteen months, the Bolingbrook police made numerous stops at either 6 Pheasant Chase Court or 392 Pheasant Chase Drive, as the battle of the Petersons ebbed and flowed. There was the combat in the courtroom, and there were the calls to the cops. There was pushing and shoving all around, and insults—Kitty of Stacy, Stacy of Kitty, and Kitty of Drew. Derek Armstrong later claimed to have documented nineteen calls to the police, ten from Kitty complaining about Peterson, nine from Peterson complaining about Kitty. Hosey reported that there were seventeen calls, but didn't break them down as to the identity of the initial complainant. Both Hosey and Armstrong agreed, however, that the bulk of the complaints were over child visitation issues. Either Peterson was late returning the boys from his twice-weekly court-authorized visitation, or Kitty was refusing to let Peterson see them.

Yuck! When two adults begin to act like third graders fighting over the crayon box—the crayons in this case being two impressionable pre-teenage boys—it can't get much worse, at least for the innocent bystanders; in other words, Thomas and Kristopher Peterson, then nine and eight years old.

9.
Follow the Money

Judging from the subsequent filings in the case of *Peterson vs. Peterson*, by the late spring of 2002, it's apparent that Kitty had become convinced that her husband was cooking the financial books—that is, he was hiding assets and income that should be part of their marriage. On June 10, 2002, Kitty was awarded a monthly payment of $2,000 from Peterson as "unallocated family support" for Kitty and the boys. By this point, Kitty had listed her minimal monthly expenses as about $3,530 a month, including the mortgage on 392 Pheasant Chase Drive. (On March 22, 2002, she told the court that the Petersons still owed a balance of $6,500 on that mortgage of $278,000. In addition, Kitty said on that date, the Petersons had $20,200 in joint bank accounts and investments. It was from this money that Kitty had paid the $11,000 income tax bill.)

Yet, on June 10, 2002, when Peterson completed an affidavit specifying his monthly income and expenses—a requirement for a divorce case in Illinois—he claimed that the estranged couple no longer owed a cent on the 392 Pheasant Chase Drive house. In other words, somehow the $6,500 Kitty had cited in March as still owed on the mortgage had been paid off.

But that wasn't all. Kitty and Drew had taken out the mortgage—actually, a first mortgage and a second, both secured by the house, in December 1999 and January 2000—in the total amount of $274,000. Yet somehow, a little over two years later, by June 2002, the entire mortgage had been retired, according to Peterson's sworn affidavit on June 10, 2002.

How was this possible? To retire more than a quarter-million-dollar debt in a little over two years would have likely required payments of almost $10,000 a month, not including interest. On the surface, it seemed incredible. Peterson, by his own affidavit, claimed that his gross monthly income from the Bolingbrook Police Department was $5,459, along with $1,000 a month in "other income from all sources," presumably meaning Suds Pub, which he and Kitty still owned, and which he valued at $410,000, and on which the Petersons still owed a mortgage of $195,000.

On paper, it doesn't seem like these numbers add up, and clearly, at the time, Kitty didn't think so either. Her lawyer, Harry C. Smith of Wheaton, Illinois, soon demanded that Peterson produce a more definitive "financial declaration" of assets, and produce answers to written questions, under oath, as to his income sources and his assets. But, Smith would later complain in a formal motion to the court, filed almost a year later, on April 10, 2003, Peterson never cooperated. It wasn't hard for Kitty to conclude that her former husband was trying to conceal something.

Years later, Peterson's criminal defense lawyer Brodsky would offer the suggestion that his client had paid this mortgage off by selling his printing business in DuPage County before he and Kitty divorced. Whether that business was really worth more than a quarter-million dollars is doubtful, and in any case, none of the records filed by Peterson in connection with his divorce from Kitty show that he had anywhere near that amount of cash after such a sale. Moreover, DuPage County records don't seem to show any such transaction. Thus the question remains: How did Peterson get the money to pay off a $274,000 mortgage just two years after its inception, by June of 2002? It's just another mystery of the Peterson tale.

Whatever this was, or if there even was anything to conceal, it wasn't something that either Hosey or Armstrong paid much attention to in either *Fatal Vows* or *Drew Peterson Exposed*. True, Hosey broadly suggested that Peterson's possible motive for murdering Kitty—the crime for which he was eventually charged—stemmed from greed: In this scenario, Peterson was supposed to have murdered his third wife in order to reclaim the equity in the 392 Pheasant Chase Drive house (which he valued at $350,000 in June of 2002, an all-cash asset if Peterson's affidavit of June 10, 2002 was accurate), to eliminate the court-ordered "unallocated" family-support payments of $2,000 a month, and to cash in on several life insurance policies on Kitty. These were all powerful possible motives, to be sure.

But at the same time, Kitty's persistence in trying to document the seemingly undeclared sources of Peterson's income from Suds Pub might well have been an even *more* powerful motive. After all, Kitty had worked in the saloon, had helped manage it, and she certainly had some idea of how Peterson had managed to reduce a $274,000 mortgage to zero in just over two years. The trick, for Kitty, was to get it on paper.

Over the next year, Kitty and her lawyers would try repeatedly to coerce Peterson to cough up financial details, to no avail. But then, it's always possible that Peterson knew as well as Kitty herself that for him to open the books might well prove literally fatal for himself, if not her. He had only to remember the death of his former brother-in-law, Gerry O'Neill, to realize that it only took an instant's doubt to make a trusted accomplice into a perceived snitch, severely ventilated by rounds from a .357 magnum, as Gerry had been in Calumet City in 1994. He knew that much from his former life as a narc. Bindy Rock could probably have told him the same. So Kitty could well have put her ex-husband in an impossible bind—the lady or the tiger.

Whatever the reality of the Peterson money, wherever it came from, by July of 2003, Peterson claimed he had sold Suds Pub. The sale had actually closed escrow at the end of October 2002, according to real estate records in Kane County, where it was soon renamed "The Dog House." Kitty had the idea her estranged husband had run off with this money, or at least used its promised sale price to buy the house at 6 Pheasant Chase Court, the salt in her open wound of pride. But by early October 2003, Kitty agreed to a "bifurcated divorce," freeing Peterson to marry Stacy in late October, a few months after she gave birth to Anthony, her first child with Peterson. Stacy was then nineteen years old. The matter of the pub, and the money, was put into abeyance, pending a later trial on the property settlement issues.

But all this was still in the future. A year before Peterson married Stacy in late October 2003, Kitty, while still legally married to Peterson, had sent a damning letter to the Will County State's Attorney's Office, complaining that her estranged husband might possibly kill her in order to remove her from his life and to get custody of their two children, as well as all the money. Reading between the lines—being open to the suppressed emotional subtext—it's fairly clear that despite the anger Kitty had for Peterson, she at some level still wished he would come home.

Although this letter was sent around the middle of November 2002, more than fifteen months before Kitty's death on or about February 29, 2004, and before Kitty herself found a new love interest, it would become Exhibit A in the murder case against Drew Peterson over five years later, when that case was finally filed in May of 2009. And eventually, a single sentence in the letter would echo from coast to coast as an accusation "from the grave," as the media as well as the prosecutor somewhat luridly described it.

10.
The Letters

In retrospect, it's difficult to evaluate the evidentiary weight of the missive dated November 14, 2002, and sent to an assistant state's attorney in Joliet, just as the divorce between Kitty and her former husband was reaching its lugubrious nadir. The letter was long; it rambled somewhat, and it was loaded with misspellings and gross grammatical errors. It was almost as if it had been written by someone who spoke English as a second language. Yet other letters written by Kitty were far better composed—much more coherent and grammatical. After all, Kitty had three years of college education, and was studying to be a nurse, so she was hardly illiterate.

It thus appears that the November 14, 2002, letter, which was to play a pivotal role in the indictment of Drew Peterson in May of 2009 (almost seven years later), was typewritten by a woman feeling enormous stress and bitterness, and possibly under the influence of drugs or alcohol. Peterson would later claim, at least to Derek Armstrong, the Canadian author, that it represented Kitty's unstable mentality, with which he had put up for years. He complained to Armstrong that his third wife's behavior in public "was embarrassing."

All of his later actions toward Kitty, Peterson would later insist to Armstrong and others, were predicated on his desire to keep her from harming herself or their children. Of course, this glossed over his trysts in the basement with his teenage paramour.

By the time she sent this damning letter to Elizabeth Fragale, an assistant state's attorney in Will County, on November 14, 2002, Kitty and Peterson had had a number of physical confrontations. It appears that sometime in the spring of 2002, after Peterson had decamped with Stacy to 6 Pheasant Chase Court, Kitty had discovered some things missing from the house at 392 Pheasant Chase Drive, and assumed that her departed husband had taken them, the better to enjoy them with his new "girlfriend," as Kitty referred to Stacy. Among these allegedly pilfered items was a video camera.

Then came several other confrontations between husband, wife, and husband's girlfriend, in which names were called, slaps were exchanged, fingers were gestured, and bad vibes emanated, much to the confusion and consternation of the two young boys of Drew and Kitty, Thomas and Kristopher.

After the spring and summer of unhappiness in 2002, Kitty addressed her November 2002 letter to Elizabeth Fragale. It is here reproduced verbatim, errors of spelling and grammar included, insofar as they are indications of her state of mind at the time she wrote the letter:

Ms. Fragale,
    On three different occasions I have tried to reach you over the phone regarding charges I filed against Drew Peterson, on the date of July 5, 2002.
    Note, I did contact the Police Department, and talked to the assistant Chief Mike Calcagno, in reference to Drew['s] Break[-]in that same weekend. I than filed a report in regards to my safety, from Drew by two officer that arrive at my residents 392 Pheasant Chase, Bolingbrook, Il, 60490.

When I found out Mr. Peterson was having an affair with a minor at the police department, he began to get very violent. By striking me with his hand and chasing me through the house with a police stick. At that time on record, I had to get an order of protection from him.

(Kitty did in fact obtain a protective order preventing her estranged husband from contacting her. But according to Hosey, she later withdrew it. Hosey asserted that the order was withdrawn after Peterson protested that it would prevent him from working as a police officer, because it prevented him from carrying a firearm.) Her letter to Fragale continued:

Their has been several times throughout my marriage with this man where I ended up at the emergency room in Bolingbrook for injuries, and I have reported this only to have the police leave my home without filing any reports.

On July 5 [2002], Mr. Peterson got into my home with a garage door opener he programmed for himself, while I was out of town with my son's. I was unaware of his presents, and was very afraid for my live. This man pop out from our living room while I was walking down stair, with a basket of laundry. I was shocked and dropped all the cloths and stood their, asking him to get out. Drew was in uniform (Swat Uniform), with his police radio in his ear. He yelled, for me to sit down and be quiet I refused and he pushed me on the stairs. He told me to move down to the third step and not to move or speak. He was very angry that in our divorce the judge ruled he would have to pay me child support. He told me he didn't want to pay me anything. (He left my boys 8 and 9, and I with many bills, up to 2,000.00 and with an 11,000.00 income tax bill, as well as 6800.00 property tax bill for us to pay. Needless to say we are without money or any credit.) He kept me in a position for a very long length or time, while trying to convince me how horrible I am, and I just need to die. He asked me several times if I was afraid , I started to panic! He pulled out a knife, that he kept around his leg and brought it to my neck. I thought I'd never see my boys again. I just told him to end this craziness and he for some reason pulled back. I didn't tell the police because I know they can't protect me from him. I know he will; be back; he's now attempting to try to make me look like the bad guy, with untrue charges of Battery against him, and his 17 yr. Girlfriend. The sick thing is I really think they're enjoying this. Over the summer they went out of their way to roller blade right in front of my home, drive by and stop for long lengths of time in front of the house. Childish things like his girl friend flipping me off if I was out in front with the kids while driving by.

At the present time my children have been in a program at school called rainbows, in efforts to repair some of the damage Drew and his girlfriend has created. One of which Drew falsely arrested me in fron[t] of my children with my face in the grass and calling me a criminal for hitting his girlfriend, which didn't happen. Instead she called me a bounce [bunch?] of inappropriate name in front of my children, so I felt it was necessary to get them back in the house away from this. When I ran to the truck, it being very high up I notices Stacy his girl friend taping me, with the stolen camera Drew took from out home. I attempted to take the camera and my next goal was to return to the home with my children. But I was thrown to the ground and treated like an outlaw, and booked and arrested for no reason. My wrist was sprained, when I was thrown to the ground and held down by Drew, who was not on duty at the time. While this was happening my children were being held against their own will, by [Stacy], while she told them to sit down and be quiet. My son's [psychologist] is working with them but states, "she can't fix what continue to happen on an on-going basis." My eight year old come home from spending 1 hour with his dad, because he really is never there, and pushes his sons and girlfriend on my son all the time, and expressed to me that he was confused. It seemed that Drews live[-]in girl friend showed both my sons her wedding dress and ring, and told them she was going to marry their father. Of course, that's okay, for Adults, but when my boys come home with tears in their eyes, still hoping for mom and dad to get back together again, it become heart breaking and very confusing to them. They don't understand how dad can get married if he's still married to their mommy. The list goes on, and I understand it's just part of it, but it need to stop. My sons and I would like to move away from this area, for our safety and sanctity. I am a full time Nursing Student and Drew left me while in the middle of the program. I don't want my career or my sons to suffer this nightmare anymore.

He knows how to manipulate the system, and his next step is to make my children away. Or Kill me instead.

I would really like to know why this man wasn't charged with unlawful entry, and attempt on my life. I am willing to take any test you want me to take to prove my innocents of charges against me, and also any lie detector test, on my statement that I filed against him. I really feel Drew is a loose cannon, he out on the streets of Bolingbrook patrolling, and just taking the law into his own hands. I haven't received help from the police here in Bolingbrook, and asking for your help now. Before it's to late. I really hope by filing this charge it might stop him from trying to hurt us.

Sincerely,
Kathleen Peterson

Kitty made a copy of her letter to Fragale and sent it to Walter Jacobson, a former anchor for Fox News in Chicago

and host of a political news talkshow. She provided a second
letter to Jacobson:

Walter Jacobson
Fox Chicago News
I have tried to reach you in effect to tell my story of
corruption in Bolingbrook and Will County. Here is a
letter to the State's Attorney in reference to another
matter that the Justice Department is over looking. My
husband is a Police Officer with Bolingbrook and has
directed all of you is employed by the Department to
do what he says. This goes from the Major to the Chief
of Police. His affair with a seventeen-year-old employee of Bolingbrook has raised some heads. It seems
everyone needs to cover this up, based on the way it
was handled. That only the beginning of looks the
other way clause. In this particular case the lack of filing police reports due to the fact that Officer Peterson
is our friend is going to destroy my sons and my life. I
would like to talk or meet with you, to explain my story.
This man is manipulating the system, to destroy mine,
and benefit his. How many times has this happen to
others?? At the present time I am a fulltime nursing
student struggling to finish my goal, but because of Officer false allegation he and his girlfriend are charging
me with Battery. This isn't your typical domestic.

My court is at Will County courthouse on November
21st room 306 9:00 am
    And January 6 1:30 2003 this is INJUSTICE in
action
    Please call . . .
    Thank-you for your time
    Kathleen Peterson

There were some interesting aspects to these November
2002 letters from Kitty. The misspellings and bad grammar
seem to indicate that they were written, first of all, in haste,

if not inconsolable bitterness; and second, in a desire to implicate her estranged husband in some sort of corruption larger than himself. But the details of the supposed bad conduct she related seem only to do with her, Stacy, and the two boys, not the cops, or crooks, or politicians—in other words, nothing an ambitious assistant prosecutor might get excited about.

If Kitty in fact had information about Drew's possible dealings with the netherworld of bikers and druggies, or crooked politicians, why didn't she spill it? She hinted at it, but didn't give up any goods. The chances are, she didn't know any real facts, but was only suspicious—whatever was going on as to his sources of extracurricular income, it appears that Drew had kept his third wife in the dark. Based on her claims in their nasty divorce, it seems as though she believed something was there, but she just couldn't get a grip on whatever it was.

As for Fragale and Jacobson, the chances are also that if both actually read the letters—assuming they weren't shortstopped by clerical personnel as the usual dross they routinely received from the aggrieved public—they likely perceived them as sour grapes from a woman scorned. True, the idea of a suburban cop bedding a teenager employed by that very same suburb seemed pretty sleazy. Also true, the allegation that Peterson had been having sex with "a minor" and had abandoned his legal wife and children to do so was an eye-opener—although, under Illinois law at the time, at seventeen, Stacy was over the statutory limit, unless a prior "protective" relationship could be proved (if, for instance, Peterson had used his authority to compel her in some fashion, say, by *not* arresting her in return for her favors).

Beyond that, however, there was Kitty's assertion that her separated husband had actually broken into her house and held a knife to her throat. *That* had to be a crime, even if running off with a seventeen-year-old wasn't.

Well, not necessarily—it all depended on who you believed. It would have been relatively easy for Fragale and Jacobson to dismiss Kitty's assertions as the overheated imagination of a woman who had been replaced by a Lolita, if indeed they'd actually read the letters. Yes, Peterson was a dirty dog—everyone knew that. It wasn't necessarily illegal. And once anyone asked, there was Peterson's side of the story: As he put it, his estranged wife had mental problems—bipolar disorder, or whatever—and when he had confronted her on various occasions, it wasn't because he was trying to intimidate her, but only because he was concerned with her capacity to take care of their children, or worried that she might do herself harm. After all, he was a cop, sworn to protect and serve.

Kitty's seeming paranoia—that Peterson would kill her someday—only seemed to bear out Peterson's contentions that his estranged wife was around the bend. In a sense, her call for help served to make sure no one listened to her. Certainly the very fact that she waited until mid-November of 2002 to send her letters undercut the credibility of her allegations against Drew. The delay from July to November made the charges seem fantastic, vindictive, and the fact that the allegations surfaced only a week before a court hearing in the divorce case had to make anyone reading them suspicious of bad faith, or at least exaggeration on Kitty's part. So they were easy to discount.

Nevertheless, when *Stacy* Peterson vanished a little more than five years later, one line from Kitty's 2002 letter to Fragale would become the mantra of the national news media, and it would be repeated over and over, as the justification for the story:

> He knows how to manipulate the system, and his next step is to take my children away. Or Kill me instead.

This single sentence would eventually become the predominant public depiction of Drew Peterson, and at the same time the justification for the news media circus that would eventually play out across the small screens of America. Quoted over and over, from the time of Stacy's disappearance in October 2007, to the time of his arrest nineteen months after that, in May 2009, it would consume Peterson's life, as well as that of his children. In the back-shadow of Halloween of 2007, it seemed as though Kitty Peterson had, five years earlier in 2002, prophesied her own death, and in a way, had also forewarned her successor, the girl she hated, Stacy.

Once Stacy Peterson was suddenly amongst the missing in the fall of 2007, this letter of Kitty's from 2002 took on a much more ominous meaning, and by the time Peterson was finally charged with Kitty's murder, there were very few people in the United States of America who hadn't heard of Kitty's claim of the murderous instincts of her estranged husband, the rogue cop. Or his alleged manipulative nature. But very few realized that the letter had been sent more than a year before her actual death. The way it was portrayed on the cable channels of Fox and CNN, it seemed like the letter was followed almost immediately by Kitty's demise, when this was hardly the case.

11.
Divorced Again

The nasty divorce between Kitty and Drew Peterson made its melancholy way through the Will County court system through the rest of 2002 and on into the next year. By the fall of 2003, Peterson had become increasingly anxious to sever the marital bonds he had shared for a decade with Kitty—Stacy had given birth to their first child, Anthony, in July of 2003, nine months after Kitty's letter to assistant state's attorney Fragale. By September of 2003, Peterson's lawyers were proposing a so-called "bifurcated" divorce, one in which Kitty would agree to the marriage's legal dissolution, while setting aside the more contentious property issues for a later trial.

Those issues were proving to be the major sticking point in the divorce. Kitty's lawyer, Harry C. Smith, kept pressing Peterson's side to cough up his financial details, but Peterson seemed to be dragging his feet. And Kitty was adamant: Her estranged husband had to account for exactly how he had been able to buy the love nest he was sharing with Stacy at 6 Pheasant Chase Court. Kitty had the idea that Peterson had somehow run off with a portion of community property, perhaps equity from the saloon, to buy the house he was now sharing with Stacy.

By April 2003, Kitty's lawyer had asked the divorce court to order Peterson to provide details of his finances, contending that beyond the bare-bones declaration of income and assets of June 10, 2002, nothing else had been provided, not the least how he had been able to buy the house at 6 Pheasant Chase Court. That was still apparently the case by July 31, 2003, when Smith demanded that the court find Peterson in contempt for failing to provide the demanded financial documents; that he be barred from testifying at any trial; that any witnesses he might call be disallowed; that all of his pleadings in the case be thrown out; and that judgment in favor of Kitty be granted. This, indeed, was the nuclear option—in effect, Peterson would be left at Kitty's mercy, because whatever defense he might have would be disallowed by virtue of his failure to comply with Smith's discovery demands.

Smith also asked that Peterson be made to pay all of Kitty's attorneys' fees, which were piling up as a result of the long delay. It's fairly clear from the court file in the case of *Peterson vs. Peterson* that Smith was focused on Blue Lightning and Suds Pub as the source of Peterson's potentially undeclared income, possibly much more than the declared (if unauditable) $1,000 a month he had claimed in his income declaration of June 10, 2002. Peterson's recalcitrance seems only to have whetted Smith's determination.

Smith's threat to lower the legal boom on Peterson seems to have produced some results. By early September of 2003, Smith was poring over documents related to Blue Lightning, the pub, and other financial information. From Smith's billing accounts, later provided to the court in support of his demand that Peterson pay his fees, it appears he still wasn't satisfied: He had listed a $200 charge for spending an hour identifying "deficiencies" in the financial accounting in early September of 2003.

More time was spent in court wrangling over the motion to bar Peterson from testifying, and, at length, it appears Smith was somewhat satisfied.

Much later, after the aborted divorce case of *Peterson vs. Peterson*, it would be asserted that on the day after her disappearance, *Stacy* Peterson was scheduled to meet with Smith to discuss her own supposed divorce of Drew Peterson. If so, it seems likely that Stacy might well have appreciated aspects of Drew Peterson's potential vulnerability as to the validity of this property settlement, possibly due to pillow-talk admissions of Drew Peterson himself in the aftermath of Kitty's death. In October of 2009, Smith was "out," according to his secretary, when asked for an interview by this author. He never returned a telephone call. Thus, what Smith finally discovered about the pub and Blue Lightning remains undisclosed, at least pending Peterson's murder trial. It is likely, of course, that Smith will be called as a witness in the murder case of *State vs. Drew Peterson*, and this might well have explained his reluctance to be interviewed. What Stacy might have disclosed to Smith in supposedly asking Smith to represent her was not initially revealed after her disappearance, although by the time Peterson was eventually charged with Kitty's murder, Stacy's conversations with Smith were seen by prosecutors as potentially vital evidence.

In any case, by late September of 2003, Peterson's lawyer, Alexander H. Beck, responded to Smith's legal exertions with a motion asking that Peterson's child support payments of $2,000 a month be reduced. "Suds Pub has been sold and the plaintiff [Peterson] is receiving fewer payments," Beck asserted to the court. In fact, real estate records from Kane County, where the pub was located, seem to show that the pub had been sold more than a year earlier.

Just how much Peterson netted from the sale of the saloon wasn't entirely clear, but based on his own June 10, 2002 estimate of its $410,000 market value, and its $195,000 debt, it seems possible that Peterson cleared around $200,000 from the sale. How much of this was split between Peterson and Kitty, or any other partners, wasn't clear either, although Smith later contended that Kitty never got a cent from the sale. The Illinois Liquor Control Commission doesn't keep records as to corporate owners, only licensees, which aren't always the same.

On October 10, 2003, the divorce court granted the "bifurcated" divorce, and also ordered Peterson to pay $15,000 in attorneys' fees to Smith. The court set a date for trial on the property issues for January of 2004. A little over a week after the 2003 divorce was granted, Peterson married Stacy Cales, then nineteen years old. Peterson was forty-nine.

The trial that was supposed to begin over the finances of the former Mr. and Mrs. Peterson in January of 2004 did not come off as scheduled. The court record isn't entirely clear as to the reason for the delay, but by this point, Peterson had replaced Beck as his lawyer with Joseph Mazzone, who practiced law in Joliet, so perhaps Mazzone needed more time to prepare. A new trial date was set for April 6, 2004.

But by then, Kitty Peterson would be dead.

Later, one of Kitty's sisters would claim that only a few days before she died, Kitty had told her that she was afraid her ex-husband would kill her "and make it look like an accident."

"Take care of the children," Kitty was supposed to have told her sister, Susan Savio Doman. Of course, Susan reported this during an interview on the television program *Good Morning America* in November of 2007, more than three years later, during the media frenzy over the disappearance of Stacy Peterson. There was no evidence that either Kitty or Susan reported Kitty's concern about Drew Peterson to the Bolingbrook Police at the time. But then, they wouldn't—by then, all of the Savios were convinced that the suburban department would do whatever it had to do to protect one of their own, Peterson. After all, hadn't Kitty suggested as much to Fragale and Jacobson, in her November 2002 letters? So it appears that the Savios had no faith back in 2003–04 that the Bolingbrook police would ever call Peterson to account.

The death of Kitty was fairly well documented—that is, within the limits of the subsequent official investigation, which by most accounts was rather cursory. It wasn't until Stacy Peterson vanished in late October of 2007 that the pieces were reassembled, and then only because suspicion had fallen on Peterson in connection with that event.

Still, for all her apprehension over the threat seemingly posed by her former husband, it appears that life was beginning to calm down a bit for Kitty by February of 2004. True, there was still the second half of the divorce case looming—the trial on the property settlement—but Harry Smith had done a fairly good job of collecting the financial details necessary to obtain an adequate decision. Then, too, Kitty had begun a new romantic relationship, with a man named Steve Maniaci, who also happened to be a longtime friend of Kitty before her marriage to Peterson. Both had once worked for a company that provided jukeboxes and pinball machines to Chicago-area taverns, according to *Herald-News* reporter Joseph Hosey. Hosey would report, in *Fatal Vows*, that an Illinois State Police investigator told him that Maniaci and Kitty were talking of marriage by February of 2004. Once the property settlement with Peterson was finished, Kitty stood to have some substantial assets.

"Drew was already skinned alive in the preliminary," Hosey quoted Kitty's sister, Anna Marie Savio Doman, as telling him after Kitty's death. (Anna Marie divorced her husband. Later, her sister Susan married the same man, according to Hosey, which is why the two Savio sisters had the same last name.) "She was going to get the majority." Kitty, Anna Marie thought, was probably going to get the 392 Pheasant Chase Drive house free and clear of any mortgage, as well as a part of Peterson's police pension. "She was going to do pretty well. She wouldn't have to work after that. But she never got it. Quite a miracle," Anna Marie told Hosey.

Anna Marie was being bitterly sarcastic, of course—the "miracle" benefited Peterson, because Kitty's death, fortuitously for him, wiped out the looming trial on the property settlement. After Kitty's death, Peterson would keep the house at 392 Pheasant Chase Drive, the entirety of his police pension, and any other assets he might have had to split with his ex-wife. And then there was, it soon appeared, a $1 million life insurance policy on Kitty. To prosecutors, later, all of this would be a motive for murder: As they saw it, Peterson was greedy and wanted it all, every last bloody cent.

12.

The Tub

In the preliminary divorce ruling of June 10, 2002, Peterson had been granted regular visitation hours with Thomas and Kris, Tuesday and Thursday evenings, and every other weekend, from 5 p.m. Friday to 7 p.m. Sunday. On Friday, February 27, 2004, Peterson arrived at the 392 Pheasant Chase Drive house to pick up the two boys. According to Peterson's account to Armstrong, Kitty seemed relaxed, happy, and even made a joke: After she answered the door, Peterson pointed out that there was a dead crow on the porch.

"Probably because *you're* here," Kitty told him, Peterson later recounted to Derek Armstrong. Peterson and the boys left for the regularly scheduled weekend visitation. Peterson had the idea that Kitty was getting ready to go on a date, he later told Armstrong. He told Armstrong Kitty was "dressed to the nines."

Back at 6 Pheasant Chase Court, a half-mile away, Peterson and the boys stayed in with Stacy, infant Anthony, and Peterson's son Steve from his first marriage, along with Steve's girlfriend. At the time, according to both Hosey and Armstrong, Stephen and his girlfriend were living at the 6 Pheasant Chase Court house with Drew, Stacy and baby Anthony. (According to Peterson's later account to Armstrong, Peterson's eldest son Eric disapproved of his father's marriage to a wife younger than he was, and thereafter limited contact with his father.)

According to Armstrong, Peterson told him that the group had spent Friday and Saturday nights eating popcorn, playing video games and table tennis, and going to see a movie at a local theater.

Meanwhile, late Saturday night or early Sunday morning, Kitty had a telephone conversation with her current paramour, Steve Maniaci. They had spent Friday evening and possibly part of Saturday together, and, again according to Armstrong, had had some sort of dispute. But late Saturday or early Sunday morning, February 29, 2004, Kitty had called Maniaci, and asked him if he wanted to come visit her at the house at 392 Pheasant Chase Drive. Maniaci, according to Armstrong, declined, saying he was tired. This was the last time anyone spoke to Kitty, as far as anyone knows.

On Sunday, Peterson and the two boys went to Shedd Aquarium in Chicago, along with, possibly, Stacy. There was evidence from Stacy, Steve Peterson, Steve Peterson's girlfriend, and the two boys, Thomas and Kristopher, that Drew Peterson was present at the 6 Pheasant Chase Court house on Sunday morning prior to the trip to Shedd Aquarium, and that he was with his two young sons all that day in Chicago.

According to Armstrong—again, from Peterson himself—Stacy accompanied the two older boys to the Aquarium with Peterson. The whereabouts of seven-month-old Anthony on this particular day weren't explained. The question of just why the teenaged mother of a still-nursing, seven-month-old infant would carry him to a potentially germicidal place like a popularly attended public aquarium seemed not to occur to either Hosey or Armstrong in their questioning of Peterson, but of course, it could have happened.

That evening, Peterson arrived at the 392 Pheasant Chase Drive house to return custody of Thomas and Kristopher to Kitty. He rang the bell, he said later, but no one answered the door. Concluding that Kitty had for some reason been delayed—perhaps off with her supposed boyfriend, Maniaci—he drove the boys back to his house at 6 Pheasant Chase Court.

The following day, Monday, March 1, 2004, Peterson

started his regular uniformed patrol shift for the Boling-brook police at about 5 p.m. According to his account to Armstrong, he had called Kitty several times Sunday night and apparently on Monday, leaving "bitchy" messages each time, tolling her for her failure to be available to reclaim her scheduled custody of Thomas and Kristopher, but was unable to reach her.

Around 7 p.m. on Monday, March 1, 2004, the uniformed Peterson pulled up in his marked police cruiser in front of the house at 392 Pheasant Chase Drive. According to the accounts reported by both Joseph Hosey and Derek Armstrong in their 2008 books, Peterson's first maneuver was not to the front door of 392 Pheasant Chase Drive, but to a nearby neighbor, the house occupied by Mary Pontarelli. Peterson asked Pontarelli if she had seen Kitty on Sunday or Monday. When Pontarelli said she had not, Peterson said he was worried about his ex-wife's welfare.

While essentially the same in their descriptions of the factual events, Armstrong and Hosey's accounts differ somewhat in that Armstrong includes quotes from Peterson as to what he said at the time, at least in Peterson's own recollection, four years later.

In his version, Armstrong has Peterson suggesting to Mary Pontarelli that she telephone Kitty, and then that she telephone Maniaci, Kitty's male friend. Peterson subsequently explained this request of Pontarelli—and to Armstrong—by saying that he and Maniaci didn't get along with each other, so he wanted Pontarelli to call.

Then, according to both Hosey and Armstrong, Peterson went to the house of a second neighbor, Steve Carcerano. While at Carcerano's house, Peterson was called by Mary Pontarelli, who, according to Peterson's account to Armstrong, told him that she thought they needed to get inside the house at 392 Pheasant Chase Drive—Maniaci had told her that he hadn't spoken to Kitty since late Saturday night. Peterson said he thought so, too, but was afraid to break in for fear that Kitty would make another complaint about him to his own department.

Shortly after 7 p.m., Peterson, Carcerano, Pontarelli, and Pontarelli's teenage son Nick returned to Kitty's house. Peterson declined to break in. Instead he called a locksmith. After some delay, the locksmith arrived, and soon had the front door open. Peterson hung back on the porch, while Carcerano, Pontarelli, and her son went inside.

According to Peterson's account, later reported by both Hosey and Armstrong, the next thing Peterson heard was shrieking from inside the house. Abandoning his on-the-porch-only posture, he ran into the house and up the stairs, where he encountered Carcerano and the two Pontarellis staring at the naked form of Kitty lying on her side in an empty bathtub. Carcerano had at first thought the pink orb in the oval tub was a beach ball. It was only when Mary Pontarelli began screaming that he realized what he was looking at. The next thing Carcerano knew, Peterson was at his side.

Both Hosey and Armstrong quoted Peterson's reaction: "Oh my God," then trying to find a pulse in the cold body. And shortly thereafter, "What am I going to tell my boys?"

Someone called the paramedics, then the Bolingbrook cops. And the Bolingbrook cops, having had two years of push-you/pull-me from their night sergeant and his estranged former wife—it was on the official record—soon realized that the better part of police procedure was to recuse themselves from this stinky situation. Conflicts of appearance, maybe even actual conflicts, were smeared all over this, with the dead ex-wife of a controversial Bolingbrook police officer lying dead in an empty bathtub in a piece of disputed real estate worth around $300,000 or more, and two years of back and forth domestic complaints, a quasi-legal seventeen-year-old girlfriend, now twenty-year-old wife, in the background; old, maybe corrupt associations with alleged mobsters and biker gangs, including a shot-dead former biker brother-in-law, as well as politicians. It was enough to make any local cop back away if they knew any of the players personally, as they all did with Drew and Kitty Peterson. So the suburban

Bolingbrook cops called in the Illinois State Police, never Peterson's biggest fans, not since the later MANS days and the fiasco with Bindy Rock.

The next day, a pathologist for Will County conducted an autopsy on Kitty's mortal remains. Peculiarly, the autopsy report asserted that the postmortem took place at 2:20 p.m. on March 1, 2004. This, of course, was five hours before Carcerano and the two Pontarellis found Kitty Peterson's body in the empty bathtub, so the reported time of the postmortem had to be in error. The sloppiness in recording the time of the autopsy by the Will County coroner only foreshadowed later doubts as to the validity of the first examination. A few years later, there would be two more autopsies, both with radically different conclusions as to the cause of death.

Still, on paper, this first autopsy would be equivocal, to say the least. That is, there were some indications of murder, and yet other indications of accidental death. Overall, there was a general failure to follow up on potential forensic leads that the autopsy provided. Some led toward murder, others toward accident.

The postmortem examination of March 2, 2004 (despite the date of the official report), was conducted by Dr. Bryan Mitchell, a pathologist under contract to Will County. Two Illinois State Police investigators, Bob Diehl and Bill Belcher, attended as observers.

Mitchell quickly discerned the cause of Kitty's death: drowning. He found water in the sinuses, as well as lung damage typically associated with drowning. Those factors, coupled with the fact that Kitty's long dark hair had been damp at the time the body was discovered, suggested that the drowning had occurred in the bathtub. The fact that the tub had been empty of water at the time of discovery suggested that the bathwater had drained out in the time between the death and the discovery, which appeared to show it had taken place many hours before.

Of rather more significance, however, was a one-inch

bloody laceration to the left rear of her scalp. In addition, there were numerous other bruises on various areas of the body, some red, indicating recent origin, other purple, which suggested somewhat older injuries. One red bruise was on the buttocks, three purple bruises were on the lower left abdomen, another purple bruise was on the left thigh, and purple bruises were on each shin. There were two fresh abrasions on the right wrist, another on the right index finger, and another red abrasion on the left elbow.

Mitchell suggested that Kitty might have slipped while getting to her feet in the tub, falling backward to crack the back of her head against the rear of the tub, knocking herself unconscious, then submersing herself insensibly in the water, thereby drowning.

He concluded: "In consideration of the circumstances surrounding her death, the available medical history, and autopsy findings, the death of this 40-year-old white female, Kathleen Savio, is ascribed to drowning.

"Comment: The laceration to posterior scalp may have been related to a fall in which she struck her head."

Mitchell did not make much of the remaining bruises, however, perhaps a curious omission. Years later, the other pathologists would point to the totality of the bruising to suggest that this was evidence that Kitty had been in a struggle and forcibly drowned. While it was true that the most significant injury, the bloody bruise on the rear of the head, could have been caused by falling backward, what explained the bruising to the lower left abdomen, both shins and the injuries to the right wrist and index finger? Those were frontal injuries, probably not the result of falling backward.

But if it was a murder, how could it have happened? And when? Kitty was alone in a locked house when discovered. For murder, someone would have had to gain access to the house, surprise Kitty, get her clothes off, get her into the bathtub, and hold her underwater. Surely Kitty would have resisted such an attack. But there was no evidence of any such resistance—no scrapings of skin under her nails, no evidence of disarray in the bedroom or other areas of the house. There was no evidence of forced entry—all the doors and windows were locked. Peterson, the most logical suspect given the marital history, had no keys to the house, because Kitty had changed all the locks after he moved out.

And as to when: because Kitty had spoken on the telephone with Steve Maniaci late Saturday night or early Sunday morning, and because she had failed to answer Peterson's knock at the front door Sunday evening, when he was returning the boys to her custody, that seemed to suggest that the death had occurred between, say, 1 a.m. Sunday morning, and 7 p.m. Sunday evening. As Peterson was at the Shedd Aquarium throughout much of the day, that further suggested that if Peterson had somehow gained entry to the house to commit murder, it had to have been in the middle of the night, sometime between 1 a.m. and 8 a.m. Of course, Peterson soon asserted that he was asleep at 6 Pheasant Chase Court during those hours, and Stacy backed him up. Thereafter, he was busy taking the boys and apparently Stacy (and infant Anthony?) to the aquarium in Chicago.

Well, there were other possibilities. It didn't have to be Peterson, of course, although a wandering burglar who left no evidence of entry and even locked up after himself seemed patently ridiculous. Or Peterson could have hired someone to do the job; doubtless he had met people capable of doing such a thing during his long, colorful career as a cop. Or perhaps there was someone else—but who?

But on balance, to Mitchell, it seemed a simple, if tragic slip-and-fall. Perhaps Kitty had been taking some sort of medication that had made her dizzy. There were various medications in the house that, when combined with alcohol, might cause someone to lose equilibrium or even pass out. But a toxicology screen showed that Kitty had no alcohol in her system, nor any commonly tested-for drugs, either pharmaceutical or recreational.

Within two weeks of Kitty's death, Peterson was back in court, this time to ask that he be granted full custody of Thomas and Kristopher, and that his family-support payments be terminated. The judge, having been presented with a copy of Kitty's death certificate dated March 11, 2004 (with the cause of death listed as still under investigation), promptly granted both requests. Next, Peterson moved to have his uncle, James B. Carroll, appointed as executor of Kitty's estate, under terms of a will Peterson produced, one that appeared to be in Peterson's own handwriting.

This document, dated March 2, 1997, essentially made husband and ex-wife the inheritors of each other, depending, of course, on who died first. The will also named Carroll as executor. The document listed the couple's assets as of that date: three life insurance policies totaling $533,000 in benefits, although $308,000 of that was mortgage insurance for Suds Pub, and since the pub had been sold, that probably was void. The document also listed real estate that the Petersons had sold in 2000 and interests in two printing businesses, one in DuPage County. The document also listed the stock in Blue Lightning Corp., which Peterson had wound up with the previous fall after the sale of the saloon.

Although some would later suggest that this will was "conveniently" produced by Peterson shortly after Kitty's death, the contents seem to accurately reflect what would have been the couple's assets back in 1997. For one thing, the will did not list the disputed house at 392 Pheasant Chase Drive. Surely if Peterson wanted to end that controversy, he would have listed that property, too, in a fake will, and would have dated it later than 1997. It appears that the main reason Peterson proffered the will to the probate court was to have his uncle recognized as Kitty's executor.

There was something a bit unseemly, though, in Peterson having his own uncle become the executor of his ex-wife's estate. After all, the estate survived Kitty, and the estate at least, through the still-unresolved divorce case, was in litigation with Peterson over the value of various assets, not the least the house, as well as the money from the sale of Suds Pub, not to mention a portion of Peterson's police pension. Whatever the eventual property settlement, some of the assets might belong to Kitty's heirs. Making his uncle the executor of the same estate that was suing him presented a possible conflict of interest—it was like having your own fan club calling the other side's plays.

And soon Carroll discovered the biggest asset in Kitty's estate—a $1 million life insurance policy that named Thomas and Kris as beneficiaries. The money, once collected from the insurance company, was soon placed into a trust for the boys' future, with Carroll the trustee. The arrangement made the Savio family, already deeply suspicious of their former brother-in-law, convinced that he was responsible for Kitty's death in order to keep all the money, all for himself.

The Illinois State Police investigation into Kitty's drowning lasted through March and into April. According to Hosey, the investigators talked to Peterson, Maniaci, Kitty's neighbors, the Bolingbrook police, and, of course, Stacy. According to Hosey, Stacy told the state police that Peterson had been with her the night that Kitty died. "She was his alibi," Hosey said an investigator told him, years later, after Stacy vanished.

13.

Inquest

A coroner's inquest into Kitty's death was convened by Will County Coroner Patrick O'Neil on May 1, 2004, to determine the manner of Kitty's death—whether accident or murder. A jury of six citizens was empaneled to hear the evidence, and render a finding as to the cause and manner of death. Peterson did not attend.

As his first witness, O'Neil called Kitty's sister Susan Savio Doman.

After having Susan provide some background details about Kitty, O'Neil asked: "Was your sister in good health?"

"Yes."

"Was she seeing a doctor for any condition that you're aware of?"

"No."

"Taking any medications that you may have been aware of?"

"No."

"When was the last time that you or someone in your family talked to Kathleen prior to her being found deceased?"

"I actually talked to her Thursday [February 26, 2004]. She called me Saturday and left a message. I believe her boyfriend spoke to her at midnight."

"Okay, and when did you learn of your sister's death, ma'am?"

"One o'clock in the morning on . . ." Here Susan seemed

momentarily confused, and suggested it had been on a Friday, but was corrected by someone from the audience, presumably her sister or brother. "Sorry," she amended, "Monday night . . . Tuesday morning."

"She was found on Monday, March first, in her residence, in her bathtub, is that what you were told?"

Susan agreed, that's when she'd found out her sister was dead.

"What were you told?"

"I was told that my sister was dead. I asked her [Susan didn't say who had told her, and O'Neil didn't ask] if her ex-husband had killed her, and she told me she didn't know. And the reason I ask that is because they haven't settled—they were divorced, but they did not settle anything, and that actually was coming up. And she was terrified that . . . [of] him, and him threatening her."

"And what was his occupation?"

"A police officer."

"In that same town?"

"Yes."

"Have you been to the residence since your sister's death?"

"Yes."

"Anything unusual, find anything unusual?"

"Yes, everything was cleaned out. Before my sister was even put in the grave, everything was cleaned out of the house, everything—pictures, everything."

"And her and her ex-husband were legally divorced at the time? He had since remarried?"

"Yes, to an eighteen-year-old."

"Is there anything else you'd like to add?"

"Yes. I just . . . it's very difficult for my family, because of my sister telling us all the time . . . that if she would die, it may look like an accident, but it wasn't. She just told me [that] last week, and she was just terrified of him. He always threatened her. He had her in the basement one time. He did many, many things to her. He wished only for her to go away. And it's just very hard for me to accept that, what happened. His reactions were a laughing matter. Cleaning everything out, getting ready to get rid of the house. It's very hard."

"They still owned the house together?"

"Yes. Actually he requested the divorce because he wanted to marry this young girl . . . he said he wanted to settle after. And the settlement was actually coming up in April . . . and what the settlement was going to be was, she was going to be getting the house, and he didn't want her to get the house. He absolutely did not want it. And she was going to get the house, sell the house, and move away."

O'Neil next called Herbert Hardy, an agent for the Illinois State Police. Hardy had been among those assigned to investigate Kitty's death, although he was not the primary investigator.

Hardy said the state police had been called in to handle the matter about midnight on March 2 by the Bolingbrook police. "In this particular case, it involved a young lady, and her husband was a sergeant on the Bolingbrook Police Department, her ex-husband," Hardy explained.

Just why the ISP put Hardy forth as their principal witness at the inquest wasn't clear from the record. He readily admitted that he'd never gone to the scene of Kitty's death, although he claimed to be familiar with the details of the subsequent investigation. (The principal investigator, it was disclosed much later, was on vacation the week O'Neil scheduled the inquest, though why O'Neil scheduled the inquest without the availability of his most important witness seemed peculiar, to say the least. It might have made more sense for O'Neil to have called someone from the Bolingbrook police, or any other ISP agents who had actually come to the scene, to get more details as to what had happened that night—for instance, any ancillary evidence as to whether the bath was voluntary or forced, such as the presence of a bathrobe or if any lights were on, or similar indications.) But O'Neil apparently was satisfied with asking Hardy to explain the circumstances. Hardy, of course, knew only what he had been told by others.

"Her ex-husband was trying to locate her in order to return the children after his visitations," he said. "He had talked to the neighbors and asked, have they seen her, and he was trying to locate her without being able to do so. Finally her ex-husband and the neighbors went to the house. Her ex-husband called a locksmith who opened the home, at which time a couple of neighbors entered the home while the ex-husband and the locksmith stayed outside.

"They entered the home, went upstairs, they found Kathleen in the master bedroom, in the bathtub. At that time, to them, she appeared to be deceased. The one lady screamed, and at that time, the ex-husband entered the house."

"Any indication [of] why they had to call a locksmith? Wouldn't the ex-husband have had a key to the residence?"

"He did not have one."

"So the locks were changed at some point?"

"They may have been. I don't know that."

"Okay. And he was there in uniform and the kids with him, or . . ."

"I don't know if he was there in uniform, or if the children were there at the time."

These were rather surprising statements from Hardy, who had just said that he was familiar with the investigation that had been conducted over the previous two months. If he was familiar with the reports of the investigation, why didn't he know that Peterson was on duty, in uniform, at the time of the discovery? And why didn't he have any idea of where Thomas and Kristopher had been? Surely he should have known they weren't in the house with Peterson, if he was actually familiar with the reports of the investigation.

"Was there any water in the tub?"

"No, there was not."

"Was the—I guess you'd call it the plunger—was that closed?"

"Yes, it was down."

"Okay. Any indication from the reports of who had last seen or spoken to her?"

"From what I gather from the reports, her boyfriend was the last one to talk to her."

At that point, it appears that Steve Maniaci was in the audience, and that someone directed O'Neil's attention to him.

"Sir," O'Neil asked, "do you believe that you were the last person that she spoke to?"

"Yeah," came the response from the unnamed member of the audience.

O'Neil turned his attention back to Hardy. "And the police had the opportunity to speak with many people, maybe to some neighbors, and [like] that? Did you head up that investigation?"

"I didn't talk to the ones who were really close to her," Hardy said, not actually answering the last question.

"Did anyone speak with—is his name Drew Peterson?"

Hardy said he thought someone from the ISP had indeed talked to Peterson, implying by his answer that he himself had not.

"And what did he relate to the department about some of his activities in the days prior to her death?"

"Well, prior to that, he had the children," Hardy said. "They got up that weekend, they went to the Shedd Aquarium, I believe it was. His—his whereabouts were totally accounted for that whole weekend."

O'Neil asked Hardy about Maniaci. "Your department had the opportunity to speak with Kathleen's boyfriend?"

"Yes, they did."

"And what did he relate to the state police?"

"He stated that he was with some friends, they had some drinks. He spoke with Kathleen on a couple of times over the weekend. She tried to get him to come over. She called him, I believe, at midnight right before that. She again tried to persuade him to come to her house. He said no, he was too tired, he was going to stay home. At which time they got into a conversation about getting married."

Here the testimony fairly shrieked for a follow-up question from O'Neil: What was said about "getting married"?

But O'Neil swerved away from this line of inquiry. "Okay,"

he said, "is your department aware of any domestic disturbances between Kathleen and Drew while they were still
married?"

"Yes, according to the reports from Bolingbrook [police
department], there were many instances of where the police
had to show up."

"Physical altercations and things?"

"I don't know if so much physical. It was more, he's late
in bringing the children, he won't leave, that kind of thing."

"Any domestic disturbances with the boyfriend?"

"None that I'm aware of."

O'Neil turned to Maniaci in the audience.

"What was your first name again, sir?" he asked.

"Steve."

"And what the family [Susan] related about the divorce,
is that what you learned, or was there another woman involved?"

"Yes, he married another young lady, which they now
have a child together."

O'Neil returned to Hardy.

"And, no water in the tub, can you explain?"

"There was no water at the tub when our agents arrived.
It must have drained out after setting for such a long period
of time."

"Okay. Was she wet?"

"Her hair was wet."

"Her hair was wet?"

"Yes."

"Any pruning of the skin at all?" O'Neil wanted to find
out if there was any physical evidence of prolonged immersion in water.

"On the fingertips," Hardy said. "I understand there was
wrinkling of the skin." This was a peculiar fact. Had Kitty's
body been underwater for any substantial period of time—
say, hours—there should have been far more pronounced
wrinkling of the skin, the so-called "washer-woman" effect
that accompanies prolonged immersion. O'Neil skipped
over this peculiarity, seeming to not understand its possible

significance—that the water had actually drained quite rapidly from the tub, which suggested a second person's presence at the time of death.

"So there was water in that tub at one time, it's believed, correct?"

"Yes."

"And there was an autopsy performed on Kathleen?"

"Yes, there was."

"Did you go to the autopsy?"

"No, I did not."

"And do you recall what the cause of death is going to be, [as] listed on her death certificate?"

"I believe it was listed as drowning."

O'Neil's tortured sense of tense—recalling something that "is going to be"—seemed to suggest that he already knew what the result of his inquest was, even before he'd completed it. He'd already issued a preliminary death certificate, on March 11, 2004, which said the cause of death was pending further investigation. Of course, the cause of death was drowning. The issue the inquest had to determine was the *manner* of drowning: accident, suicide, or murder.

"Any injury noted to the decedent?" O'Neil asked Hardy.

"Yes, she had a laceration to the back of her head."

"Okay. Any signs of a struggle noted at the scene that you're aware of?"

"No, there was not."

"And there was a little bit of blood in the tub from that laceration of the back of her head, right?"

"That's correct."

"And a toxicology report was prepared for the decedent, Kathleen Savio?"

"Yes, there was."

"Do you know what the results were?"

"All negative."

"Are you aware of perhaps any medications that she might have been taking or seeing a doctor for, for any particular condition?"

"From the reports, there was indications that she took some kind of antidepressant."

"Okay." O'Neil turned back to Maniaci. "Steve, did you ever see those medications?"

"Yeah," Maniaci said. "She also took a little anti-anxiety . . . a generic form of Xanax, also."

"Was she seeing a doctor for that condition, Steve?"

"I don't believe so."

O'Neil wrestled with this, noting that antidepressants and antianxiety medications required a doctor's prescription. But Maniaci suggested that while she had once seen a physician and had been prescribed the medications, she had simply called the pharmacy to have the prescriptions refilled, without seeing the doctor again.

"Any insurance, big insurance policies that Drew would have been able to profit by, that you're aware of?" This to Hardy.

"None that I'm aware of," Hardy said.

Someone from the audience interrupted—the record isn't clear who, but it was likely Susan Savio Doman.

"Yes, there was actually a very large—it was a hundred—Drew took out a hundred-thousand-dollar policy. She also had a one-million-dollar policy that I'm not sure if he knew that she had changed. He was the original beneficiary. She did change it to—down the road, to put her boys [as named beneficiaries, instead of Peterson]. Plus her equity in the house, which was worth a little over three hundred thousand dollars. It was paid for. But he was trying to claim the whole house on joint tenancy, which should have been hers. It was pretty much a deal that was cut between them. Yeah—so there was a lot of financial gain."

"So the boys—they stand to inherit a million dollars on a life insurance policy?"

"Well, if they get everything that she should have gotten in the divorce, probably close to one point five."

Susan tried to explain: After Kitty's death, Peterson had filed probate claims that would have given him control over everything; through the 1997 will and with his uncle, Carroll, as executor, Peterson could get access to the funds from all the insurance policies, all of the equity in the disputed house, and retain all of his pension. She'd tried to challenge all this in court, but hadn't gotten very far. All of Kitty's assets—the house, the money from the pub, the insurance, whatever equities that might have been awarded to her from the aborted divorce settlement—should be placed in a trust for Thomas and Kristopher. And most important, they should be kept out of the control of Peterson and his allies, including his uncle, and his divorce lawyer. By this point, Peterson had replaced Beck with Joseph Mazzone. Peterson wanted Mazzone to be appointed Kitty's conservator. With his uncle as the executor, and his own lawyer the conservator, Peterson might have total control of all of Kitty's assets, due to her death. That, to Susan, was a powerful motive for Peterson to kill her sister.

"What did he, right now—what does he have to gain as a result of her death?" O'Neil asked.

"He wants the whole house," Susan said, "wanted to be named executor of the assets, which means he would have controlled the one-million-dollar policy, and plus, he also took out a separate policy himself on her, the one hundred thousand [actually, two policies, as noted above]. He said he wanted to sell her house, pay his [house at 6 Pheasant Chase Court] off, and open a bar. That's what he said at the wake, anyway." To Susan Savio Doman, it was obvious: Drew Peterson had somehow drowned her sister for the money.

"You saw this insurance policy?" O'Neil seemed skeptical.

"I talked to the company. I talked to the agent."

"Did you tell the police about that policy?"

"I called and left messages. Nobody ever called me back." She named the insurance company.

O'Neil asked if anyone else from the Savio family had contacted the insurance company. They had, came the response. But again, O'Neil seemed to veer away from the obvious question: What had the insurance company, on the hook for a cool million, told them? Unasked, it went unanswered. Instead O'Neil veered back to a more preliminary issue, one he probably knew would generate a response in the negative.

To Hardy: "Were there any signs of any break-in or anything?"

"No, there was not," Hardy said.

"Any weapons discovered, blunt-force type weapons, anything found?"

"No, there was not."

"Any signs of a struggle in the residence, in other parts of the house? I know she had this laceration on the back of her head. Does it appear as though her death occurred right in the tub?"

"Yes, it did."

"Right there? Even where the laceration occurred, it would have bled if it occurred in another part of the house?"

"Yes, it would have."

"Did you find any signs of foul play during the course of your investigation?"

"No, sir, we did not," Hardy said.

After a few desultory questions from the jurors, O'Neil moved to bring the inquest to a close. He summed up:

"Toxicology report, St. Louis University Toxicology Laboratory. Subject analyzed, Kathleen Savio, is negative. A report from Dr. Bryan Mitchell, forensic pathologist employed by this office in his examination of Kathleen Savio. It's his opinion that the immediate cause of death on her death certificate be listed as drowning. In this pathological report he says, on the left occipital scallop, there is a one-inch blunt laceration associated with that wound. There is no skull fracture. It's not a life-threatening blow that was to her head. It could possibly, though, have rendered her unconscious.

"There are six—or there are seven other bruises to the decedent, all of which are old. There are no new bruises noted to the decedent.

"In consideration of the circumstances surrounding her death, the available medical history and autopsy findings, the death of this forty-year-old white female, Kathleen Savio, is ascribed to drowning . . ."

It's difficult to make anything from this inquest, other than an attempt to mollify the suspicious Savios. The very nature of the proceeding, the failure to ask obvious questions made pregnant by the testimony, seemed to suggest that Coroner O'Neil was simply going through the motions. He had, after all, the results of the autopsy, and maybe even a possible manner: not murder, but maybe medication, despite the negative toxicology results. Yes, Drew Peterson might have had a motive—money—but he also had an alibi. There was no evidence of forced entry, no evidence of any struggle, no blood anywhere else in the house. And Kitty had been known to take antidepressants and antianxiety drugs, even if the toxicology screen seemed negative. It seemed to some that O'Neil had already reached his conclusion: death by accidental drowning. Now all he needed was for his coroner's jury to rubber-stamp it, and the case could be closed.

But still, this was a rather peculiar procedure. For one thing, no one was sworn to tell the truth. No oath was administered to any witness, not even Hardy, who seemed remarkably vague about crucial details. The transcript of the proceeding doesn't identify many of those responding to O'Neil's questions, using the term "audience member," as if that was sufficient to determine who knew what or when. True, O'Neil had invoked the Illinois statute's caveat in the very beginning, intoning that the inquest was neither a criminal nor a civil proceeding. But it was still a legal proceeding, even if one that was relatively useless without sworn testimony, and with an official transcript that identified various speakers merely as an "audience member."

And there were other problems with the inquest: apparently because it was neither a criminal or civil proceeding (neither fish nor fowl, so what was it, exactly?), O'Neil had no power to compel vital witnesses such as Carcerano, or the Pontarellis, or the insurance agent referred to by Susan, or Susan's divorce lawyer Harry Smith, or Peterson himself, to say nothing of Stacy, who had provided Peterson with his alibi. That left a lot of room for inexactitude, to put it mildly.

Conducted as it was, it was hardly surprising that the Savio contingent concluded that the fix was in, or that, at the very least, no one was taking their suspicions very seriously. Hadn't Kitty always said that her ex-husband knew "how to manipulate the system"?

14.
Money, Money

As expected, the coroner's jury soon came back with a verdict sustaining Dr. Mitchell's opinion, death by accidental drowning, and the final death certificate was signed that same day. This did not end the conflict between the Savios and their former in-law, however. As Susan Doman had told the jury, she and her siblings were attempting to derail Peterson's access to the money he stood to receive, now that the divorce case was moot. This primarily meant Kitty's share of the equity in the paid-for house at 392 Pheasant Chase Drive, possibly part of Peterson's pension, any proceeds from the still-unaccounted-for (at least it had been to Kitty) sale of the pub, and any money Peterson had used to buy the house he had with Stacy. In addition, there was the million-dollar life insurance policy that listed Thomas and Kristopher as beneficiaries. The 1997 will that made Peterson's uncle James Carroll Kitty's executor was viewed with deep suspicion by the Savios. While the million—paid out in two equal checks of $504,820 to Drew Peterson as "guardian of the estate" of Thomas and Kristopher even before the inquest, on April 23, 2004—was for the benefit of the boys, it had to pass through Drew's hands first, and the Savios came to believe that some of it, perhaps even most of it, might stick there.

But the million-dollar payout wasn't part of the probate of Kathleen's estate. Because the Savios disputed the independence of Peterson's uncle as Kitty's executor, the probate court appointed the Will County Public Administrator, Richard Kavanaugh, as an independent administrator. Kavanaugh soon met with Kitty's divorce lawyer, Harry Smith, to find out what issues remained to be resolved from the aborted divorce case.

These issues, according to Smith, concerned the division of the value of the 392 Pheasant Chase Drive house, the pension, and most contentiously, the proceeds from the sale of Suds Pub. Kitty believed, before her death, and Smith was inclined to agree, that Peterson had pocketed all the proceeds from the sale of the pub—probably around $200,000—for himself. Kitty had believed that in return, Drew should forfeit his portion of the equity in the house, and probably a little more, just to even things out.

Kavanaugh, thus enlightened by Smith as to the state of contention just before Kitty's death, delayed filing a final report on the assets and liabilities of Kitty's estate until these matters could be resolved. In Kavanaugh's mind, any money owed to Kitty from the divorce had to pass to Thomas and Kristopher, not Drew. But, said Drew's lawyers, Drew was the boys' guardian, and as such, he should be responsible for safeguarding the funds. Kavanaugh thought the boys needed an independent guardian.

The stalemate over the proceeds from the sale of the 392 Pheasant Chase Drive house continued through the summer and into the fall of 2004. The house was finally sold for about $287,000 in October 2004. Still Kavanaugh declined to release the funds, a position he maintained throughout 2005. Finally, in February of 2006, apparently at the insistence of the probate court, prodded by Carroll, Kavanaugh filed his "first and final" report on the assets and liabilities of Kitty's estate.

After listing the amounts he had received on Kitty's behalf—mostly tax and utility refunds and minor bills—Kavanaugh recapped the issues involved in the contentious divorce case that made the probate so complicated:

Kathleen (Savio) Peterson was represented by Attorney Harry Smith of the firm of Rice & Smith, Ltd., while Drew Peterson was represented first by Attorney Alex Beck and subsequently by Attorney Joseph Mazzone.

After my appointment as Administrator, I conferred with Attorney Harry Smith with respect to the status of the property settlement portion of the divorce proceeding, and also attended several status hearings before Judge [Susan] O'Leary. Attorney Smith continued to represent the Estate of Kathleen (Savio) Peterson in the divorce proceedings.

Attorney Smith advised me that there were three (3) major issues with respect to the division of property, vz.: (1) whether Kathleen's estate would be entitled to any portion of Drew Peterson's pension; (2) the valuation of the business known as the Blue Lightning Corporation, which had been sold with all the proceeds going to Drew Peterson; and (3) the value of the house, and whether Kathleen (Savio) Peterson's estate would be entitled to receive not only her one-half of the proceeds from any sale, but an additional portion of the remaining one-half as an offset for the cash taken by Drew Peterson from the sale of the business.

Attorney Smith further advised me that it was his opinion that after a full and complete hearing on the property settlement, the estate of Kathleen (Savio) Peterson would be awarded: (1) Kathleen's one-half of the proceeds from the sale of the residence; and (2) most, if not all, of Drew Peterson's one-half of the proceeds from the sale of the residence as an offset for the business sale proceeds retained by Drew Peterson.

On March 23, 2005, after a hearing, Judge Lechwar entered an order admitting the Last Will and Testament of Kathleen Peterson to probate and appointing James Carroll, the uncle of Drew Peterson, as executor of the estate of Kathleen (Savio) Peterson. The new representative immediately fired Harry Smith as attorney for the estate of Kathleen (Savio) Peterson in the divorce proceeding.

Sixteen days later, on April 8, 2005, a "Judgment for Dissolution of Marriage" was entered in case 02 D 420 by Judge Michael Powers "upon the agreement of the parties as to all issues." The judgment awarded Drew Peterson not only the business known as the Blue Lightning Corporation, but also all the proceeds from the sale of the marital home, and further provided that Drew Peterson would not be obligated to fund any college expenses for the minor children of the parties due to the fact that life insurance on the life of Kathleen in the amount of $1,000,000 had been payable to the children. A copy of the judgment is attached hereto as Exhibit "A."

The Estate was represented by the Executor, James Carroll, who appeared pro se. No one appeared for the residuary beneficiaries of the estate, who were the two minor children of the decedent, Kathleen (Savio) Peterson, and the two step-children of the decedent [Eric and Stephen, adults from Drew Peterson's first marriage, named as beneficiaries in the 1997 will]. The effect of the judgment was to transfer anywhere from $144,117.65 to $288,235.31 (one-half to all of the proceeds from the home sale) from the four children who were the beneficiaries of the estate of Kathleen (Savio) Peterson to Drew Peterson, the former husband of the decedent and the father of the four children. The actions of the Executor were not in the best interest of the Estate or its beneficiaries.

Kavanaugh's "first and final report" was approved by Will County Judge Herman Haase on February 15, 2006. Despite Kavanaugh's concerns about the potential conflict of interest between Carroll and the estate, the money from the sale of the house was soon released.

So there it was: Peterson would get all the money from

the sale of the house, retain his full police pension, and keep the proceeds from the sale of the saloon. In dollars and in every other sense, it was win-win-win for Drew: the money, the new young wife, the end of a contentious marriage. No wonder Anna Marie Savio Doman so sarcastically described the death of her sister as "quite a miracle"—for Peterson, that is.

Stacy and Drew

15.
At Home With Stacy

While this battle over the probate of Kitty's estate was unfolding, Stacy had given birth to a second child, daughter Lacy, in January of 2005. Thomas and Kristopher moved in at 6 Pheasant Chase Court, and apart from the continued enmity from the Savio clan, the Peterson family, Version 4, settled into a form of what could pass for domestic tranquility under such circumstances. (Peterson's oldest son, Eric, however, continued to absent himself from family gatherings.)

During this time, Stacy made a close friend of her next-door neighbor, Sharon Bychowski. Sharon, married and the mother of adult children, was a regional sales supervisor for Avon. She took particular delight in the way Stacy doted on her two babies, and in how she dealt lovingly with Thomas and Kris. As far as Bychowski could see, Stacy was born to be a mother, and was devoted to her family. And under Bychowski's influence, Stacy began to mature quite rapidly.

"She went, in the short time I was with her, from dressing in junior sizes to dressing elegantly and changing the way she looked," Bychowski told Hosey, later. "She really, I feel, in three and a half years, she went from dressing like a kid to dressing like a mom."

According to Hosey, Bychowski first met Stacy in April 2004, when Stacy came next door to introduce herself. This was, of course, a little over a month after Kitty's death. Bychowski told Hosey that she first met Drew Peterson a few weeks after that. Talking with Stacy over the fence that separated their properties one day, Bychowski saw Stacy's husband approach.

"You know," he said, according to Bychowski, "my last wife died."

Nonplussed by the remark, Bychowski actually laughed, she told Hosey.

"I'm like, 'Okay, are you serious?' And he goes, 'Oh, yeah, yeah. It was ruled an accident. That was close.'"

This seems to be typical Peterson humor—implying he might have been arrested for murder, ha ha!—as a means of shocking his audience. Stacy seemed to take it in stride, however; she invited Bychowski to go look at the house at 392 Pheasant Chase Drive. This was at the time that Stacy and Drew were cleaning the place out, complained of the following month by Susan Savio. It was while looking at the house that Stacy told her of the basement trysts of late 2001.

It appears from Bychowski's account to Hosey that Sharon began to think of herself as something of a mentor for Stacy, a guide from the ways of teenage nymph to adult. According to Bychowski, they often visited each other's homes, and Sharon often babysat the children while Stacy was out. Over the years between 2004 and 2007, Stacy frequently confided in her, Bychowski told Hosey, including the problems that came with marrying a much older man.

Bychowski came to believe that Stacy's devotion to motherhood and her family circle was the inevitable result of her own chaotic family history—parents with drug and alcohol problems, punctuated by periodic disappearances of either her mother or father, or both. Bychowski told Hosey of once riding in a car with Stacy. Stacy pointed out a neighborhood where she had once lived as a teenager with her brother Yelton and sister Cassandra—unsupervised by any adult. This was probably around the time in 1997 when Anthony Cales had signed the paper granting guardianship of Stacy to Tina and her then-fiancé, Todd Ernest.

By most accounts, Tina was probably the most stable force in Stacy's life just before and during her relationship with Drew Peterson. Tina had had her own share of domestic difficulties, but she seems to have been fairly level-headed, at least compared to Yelton and Cassandra. Yelton was in and out of jail, once on a sexual assault charge involving a minor, according to Hosey, while Cassandra tended to be emotional and combative, or so Bychowski thought. In contrast, Stacy seemed like a paragon of stability, whose anchor was Tina. Tina did not like Drew, according to Bychowski, and thought him to be a sexual predator for his seduction of her younger half-sister.

That there were conflicts between Stacy and Drew seemed obvious to Bychowski, she told Hosey later. Sometimes the conflicts were violent—she could hear raised voices, and occasionally sounds of physical confrontation.

"When I first moved here," she told Hosey, "they were more physical. But, see, she would hit him back. So stuff started breaking in the house. Then he realized, *She's going to hit me back and it's going to spin out of control.* Then he started following her."

This was almost a non-sequitur, but what Bychowski meant was that—in her opinion—when Peterson realized that he couldn't control Stacy by physically manhandling her, he substituted that form of control for keeping her under observation, even while he was supposed to be at work. Sometimes he would trail Stacy to the shopping mall, or the supermarket, according to Bychowski. At other times he would call her on his cell phone to determine where she was and who she was with.

In contrast to the well-documented dust-ups between Peterson and Kitty, there were no reports of police coming to 6 Pheasant Chase Court to separate Peterson and Stacy. Bychowski never reported any conflicts at the time—neighbors usually don't, unless the domestic disputes turn exceptionally hair-raising.

"I mean, that's not my place," Bychowski told Hosey. "[She] was willing to sort everything out herself."

In interviews with Hosey after Stacy's disappearance, Peterson denied ever striking or assaulting Stacy. As with

Kitty, he claimed that the physical confrontations all came from Stacy—it was Stacy attacking him, he said, then him attempting to calm her down.

Of course, Hosey was interviewing Sharon Bychowski in 2008, after Stacy's disappearance, and after relations between Drew and the Bychowskis had thoroughly ruptured, as we shall see. So there is a chance that Bychowski's recollection of the marital discord between Stacy and Peterson could have been selective.

That there were some happy times between the Petersons seems fairly clear, at least in the version of the marriage Peterson provided to Armstrong. In this version, Peterson told of taking Stacy on various vacations: Disney World in Florida, Puerto Vallarta in Mexico, Arizona, California. Then there were the toys: his and hers motorcycles, an ultralight aircraft for Drew, a camper, a gun collection. On top of this came several expensive cosmetic surgeries for Stacy: breast augmentation, corrective eye surgery, liposuction, and just before she vanished, a tummy tuck. These changes were sought by Stacy herself, according to Hosey, quoting Bychowski.

In Hosey's assessment—based on interviews with Bychowski and members of Stacy's family—there seemed to be two main areas of contention between Peterson and his fourth wife. One was money: Bychowski recalled that Peterson frequently complained about Stacy's spending. The other seemed to be sexual jealousy. Stacy, some thought, seemed to be a natural flirt, comfortable with double entendres, or suggestive remarks, even if innocent. But if she paid much attention to another man, Peterson was unhappy. At some point, in fact, Peterson convinced himself that Stacy was having affairs behind his back, although one would wonder how she found the time while taking care of four children, having repeated cosmetic surgery, and then, later, enrolling at a nearby junior college for nursing studies, so an affair seems unlikely. But Bychowski recalled, to Hosey, Peterson making repeated calls to her own telephone, trying to enlist her in checking up on his young wife's whereabouts.

By most accounts, however rocky the marriage might have been before, it began to deteriorate even further after Stacy's half-sister Tina died of cancer in September of 2006. According to Hosey, Peterson told him that Stacy went into a period of prolonged depression. He told Hosey later that the marriage became "an emotional roller coaster." This seemed to echo what Peterson had said about Kitty, however.

Probably one breaking point in the marriage came at Tina's funeral service, according to Bychowski. Bychowski told Hosey that the day after the funeral, Stacy had come over to talk to her.

It wasn't just that she had lost her big sister, Stacy told Bychowski; she'd had a big fight with Drew. As Bychowski recounted the story to Hosey, Stacy had told her that at the end of the service, she and Tina's husband had stayed after, standing around Tina's casket to say good-bye. After some minutes, they walked out together. That was when Peterson asked Stacy if she was having sex with Tina's husband.

"My God," Bychowski told Hosey, "she was absolutely devastated by that." Stacy, according to Bychowski, was utterly appalled at Peterson's insensitivity. The argument between husband and wife went on into the middle of the night.

That was when, Bychowski said, Stacy first began talking about divorce.

One interesting contrast between Peterson's first three marriages and his fourth had to do with Peterson's own self-admitted penchant for extramarital skirt-chasing. Despite convincing Armstrong, and to a lesser extent, Hosey, that he was a lothario extraordinaire during his first three marriages, Peterson seemed to downplay this aspect of his character in his interviews with them as to his marriage with Stacy. Whether this was because his libido had finally begun to ebb—he was, by the time of Stacy's disappearance, fifty-three years old—or if he thought discretion demanded a profession of fidelity in the wake of Stacy's disappearance, in order to avoid still more negative publicity, he made no boasts to either Armstrong or Hosey of his seductive prowess while married to Stacy. In other words, Peterson made no claims to having another woman on the side.

But it seems very clear that Stacy was talking openly of divorcing Peterson as late as October 2007. "She told me when I was there," Stacy's aunt, Candace Aiken, later told Hosey, "she was trying to find a way to get out and take the children." Stacy was thinking of moving to California or Arizona, Aiken told Hosey, without Drew.

Aiken said Stacy also told her, just before her disappearance, that she wanted to take not only her own two children, Anthony and Lacy, but also Kitty's two sons, Thomas and Kristopher. Such a development was highly unlikely, given the lack of legal or blood relationship between Stacy and the two boys, not to mention Drew's indirect control over the boys' million-dollar trust fund. Somehow, Drew was just going to let her walk away, and with the two golden ganders?

But of course, there *was* a way to make this happen: What if Stacy were to recant her story from 2004, and accuse her husband of having murdered the boys' mother, Kitty? After all, it had been Stacy who provided Drew with his crucial alibi for the time of Kitty's death. If she were to change her story—if she were to say she didn't really know where Drew was that night, and if Drew was then arrested and convicted of Kitty's murder—would Stacy then become the boys' guardian in his place? Would the boys' million-dollar trust fund help finance Stacy's way out of her marriage?

And here we come to the central conundrum of Stacy: If she knew that Drew had not really been with her the night Kitty died, why didn't she tell anyone? Why keep it a secret for so long? Why keep it a secret, even after she supposedly told Bychowski that if anything bad happened to her, Drew would be responsible? And most important, given this speculation as to her potential motivation—the boys and the trust fund—was it even true? Was it a possible attempt at extortion on Stacy's part? Had Peterson met his manipulative match in his twenty-three-year-old wife?

And if so, was he driven to desperate measures, no matter

what had really happened in the early morning hours of March 1, 2004, when Kitty had drowned in her bathtub? Suppose Peterson hadn't drowned Kitty—what would happen if Stacy *said* he did?

"She would just constantly say to me, 'If I'm missing, it's not an accident,'" Bychowski told Hosey in 2008, in a way echoing Kitty's own voice from the year before her death. "'He killed me.' She would say it to me all the time. Many, many, many times."

Then, of course, Stacy did go missing.

16.
Vanishing Act

Reconstructing what happened on the day Stacy disappeared is an exercise in frustration. Oh, there were witnesses—plenty of witnesses, probably altogether *too* many witnesses. Unfortunately, none of them saw what happened. They could only provide evidence of what they *didn't* see—Stacy. Worse, from an investigator's point of view, most of this anecdotal evidence popped up after the fact, usually in the midst of on-camera interviews by Fox, NBC, CNN, the newspapers, and other media outlets that were by then howling down the trail, hot after Peterson's gold-badged carcass. Much of it was contradictory, and often self-serving. Some people even took money to tell their tale. Sorting out the sheep from the goats, the bit players from the main actors, the hams from the filet mignon—that is, those who really knew anything—soon became a nightmare.

By all accounts, the mystery began sometime after 4 a.m., Sunday morning, October 28, 2007, when Peterson got back to 6 Pheasant Chase Court after his night shift at the police department. According to him, he got into bed next to Stacy. Then, according to Peterson's account to Armstrong, Stacy awakened. He said she told him she intended to visit her grandfather the following morning. "'Kay," Peterson told Armstrong he'd said, and then fell asleep.

The next thing he knew, Peterson told Armstrong, was

little Anthony coming into the bedroom to wake him up, saying he was hungry. Lacy came into the room, too, and Peterson told them to find their mother to get them breakfast. That was when Anthony told him Stacy was not there, according to Armstrong's version, from Peterson himself.

At this point, the information reported by Armstrong veers away from that reported by Hosey. For instance, Armstrong reported that Peterson told him that Stacy had said she would go to her grandfather's house that day, and was gone when he woke up. But Hosey said Peterson told *him* that when he woke up about 9 a.m., he thought Stacy was still home, although he didn't see her. While Armstrong said Peterson told him he remembered Stacy saying she intended to visit her grandfather, Hosey said Peterson told him Stacy had said she was going to help a friend of her sister Cassandra's, Bruce Zidarich, paint a house that had been rented by her brother Yelton in nearby Yorkville.

Arggh! The two stories seem to be in conflict, unless they're both true: In the early morning darkness, Stacy told Peterson that she was going to visit her grandfather, and at nine in the morning, she told Peterson that she was going to help Zidarich paint Yelton's house. On the surface, it seems like Peterson told two different versions. To complicate matters, Peterson later told *People* magazine that he recalled actually talking to Stacy face-to-face around 9 a.m. "I went back to sleep," he told the magazine, "and when I woke up, she was gone." What Peterson initially told the later professional investigators from the Illinois State Police about Sunday morning—whether he saw his wife or not—wasn't disclosed.

From then on, things become even more confusing. Bruce Zidarich later claimed that he had spoken to Stacy around 10:10 a.m. According to Zidarich, he sent and received several text messages to and from Stacy's cell phone around 10, and then she called him back—in person—about ten minutes later. According to Zidarich, she said that she was still in bed, but that she still intended to meet Cassandra, with the children, and paint the house that day. It appears, from phone records, that this call lasted a little over fifteen minutes, a rather long time. Where Peterson was during this isn't entirely clear, but if Stacy indeed was still in bed, the conversation apparently occurred while Peterson was still asleep by her side, completely oblivious, an hour after Anthony and Lacy had supposedly first awakened him, when he was alone, and at a time when little Anthony had said Stacy was already gone. From this, though, one has to conclude that either Stacy returned to the marital bed, or that she wasn't really in the house at 10:10 a.m., when she called Zidarich back.

Here, an analysis of the origin of these cell phone texts and the call from Stacy's cell phone—that is, which relaying tower was used—should be considered potentially critical evidence as to Stacy's whereabouts just before her disappearance. Another alternative is that Peterson was lying when he told Armstrong that Anthony had told him that Stacy had already left the house around 9 a.m. Indeed, she might have been dead at his own hands shortly after 10:30 a.m., and the story Peterson later provided to both Armstrong and Hosey might have been nothing more than a cover-up. After all, by the time Hosey and Armstrong got into the mystery, in 2008, Peterson had had many weeks to think over his story, and find ways to cover its potential holes. As noted, the whole thing is confusing.

That morning of October 28, according to Zidarich, Cassandra never called him to confirm the painting rendezvous with Stacy, and he heard nothing further from either sister. Around 4 p.m., Zidarich sent another text message to Stacy, suggesting that they put off the painting project until the next day, Monday, October 29. Zidarich said he received no reply to this message.

Meanwhile, Sharon Bychowski left her house to go to the store at about 9:30 a.m. As she left, she noticed both Drew's SUV and Stacy's Grand Prix parked in the Peterson driveway. When she came back, just before noon, the Grand Prix was gone.

Peterson later claimed to a variety of people that he woke

up (again?) at about eleven, and found that Stacy had already left the house.

Now matters became even more confusing. Despite supposedly noticing that Stacy's car was gone from the driveway, just after getting home Bychowski called the Peterson residence wanting either to speak to Stacy, or find out where she was. It isn't entirely clear which, although the difference is important. Kristopher answered the telephone, according to Bychowski, and put Peterson on the line. Peterson told Bychowski that Stacy had left to visit her grandfather. Just why Bychowski would ask to talk to Stacy after noticing that her car was gone wasn't clear—perhaps she had concluded that Peterson was using the Grand Prix instead of Stacy. And why would Peterson tell Bychowski that Stacy had gone to visit her grandfather, when he supposedly thought she was going to help paint Yelton's rental house, according to what he later told Hosey? The entire morning at the Peterson house is fraught with contradictions. In some ways, it has the earmarks of an accomplished liar making things up on the fly, perhaps the way a veteran undercover officer might dance between explanations to maintain his cover. This sort of dissimulation works in the field, when the viability of a lie might need to have the lifetime of a few minutes or possibly a few hours before a bust. It doesn't work so well, however, when the auditors turn out to be lawyers bent on prosecuting someone for murder.

"Drew picked up the phone," Bychowski later told Hosey, "and said, 'Hey, Shar-on'—that's what Lacy called me—'what's up?' And I said, 'Where's Stace?' 'Oh, she went to her grandpa's to run some errands,'" Bychowski said Peterson told her. So here was another statement that seemed to contradict the house-painting yarn, and this just before noon on October 28.

An hour later, Peterson brought the children over to Bychowski's house, then left a few minutes later, saying he had to run "an errand." The errand couldn't have been too far away or time-consuming, because according to Bychowski, he came back fifteen minutes later. He then returned with the kids to his own house, according to Bychowski.

That same afternoon, according to her own version of the events, Cassandra called Stacy's cell phone, but it seemed to be turned off. So she called the landline to the Peterson house, and Kristopher answered. He told Cassandra that Stacy had gone to her grandfather's house. Cassandra said she accepted this at first, but then began to wonder. She called her grandfather's number, but no one answered. She checked around, and discovered that her aunt Candace in California had talked to her father (Cassandra and Stacy's grandfather) three times that day, and that Stacy had never been there, and had never arranged for a visit. Stacy and Cassandra's grandfather lived in a retirement home, which meant that visitor arrivals were logged in. There was no record of Stacy's visit.

At that point, Cassandra began to get worried about her sister. She thought Peterson had made up the story about their grandpa, not knowing about the painting project at Yelton's house, which of course suggests he later lied to Hosey—that he'd added that detail later to conform his story with that of Cassandra and Zidarich.

Lying is probably the first red flag for any homicide investigator, and these contradictions would later fuel the deepest suspicion about Drew Peterson by law enforcement officials, as well as the public at large.

Peterson had been scheduled to work that night, beginning at 5 p.m., but at about two he called the police station and begged off, saying he was taking sick time. Around seven, Cassandra called Zidarich, saying she hadn't been able to reach Stacy all day, and asking him whether he'd heard from her. Zidarich told Cassandra he'd talked to Stacy that morning, and that he'd sent a text message to her around four, but that he hadn't heard anything back.

Peterson later said he'd tried Stacy's cell phone around eight that night, leaving a message. In this message, he later said, he apologized for bothering Stacy—if she was on a "date." If indeed he left such a message—only a trial would tell—to some it seemed he was only attempting to plant an alibi on Stacy's cell phone, and raise the specter of an alternative suspect, Stacy's supposed "date." An hour later, he said, he got a call back from Stacy. Actually, the telephone records seemed to show there were *three* calls from Stacy's cell phone to Drew. The first two lasted one minute each, and the third lasted five minutes. (The origin of these calls, as reflected from the cell phone towers that relayed them, would be potential evidence of the truth or falsity of Peterson's story.) This was when, Peterson claimed, Stacy told him she was leaving him.

Oh, by the way, Stacy supposedly told him, *I left my car at the airport,* apparently Clow Airport, whose parking lot was about a half-mile north of 6 Pheasant Chase Court.

An hour or so later that same night, Sunday, October 28, Cassandra drove to the Peterson house from her own residence in nearby Downers Grove. She wanted to confront Peterson. The fact was, Cassandra no longer got along with her brother-in-law Drew, and she was suspicious of him, especially now that her sister had seemingly fallen off the face of the earth. She thought Drew Peterson capable of anything, even murder. What Stacy had told Cassandra about Kitty Savio Peterson isn't clear, although as the law stood in 2007, it wasn't admissible against Peterson, although that would change, as will be seen.

Cassandra arrived at the Peterson house in Bolingbrook at about 11 that night to see what was up. She later said that the Friday before, Stacy had confided to her that she was afraid for her life, and that she would call her on Sunday when she got up, but never did. So Cassandra was already worried, not having heard from Stacy all day. When she arrived at 6 Pheasant Chase Court, she noticed that neither Drew's Denali SUV or Stacy's Grand Prix were in the driveway. She rang the doorbell, and Kristopher opened the door. When Cassandra asked Kris where Drew and Stacy were, she said later, Kris told her that Stacy and Drew had had a fight earlier that day, that Stacy had left, and that Drew was then out searching for her.

Cassandra soon left the house. She got into her own car,

drove a few blocks, parked in a mall parking lot, and called Peterson on her cell phone. He answered. Cassandra said she asked him where Stacy was, and Peterson told her that Stacy had telephoned him at around nine that night to tell him that she was leaving him for someone else. When she asked him where *he* was at that minute, Cassandra said later, Peterson told her he was at home. Cassandra felt that couldn't be true—she was nearby, and Peterson couldn't possibly have gotten home before she made the call. Besides, Cassandra thought she could hear the sound of Peterson breathing hard and inserting the keys into an automobile ignition during the call.

At that point, Cassandra drove to the Downers Grove Police Department to report her sister Stacy missing. The Downers Grove department, where Cassandra lived, told her they couldn't take the report, and that it had to be made to the Bolingbrook department. So Cassandra drove on to the Bolingbrook department, arriving a little after midnight, where she again reported Stacy missing. A bit after that, the Bolingbrook police called Peterson to find out what was going on. Peterson told his department that Stacy had left him for another man, someone he did not know.

The Bolingbrook police wanted to know which of the two cars Stacy might be driving, so they suggested that Cassandra drive back to the Peterson house to see which car, if any, was in the driveway. When she returned to 6 Pheasant Chase Court, she saw that *both* cars were in the driveway. In other words, Stacy's Grand Prix had come home.

At that point, Cassandra was probably mystified: Only a few hours before, Peterson had told her that Stacy had left him for another man, and had left the Grand Prix somewhere in Bolingbrook for him to find. Now, around 2:30 a.m. on October 29, both cars were in the driveway. It appears that Cassandra then called her friend Bruce Zidarich, and induced him to call Peterson. Zidarich apparently asked Peterson if Stacy had returned, and Peterson said no—she'd told him that she'd left the Grand Prix at the nearby airport. He'd gone over there to pick it up and bring it back to 6 Pheasant Chase Court, Peterson told Zidarich.

By this point, Cassandra was convinced that something sinister had befallen Stacy. She drove to the Illinois State Police barracks in Lockport to make still another missing person report.

The next morning, Cassandra and her father, Anthony Cales, met with Bolingbrook Police Chief Ray McGury. It was obvious to McGury that Cassandra and her father had no faith in his department. "It was a bitter pill," he said later. McGury had inherited Peterson—he'd only been chief in Bolingbrook since 2005, more than a year after Kitty Savio Peterson had died in her bathtub. He was no great enthusiast of Peterson by any means, but civil service rules made it hard to get rid of him. And then, of course, there were the politics to consider . . . McGury's own tenure as chief was still early; he was still feeling his way into the community. He understood that Cassandra and her father had come to believe that Peterson held, through covert political connections in Bolingbrook, virtual control over the department that employed him. McGury realized that, under the circumstances, the wisest course was to hand the investigation into Stacy's disappearance off to the Illinois State Police.

17.

In the News

By noon on Monday, October 29, the investigation into Stacy's disappearance was just getting started. Looming over everything was the ghost of Kitty. A little less than three years earlier, Kitty's death in the bathtub had been ruled an accident, fortuitous though it was to the fortunes of Drew Peterson. Now, another wife of Peterson's was potentially in harm's way. Fool me once, the saying goes, shame on you; fool me twice, shame on me. The Illinois State Police did not want to get shamed on this one.

In her subsequent account to Hosey, recounted in *Fatal Vows*, Bychowski answered her doorbell around 8:30 Monday morning and found Peterson on the doorstep. Bychowski told Hosey that Peterson took her by the arm and dragged her over to his own house next door. Once there, Peterson explained, as Bychowski said later.

"He says, 'She left me,'" Bychowski told Hosey. "I go, 'Yeah.'" Bychowski told Hosey she wasn't surprised to hear this from Peterson, given Stacy's earlier talk about divorce. "I said, 'Where are the kids?' And he says, 'They're upstairs.'"

That was when Bychowski first thought there was something terribly wrong. In her mind, there simply wasn't any way that Stacy would have walked out on Peterson without taking at least little Lacy and Anthony with her, if not Thomas and Kris. Of course, Bychowski saw Stacy in her own image—a dedicated suburban mom. She certainly didn't, at least at that point, see her in the image that would soon be painted by Peterson: a party girl, with boyfriends on the side. When Bychowski soon heard that Peterson had described his young wife in those terms, she was appalled—no, furious—with Peterson.

But on this morning of October 29, 2007, Peterson was insistent—not only had Stacy left him for another man, she had taken $25,000 in cash Peterson kept in a safe in the house, along with "passports" (Hosey used the plural, indicating more than one passport was supposedly missing), a deed to the house, some clothes, and a "favorite bikini." Peterson made it seem as though Stacy had taken off for some fun in the sun. (Just why Peterson would have been keeping $25,000 in cash in a safe in his house is another mystery, one not addressed by either Hosey or Armstrong, but one that suggests that Peterson might have had some nontaxable sources of money, a la, possibly, the earlier days with Suds Pub.)

Although Sharon Bychowski later said that police investigators from both the ISP and Bolingbrook came to her door around noon on Monday, October 29, this may have been an error in her recollection—understandable after the passage of many months after the event, and many other developments, some of them fairly traumatic. According to Hosey's account, based on interviews with Bychowski when the events were still relatively fresh, Cassandra and Zidarich came to see Bychowski later on Monday, presumably after Cassandra and Anthony Cales's discussion with McGury. Cassandra was distraught, according to Bychowski's account to Hosey.

"He killed her, he killed her," Cassandra told Bychowski, at least in Bychowski's later account to Hosey. For her part, Bychowski thought this was possible: Not only did Bychowski believe that it was totally out of character for Stacy to have abandoned her children for some man (and someone she'd never confided in Bychowski about, despite their fairly close relationship), Stacy had told her that she'd "transferred"

(Hosey's word) $25,000 to retire a home-equity line of credit debt that both Petersons owed, in preparation for an imminent separation. So when Peterson had told her that Stacy had taken $25,000 from a safe in the house, Bychowski had the feeling that Peterson was attempting to set "Shar-on" up, to influence what she might say if anyone came around asking questions. In other words, he was trying to create a scenario that Bychowski would validate in which Stacy ran off with an unknown lover, $25,000 in cash, and her "favorite bikini."

Later that day, the ISP and Bolingbrook police both put out missing person flyers on Stacy, each providing her physical description, and noting that when last seen, she'd been wearing a "red jogging suit." The origin of this information wasn't clear—if it came from Peterson himself, it suggests that he *did* see her Sunday morning, despite his later statements to Hosey and Armstrong as to his snoozing on Sunday morning. Who else could have provided such a detail? Not Cassandra, and not Zidarich, and not Bychowski, none of whom saw Stacy on the day she went missing, according to their accounts.

By the following day, Tuesday, October 30, Stacy's disappearance had made the news in fairly cursory reports in the *Chicago Sun-Times*, Hosey's parent newspaper, and in the *Chicago Tribune*. And like the biblical cloud no larger than a man's hand—at least at first—it soon became a deluge.

According to Hosey, around 9 a.m. on the morning of Tuesday, October 30, Bychowski answered her doorbell once more, and once more her neighbor, Drew Peterson, was on the stoop.

"He goes," Hosey quoted Bychowski, " 'This is what's going to happen today. The media, the media will be coming.' "

Bychowski said she asked what Peterson meant. That was when Peterson told her that Cassandra and Bruce Zidarich had told police the day before that he'd done something to Stacy to make her disappear. " 'So, now the media's going to be coming,' " he concluded, according to Bychowski, recounting this conversation to Hosey.

At that point, Bychowski told Hosey, Peterson wanted to move Stacy's Grand Prix into her driveway. Bychowski was reluctant, she told Hosey. She claimed her secretary talked her out of it—apparently Bychowski's secretary had some sort of idea that Peterson was trying to involve her in whatever was going on. So Bychowski refused to move the car. In the end, Bychowski told Hosey, Peterson did it himself.

Around noon on Tuesday, October 30, a detective from Bolingbrook, accompanied by an investigator from the ISP, arrived at 6 Pheasant Chase Court. After a short discussion with Peterson, they made a cursory search of the house, as well as Peterson's Denali. They wanted to look inside the Grand Prix, seemingly still parked in the Bychowski driveway, but, according to some accounts, Peterson wouldn't give them permission. So they went next door to the Bychowski house.

Bychowski greeted them at the door, and when the Bolingbrook detective identified himself, Bychowski said later, she declined to be interviewed—she wanted to talk to the ISP, not someone from Peterson's own department. At that point, the ISP agent identified himself. In Bychowski's recollection, the agent was the same person who had investigated Kitty's death in 2004.

Bychowski later wasn't specific as to what she told the two investigators, but it seems likely that she sketched in at least the broad outlines of the marital discord Stacy had told her about, and very likely her suspicions as to Peterson's dissimulations about the twenty-five grand, the favorite bikini, and Peterson's claims about Stacy's supposed boyfriend.

Not long after the two investigators left, the Bychowski doorbell was rung by Mike Puccinelli, a reporter for the CBS affiliate Channel 2 in Chicago. Puccinelli was apparently the first news media person to go to the cul-de-sac that would soon become nationally notorious. According to Bychowski, he was already aware of Kitty's death—Bychowski thought that Cassandra had given Puccinelli the backstory. By that point, the ISP had disseminated their missing persons flyer on Stacy, and the office of Will County State's

Attorney James Glasgow had put out a statement saying it intended to "review" the circumstances of Kitty's death, given the disappearance of Stacy Peterson. So Peterson was right, in a way—the media was now on the prowl.

According to Puccinelli's later account, Peterson's initial reaction to being in the news was fairly hostile: He warned the cameraperson to get off his property. He spoke to Puccinelli through his screen door.

"Sergeant Peterson didn't want to go on camera," Puccinelli told his viewers. "But off camera he described his last conversation with Stacy on Sunday night as 'very unusual.' He said she 'seemed snotty.' He also said her demeanor changed after one of her sisters died recently from cancer. He said she had been under the care of a psychiatrist who put Stacy on antianxiety drugs.

"He said he had no reason to suspect foul play in his wife's disappearance. But Stacy's only surviving sister, Cassandra, said her sister lived in fear of the veteran police officer.

"Sergeant Peterson said he believes she is 'where she wants to be.' He also said after she sees the media reports she'll either 'go deeper underground, or she'll surface.'

"We asked Drew Peterson if he ever thought she would leave her kids. He said that would be 'very unusual.' He also said he's lived an honorable life and now people are 'looking at' him 'sideways. That hurts.' "

The next day, of course, was Halloween.

That night, Bychowski escorted the Peterson kids—Thomas, Kris, Anthony and little Lacy—as they went trick-or-treating, Anthony as Superman and Lacy as Tinkerbell. To Bychowski, it wasn't fair that the kids should be denied the pleasures of Halloween, even if their father was a prime suspect in a possible murder of their mother and stepmother.

While Bychowski was escorting the Peterson children around the neighborhood, Fox News' Greta Van Susteren was interviewing Anna Marie Doman and her son Charlie about Peterson's previous wife, Kathleen, or Kitty, as Anna Marie referred to her sister. Just how Van Susteren latched on to the Peterson saga wasn't entirely clear, but the demographics had to have seemed promising to the cable network's programmers. In any event, she came to Chicago, and was soon stirring up a storm.

In this interview with Anna Marie, after sketching in the broad circumstances of Kitty's drowning death in the bathtub, Van Susteren asked if she'd brought a copy of Kitty's death certificate. She had, Anna Marie said.

"Did there ever come a time in those ten years that you thought the marriage was in trouble?" Van Susteren asked.

"Oh yeah, after a few years, it started."

What did Anna know about her sister Kitty's marriage to Drew Peterson?

Drew, Anna told Van Susteren, had grown increasingly "abusive" over the time of the marriage. He got telephone calls from women while at home. He'd told Kitty it was "business," Anna Marie said. But Kitty had her doubts. So Kitty started calling Drew's women callers back, wanting to know who they were, and why they were calling her husband.

Then came the anonymous letter that identified Stacy as Peterson's teenage girlfriend. That tore it, Anna Marie said—Kitty wanted a divorce.

Anna Marie tried to explain the circumstances of the so-called "bifurcated" divorce—the legal split in October of 2002, and the pending property settlement of April 2004. "She felt sorry for Stacy, even though she was very upset," Anna Marie said. Anna Marie seemed to think that Stacy was pregnant with Anthony at the time of the initial October decree, although she'd already given birth to Anthony two months earlier.

"Drew wanted to marry her before the baby was born," Anna Marie said. So Kitty had agreed to the first phase of the divorce, and also agreed to sort out the property issues later.

"And two weeks [actually more than a month] before the actual [property] settlement was supposed to take place, they found her in the bathtub," Kitty told Van Susteren.

Van Susteren asked Anna Marie if she believed that her sister Kitty had really drowned in the tub.

She did not, Anna Marie said, emphatically. It was impossible. "How does a healthy forty-year-old woman, with no drugs in her system, no alcohol, pass out in the bathtub, which is a little, oval, corner bathtub, a whirlpool tub, the bottom's not even big enough to stretch your legs out?" Kitty was taller than she was, Anna Marie said. How in the world could Kitty drown in such a small space?

Well, Anna Marie had posed a very salient question: The tub seemed far too small to account for Kitty slipping and whacking her head on the rear edge, which was rounded, anyway, not a sharp corner. The very configuration of the bathtub seemed to show the drowning could not be accidental.

Van Susteren wanted to know what the coroner's officials had told Anna Marie when she raised that point.

They'd insisted that Kitty had drowned, Anna Marie said. But from the water in her nasal cavity and lungs, it was obvious that she'd been trying to breathe while under the water in the tub.

"I don't really understand that, but they said she was trying to breathe," Anna Marie said. "I'm wondering if somebody gave her something and she passed out, or—I can't see how she stayed under the water. The tub is too small."

Van Susteren asked Anna Marie what she thought might have happened.

"I think she had some help."

"By whom?"

"I don't know, I don't want to speculate," Anna Marie told Van Susteren. "I don't know, but I think Drew knows more than he's saying. I'm not saying he did it, but I think he may know more."

Van Susteren had by this time heard about the $1 million life insurance policy. Anna Marie told her that Kitty had changed the beneficiary of the policy from Drew to her two children, Thomas and Kris.

Why did Kitty change the policy?

"Because she didn't want Drew to get it, because she said he was going to kill her," Anna said.

* * *

That same evening, after Bychowski chaperoned the Peterson children on their trick-or-treat mission, Hosey entered the cul-de-sac to talk to Peterson.

"Peterson granted me an audience as he sat behind his desk [at 6 Pheasant Chase Court] . . . he took questions and was gracious and expansive with his answers . . ." Hosey reported later in *Fatal Vows*. That evening, one of Peterson's friends, Ric Mims, was also in the house. The relationship between Mims and Peterson was never fully explicated by either Hosey or Armstrong, and Peterson himself did not explain. Mims would later claim he'd arrived at the Peterson house the previous day, to support his friend, Peterson, in his hour of need. But Mims would soon switch sides: He would suggest rather broadly but without specifics that his pal Drew was deeply involved in the mysterious disappearance of his fourth wife, Stacy.

Hosey had no way of knowing this was going to happen later, though. During his initial conversation with Peterson on Halloween, Peterson insisted that Stacy had run off with another man.

"I believe," Peterson told Hosey, "like I tell everyone, she's not missing. She's gone [off] on her own. And it's not—by nothing I did." Peterson then suggested to Hosey that Stacy was replicating the behavior of her own mother, Christine Cales, from years before. In short, Peterson was suggesting to Hosey that it was all in the family: Too much parental responsibility made people like the Cales crazy.

The next day, Thursday, November 1, the Illinois State Police arrived with a search warrant, accompanied by dogs trained to find the scent of contraband, including cadavers. The warrant gave agents the right to search the Peterson house, his Denali, and the Grand Prix, for evidence of "the offense of first-degree murder, or concealment of a homicidal death," and to seize any evidence, including any automobiles, computers, cell phones, video cameras, and any objects containing biological evidence—blood, hairs, fingernails, fingerprints, saliva, urine.

The warrant pretty much covered the proverbial waterfront,

and from that point forward, Peterson knew that the Illinois State Police weren't fooling around anymore. And with the arrival of the warrants (others were served in other locations, including a storage locker Peterson had in nearby Romeoville), Drew Peterson, by Saturday, November 3, 2007, was finally, indisputably, live on Saturday night.

18.

Don't Miss a Moment

The Thursday, November 1, service of the search warrant at 6 Pheasant Chase Court seems to have been yet another traumatic event, in least in Bychowski's later account to Hosey. She told Hosey she first heard of what was going on when a neighbor told her that the police were trying to seize the Peterson kids.

"One had Lacy in his arms," she told Hosey. Lacy, Bychowski said, was screaming, "blood-curdling screaming," outside the Peterson house. Halloween indeed! Bychowski told Hosey she went outside and rescued Lacy from the police, and brought her to her house to calm her down. Presumably Anthony came, too. Hosey did not mention the whereabouts of Thomas and Kris, but possibly by the time the warrant was served, they were already in school. According to Hosey, the police took Peterson in for questioning.

The state police, meanwhile, went through 6 Pheasant Chase Court with their dogs, and seized a number of items, including the two Peterson vehicles, the Denali and the Grand Prix. By the time the search was underway, the news media had arrived in force, including the usual circling helicopters. At some point in the afternoon, the police released Peterson, and he returned to the cul-de-sac, and joined his children at the Bychowskis'. Peterson wanted to avoid the reporters as much as possible, but some still managed to induce comments from him. In one, broadcast later on MSNBC, he admitted he wasn't happy to see his house being ransacked by the state police.

"Anytime someone searches your house," he said, "you think it's like a major violation of your rights. So, it's like, 'Okay, I have nothing to hide,' so it's like, 'Come and look.' They did it on a court order, so I didn't have a choice."

The state police also seized a number of items from the house, including computers, and, apparently, Peterson's own cell phone. Later, of course, they would ask for phone company records for the Petersons' landlines, as well as Drew and Stacy's cell phones. Stacy presumably had her cell phone with her when she vanished, but the records of any calls still existed. Any calls from Stacy's cell phone after 11 a.m. on October 28, of course, might tend to show that she was still alive, and where she was.

When Peterson reached the Bychowski house that afternoon, the search was still in progress, it appeared. Peterson must have been stunned to find the Bychowski house jammed with people—not just his children, but a pair of police officers, not to mention Cassandra and Bruce Zidarski, and even Anna Marie Doman, Kitty's sister! Bychowski said later that as the news about the search had spread, Anna Marie had rung her doorbell to introduce herself—"Hello, I'm Anna Marie Doman, and Kathleen Savio was my sister," was how Bychowski later recalled the first time they met.

But the appearance of the Savio and Cales contingents wasn't all. There in the Bychowski living room was Van Susteren, along with her entourage, including, it appears, none other than Mark Fuhrman, the former LAPD homicide detective, author, and radio host. Geraldo Rivera was also on the scene. It could have been a scene from the movie *Grand Hotel*, or even *Ship of Fools*.

Van Susteren and her outfit had already interviewed Cassandra, to follow up on the interview of Anna Marie the evening before. The tension at the Bychowski house had to be suffocating.

* * *

At some point during the later afternoon or evening, Fuhrman had a brief conversation with Peterson, according to some accounts. So, apparently, did Rivera. Then Peterson asked to speak with Bychowski privately, according to her later account to Hosey. They went into a bathroom and closed the door.

"He walks in with me," Bychowski told Hosey, "and he says, 'Well, it's been a long time since I've had a chick in the bathroom.'"

Well, there it was again—the Peterson special, inappropriate humor designed to shock, but probably, mostly to relieve the tension. Bychowski, in her account, wasn't having any of it.

"Okay," she said she told Peterson, "and we are here because . . . ?" Inviting him to state his business, no fooling around.

"Okay," Peterson said, "should they arrest me, I want to make sure my kids go to Steve [Peterson's second son from the marriage to Carol]. You've got his number. Call him right away, and he'll come and get the kids."

Peterson then told Bychowski that he expected the ISP to book him for investigation—since it was Thursday night, that might mean he might be held for as long as three days before he could get bail. But Peterson was not arrested that night, and within a few minutes, departed with the children to his own house next door, once the search was finally over.

Peterson didn't realize it yet, but the fifty-three-year-old suburban dad and self-professed lothario was about to become a TV reality show.

That evening, Fox News's John Gibson and his co-anchor Heather Nauert spotlighted the Peterson young wives' tales on their program *The Big Story*.

Gibson introduced the show by hyping it in the same tones his colleague Rivera might once have used while preparing to open Al Capone's vault:

"With us now live on the scene from Bolingbrook, Illinois, in the middle of it all, Fox's Jamie Colby and reporter

Craig Wall with the Fox affiliate, WFLD. Jamie, if we can go to you first. Describe all the action today. Very dramatic stuff, towed away the cars, executed search warrant, children taken away. Tell us what happened."

There had been a lot of excitement that day in Bolingbrook, Colby said. Her team from Fox had arrived at the cul-de-sac of Pheasant Chase Court, and within a short time of their arrival, a squad of police arrived. Colby said she thought there were as many as twenty police cars pulling up in front of the Peterson house. The police went inside, and later towed away several cars from the residence.

Then, Colby said, the police attempted to carry off the two small Peterson children. But Bychowski had swept in to rescue them.

But then things got even weirder, Colby said, describing "an incredible scene."

At that very moment, Colby said, in Bychowski's house next door to the Petersons, was the Cales family. So, too, was the Savio family—previously mortal enemies. And then: "In walks Drew Peterson!" Colby exclaimed.

After having left the house in the company of the police that day—"taken in for questioning," was how Colby described it—Peterson was released, and had returned to his house to find his children gone, and the police still searching. So he had gone next door to Bychowski's house, only to find the Cales and Savios there to greet him.

Gibson wanted to know why the police had served search warrants on the Peterson house. What was the "urgency"? he asked. He directed this to Craig Wall, the Fox affiliate reporter.

Wall said they had no idea, except, "obviously, looking for evidence of . . . foul play." The Cales family had told him that Stacy would never simply walk away from her children, Wall said.

He'd talked to Cassandra, Wall said. Cassandra had told him that her family was gratified to see all the police activity. And he'd talked to Anthony Cales the day before, who had told him that the family had hired a private detective to look into Stacy's disappearance. Anthony had told him that "every time they'd be living someplace, the cops would be showing up." (This remark made no sense—obviously Stacy and Drew had only lived together at 6 Pheasant Chase Court, and the police had never come there. Possibly Wall had become confused between Kitty and Stacy, or was thrown off by something Anthony Cales had told him about the Cales' family's distrust of the Bolingbrook police, and the Cales' family's own perambulations.)

Wall went on: Cassandra had told him that Drew was "very controlling," and discouraged Stacy from having any friends he did not approve of.

Colby broke in. Gibson should know, she said, that Stacy and Drew were going to divorce. She'd talked to Peterson briefly inside the Bychowski house, and he'd told her that he believed Stacy had left him for another man, and that the marriage was finished. Peterson, she said, was very "forthcoming." Not so the ISP, she said—they weren't saying much of anything.

Gibson's co-anchor Nauert cued Geraldo Rivera. Why did Rivera think the police hadn't questioned Peterson longer?

Rivera went right past the question. The big news, he said, was the service of the search warrants. The ISP wouldn't have gotten search warrants for Peterson's house and vehicles if they didn't have probable cause "to believe a serious crime was committed."

Cops didn't ordinarily descend on a suburban cul-de-sac in twenty cars "and seal a house and seize two vehicles on a whim, Rivera said.

"They know something, or they *think* they know something," Rivera went on. "The thing that I'd be checking to see, if this Drew Peterson is related to *Scott* Peterson. This is a guy whose previous wife was found drowned in her bathtub. She left a note when she got the order of protection in 2004."

As far as he could tell, Rivera added, Peterson was "a person who's extremely troubled. He's, by all accounts, a manically jealous person over his much younger wife." Rivera said he believed that Stacy wanted to dump Peterson, and . . . "I would be of the opinion that he is the most un-likely person in the northern hemisphere if he is innocent in this case."

This was probably a record-standing broad jump for Geraldo Rivera, who was already infamous for his leaps. Linking Drew Peterson to Scott Peterson was breathtaking. The order of protection hadn't been issued in 2004, but in 2002, two years before, and it had been canceled, apparently by Kitty herself, shortly thereafter. Rivera made it seem as though Kitty's November 2002 letter to Fragale was part of the order of protection, failing to point out that it came in the midst of the acrimonious divorce case, and that none of the supposed threats had been reported by Kitty to the police at the time they supposedly occurred.

Calling Peterson "extremely troubled" made Peterson seem like some sort of drooling monster, and adding that it was his opinion that Peterson was guilty was well over the foul board, even for a TV personality posing as a journalist.

"Apparently, Stacy told relatives that she was afraid of him and that she was afraid that she might disappear," Nauert incited.

"This guy is hinky, too," Rivera plunged on, using police vernacular for someone who is sexually perverted. Peterson had a "checkered past" as a cop, Rivera said, with accusations of "dealing with drug kingpins in his area." Peterson had "a lot of baggage," and "some real anger issues."

Gibson tried to sum up. "The hubby cop's on the hot seat, you know, the neighbors have said this," he said, apparently trying to lasso Rivera back from the abyss of possible nation-wide slander. Gibson referred to Stacy's mother, the still-vanished Christine Cales. What if Stacy had simply replicated her own mother's behavior, and had taken off for parts un-known?

Rivera was undaunted. If that was the case, he said, it would be "extremely unlucky." Rivera seemed to have meant "unlikely," however. As he put it, how often did it happen that a full-grown woman drowned in a bathtub? Babies drowned in bathtubs, he said, but "wives don't drown in bathtubs, especially when their husbands are being accused of being, you know, physically abusive."

Gibson thanked Rivera, then hyped the show to follow. "Greta Van Susteren will be live on the scene of the search for the missing mom, Stacy Peterson, that's tonight, *On the Record*, at ten Eastern, right here on Fox. Don't miss a moment!"

But in fact, this was the "moment" when the news media vigilantes first measured Drew Peterson for a noose.

19.

The Curtain Rises

Between November 2, 2007, and the end of the year, the Peterson story was featured twenty-two times on Van Susteren's Fox Cable News show, *On the Record*, and twenty times on Nancy Grace's show on CNN Headline News. John Gibson on Fox, Larry King on CNN, Dan Abrams of MSNBC, Matt Lauer on the *Today show*, and Diane Sawyer on *Good Morning America* all devoted substantial segments to the Peterson saga. The *Chicago Tribune* and the *Sun-Times* gave the topic substantial coverage, as did the local television and radio stations. *Newsweek* and *People* magazines got in on the act, and so did *The National Enquirer*—in short, the media lynch mob was in full mode. The cul-de-sac continued to be jammed by television crews, satellite dishes, trucks, hovering helicopters, and the usual mob of rubberneckers wanting to see something historic happen.

The spectacle became surreal for the Bychowskis and all the rest of the neighbors on Pheasant Chase Court. On the evening of the search warrants, Peterson had asked Bychowski to take care of the kids until Steve Peterson could come to pick them up. He didn't want them peppered with questions from the news media gaggle that had already jammed the Bychowski house. Steve arrived at the Bychowskis' the same evening. Bychowski told Hosey she sent Steve over to the Peterson house to get the kids' coats, boots, and gloves. Then Steve drove off with the kids, while Peterson barricaded himself inside 6 Pheasant Chase Court, occasionally opening the front door to grunt monosyllables at the news media whenever they dared to approach. By the next day, according to Bychowski, Peterson himself had disappeared. One can visualize Peterson crouched down in Ric Mims's backseat, a blanket pulled over himself to conceal his escape from the intruding lenses, although this may be fanciful.

Bychowski told Hosey that she didn't see Peterson again until Thursday of the following week, November 8, 2007. Neither Hosey or Armstrong reported Peterson's whereabouts during this time, but it seems very possible that Peterson also went to his son's house, to hide out, at least for a while, from the news media gaggle. On the other hand, he could well have remained inside 6 Pheasant Chase Court for the entire time, simply refusing to answer the door or the telephone, a prisoner in his own suburban castle.

For the week following the search warrants, the reports dribbled in. Fox led the charge, followed by CNN, MSNBC, and even the over-the-air broadcasters. Daily, the media gaggle assembled for the denouement. It was like waiting for lightning to strike, or the blade of the guillotine to fall.

"It was absolutely crazy," Bychowski told Hosey later. "This is the biggest thing in our life that we'll ever be through. I mean, think about it. Could there be anything bigger than somebody murdering their wife next door to your house? I don't think so." Well, it wasn't the suspicion, really, that was big—it was the news media horde camped out in front that told Bychowski it *had* to be big. And almost from that point forward, Bychowski knew she was in the middle of something that would define much of the rest of her life— her Warholian fifteen minutes of fame.

On Friday, November 2, Van Susteren had a special guest: Dr. Michael Baden, the New York State medical examiner who had a lucrative sideline as an expert witness-for-hire and as a rather celebrated "talking head" on matters medical and murder on cable television shows like Van Susteren's. Baden had just finished a rather long stint as an expert pathologist called by the defense in the Phil Spector murder case in Los Angeles, where he'd opined that it was possible that the actress Lana Clarkson had shot herself in the mouth while visiting Spector's "castle" in Alhambra, California. Baden testified he had been paid $90,000 to testify for Spector, and his testimony, while erudite, had been loaded with qualifiers intended to raise reasonable doubt—such as his opinion that Clarkson's heart might have been beating for as long as forty-five minutes after a .38-caliber bullet from a gun belonging to Spector had torn through her throat and ripped out most of the top of her spinal column, a result most pathologists agreed was highly unlikely, anatomically speaking. So Baden's credibility as an expert had dimmed somewhat, much as the crime scene analyst Henry Lee's had, by hiring on to the same defense team as a forensic expert. The fact that both Baden and Lee had billed so much money in return for their testimony for Spector's side undercut their value as objective witnesses, some thought.

In any event, on November 2, four days after Stacy Peterson vanished, and almost three years after Kitty had been found dead in the tub, Baden was offering his expert opinion on Kitty's death to Van Susteren, who said nothing of the recent controversy over Baden's testimony in Los Angeles. She referred to the 2004 inquest on Kitty's demise, and the autopsy report of Dr. Mitchell, then asked Baden for his opinion.

"The coroner said she drowned," Van Susteren told him, "but did she?"

"It is not an accident," Baden said, flatly. "The hair, her head hair, was soaked in blood, as the medical examiner says [actually, that detail wasn't in the examiner's report, and State Police Investigator Hardy had said it was water, not blood, that had soaked the hair], and she had a laceration, a blunt force laceration on the top [actually back] of her head. She had a dozen [well, eight] other black-and-blue bruises and scraping abrasions of the extremities, and of the abdomen. It looks as if she—from the description—that she was beaten up, apart from drowning. Her heart was good. Her brain was good. There were no drugs in her body on toxicology. There's no reason for her to have drowned. Adults don't drown [in bathtubs] if they're in good health." The inexactitude of Baden's description of Kitty's original autopsy, for anyone who knew the true facts, had to make one wonder whether Baden had slanted his opinion to side with the beliefs of those who were convinced that Peterson murdered his wife.

Van Susteren asked if it was a close call for the pathologist or the coroner—if it could have gone either way, accident or homicide.

"No, it's not a close call," Baden said. "It should not have been called an accident." Well, this was pretty raw—essentially, Baden was claiming that Dr. Mitchell was incompetent, along with the coroner, Patrick O'Neil. Now for the salt into the just-inflicted open wound: "And if that question had been looked into three years ago, possibly his wife wouldn't be—[wouldn't] have disappeared at this time." Baden meant that if Peterson had been charged with Kitty's death in 2004, Stacy might not be . . . what? It appeared that Baden was about to say "dead," trying to validate the still-only-hinted-at understory of the Peterson saga, already broadly suggested by those who had reportedly paid him—his host, Fox—that Peterson had murdered Stacy to shut her up about Kitty. That, after all, was where the media mob had been headed from the very beginning.

"It—and I suppose that it would make—it might be helpful—" Van Susteren fumbled for objective phrasing, despite telegraphing where she wanted Baden to go—"*would* it be helpful to exhume her, if she wasn't cremated?"

"It might be," Baden said. "It would be, and under these circumstances, to see further whether there were any fractures or other injuries that were overlooked initially. There's no evidence that they took X-rays, for example. It would be important to exhume the body and do X-rays to see if there are any subtle fractures."

But by that point, as Van Susteren doubtless already knew, the Will County State's Attorney was already preparing a petition to dig up Kitty Peterson's mortal remains—an exhumation. And it is likely that Van Susteren also knew that Baden had volunteered to do his own autopsy after an exhumation, if, as later reported, Fox agreed to pay his fees.

A few days later, Van Susteren called another player into her televised witness box. This was Ray McGury, the police chief in Bolingbrook. McGury was a veteran suburban cop, having worked as a captain in nearby Naperville for some years prior to taking the job in Bolingbrook in 2005.

Van Susteren was careful to point out that Kitty hadn't died on McGury's watch—he'd still been in the nearby suburb of Naperville when that happened. Still, she wanted to know what McGury thought about Kitty's bathtub demise, and his supervising night patrol sergeant, Drew Peterson. She replayed a snippet from her interview with Baden.

"Having reviewed the autopsy report, as a police officer," McGury said, after Baden, on tape, had said it was no accident, "not as a professional doctor, not as a pathologist, not as a coroner—yes, it has piqued my interest. And I would concur with you, Dr. Baden, and your viewers, that there are some questions in this that need to be answered."

McGury threaded his way carefully—he didn't want to say explicitly that a crime had occurred, but he also didn't want to appear to be indifferent to the storm of questions that Stacy's disappearance had raised about Kitty's death. He thought it was appropriate to "get some answers." He was glad, he said, that Glasgow, the Will County state's attorney, had announced plans to reexamine Kitty's drowning.

He'd just spoken with Glasgow, McGury added, and provided the prosecutor with a "bunch of materials that your producer was very kind enough to give to us . . ."

If Fox and Van Susteren had "turned over a bunch of materials" to McGury, who in turn gave them to Glasgow, McGury had let the cat out of the bag—then Fox had morphed into the hunter, rather than the prey. Providing "materials" about Kitty's death and her marriage to Peterson suggested that the cable network had an interest in Peterson's continued viability as a possible murder suspect, which brought the cable network's objectivity into question. In this instance, they were even trying to drive the law enforcement investigation forward by handing over materials.

Van Susteren pressed McGury: Did the Bolingbrook Police Department have records showing any domestic violence between Kitty and Peterson, or Stacy and Peterson? But McGury wouldn't bite.

"To my knowledge," he said, "as I sit here today and speak to you, there's nothing in his record . . . that indicates any type of domestic violence, excessive use of force. None of that exists. You know, again, I can't get into much detail, but I can tell you, with much certainty, that none of that exists."

Van Susteren now served up a softball to McGury:

"But when people say on our show or post comments on [Van Susteren's Fox blog] Gretawire.com [about] the good-old-boy network, they are grossly wrong about your department," she told McGury. "And it stinks, doesn't it, sir?" Here Van Susteren was referring to comments from the public to Fox and her daily website blog suggesting that the Bolingbrook force (the supposed "good-old-boy" network) was covering up for Peterson, even abetting him in murder.

"It does," McGury agreed. "You know, and again, this past week, the e-mails that I've gotten and the phone calls— some of which have been death threats, by the way—it's part of the job. It's part of being the chief of police. But it doesn't make it easy. And certainly, it doesn't make it easy, and certainly [not] easy to walk through the halls here, in [the] Bolingbrook Police Department, [to] look at the men and women . . . [that] I think are some of the finest officers, if not *the* finest officers in the United States . . ."

McGury's effort to defend his police department was understandable. Once the public thinks the cops are the crooks, a badge is worthless, and from the instant Stacy Peterson vanished, and the media discovered that Kitty was dead, the suspicion had been always that Peterson's pals in the Bolingbrook Police Department, if not the state police, had been covering up for him—letting him get away with murder. By this time, McGury had already suspended Peterson from his job—not for the disappearance of his fourth wife, or the suspicion of the drowning of his third wife, but for a relatively minor policy violation—Peterson had permitted one of the patrol officers he supervised to engage in a forbidden high-speed chase. In retrospect, this was probably the most efficient way for McGury to get rid of a bad penny. But at the time of the suspension, Peterson was already thinking of retiring—he knew he'd just been branded with the mark of Cain. And by then he had 27 years in, sufficient for a pension of a little over $6,000 a month. He didn't need the job anymore—at least, not for the money.

He already had a lot of that.

The next day, Van Susteren checked in with Ric Mims, Peterson's erstwhile friend. Mims had been at the Peterson house on October 31, and since that time the Fox folks had remained in contact with him, wherever he was. Mims seemed to be cooling on Peterson—as if he was beginning to have his doubts that Stacy had simply taken off for warmer climes with her "favorite bikini."

Van Susteren reached Mims by telephone. She wanted to know what was going on with Peterson in the aftermath of the searches, and Baden and McGury's suspicions. Mims told Van Susteren that he'd talked to Peterson by telephone only a few minutes before.

"Do you know where he is?" Van Susteren demanded.

"No, I have no clue," Mims told her.

"Did you ask him?"

"[I think he's] at the house."

"Did you ask him . . . ?"

"No . . . I asked him if he was safe . . ."

"Yes. Go ahead. You asked him what?"

"I asked him if—I asked him if he was safe, and he said, yes, he was."

"Now, Ric, you have been standing by your friend, Sergeant Peterson, since the very beginning. You thought that Stacy ran away. Do you still think that?"

Mims said yes. He still believed that Stacy had bolted—but he admitted he was now having doubts. "As time goes by, you know, everybody has their suspicions," Mims told Van Susteren.

"So do you have any—*you* don't have any suspicions?"

"I can't comment on that right now," Mims said.

It wasn't hard for Van Susteren and anyone else listening to the program to conclude that Mims was having second thoughts about his longtime friend. Either that, or becoming a sudden television personality had swayed his judgment. But if so, Mims wouldn't be the first person in the Peterson saga to succumb to the lure of the bright lights, nor, by far, the last.

The next day, November 7, Will County Coroner Patrick O'Neil surfaced, seemingly stung by Baden's criticism five days earlier. His office released a formal statement that was one part defense and second part apology:

My legal obligation as the coroner is to preside over inquests and to present testimony and evidence on all unnatural deaths to a coroner's jury in a neutral fashion. This is exactly what I did while presiding over the inquest in the death of Kathleen Savio. The six-member coroner's jury heard testimony from police and reviewed toxicology, autopsy and police reports involving the investigation into Kathleen Savio's death. In addition, the coroner's jury heard concerns voiced by Kathleen Savio's family members that they believed certain aspects of her death were suspicious.

After hearing all of the evidence, the coroner's jury convened in private and ruled that the manner of Kathleen Savio's death was an accident. The cause was listed as drowning.

Certain aspects of Kathleen Savio's death raised concerns for me as well. In my professional opinion, having served at the time as the coroner for 14 years, it was my opinion that, at the very least, her death should have been ruled 'undetermined.' The coroner's jury, unfortunately, ruled otherwise.

At the time, I had every confidence the police agency that investigated her death would present its reports to the state's attorney's office for review. Sgt. Pat Collins of the Illinois State Police obtained the assistance of State's Attorney's [Jeff] Tomczak's office on March 3, 2004 in his investigation. Any criminal charges that might have resulted against any individual would have been the responsibility of the former state's attorney.

O'Neil's statement didn't say why he'd scheduled the inquest for a day when the ISP's lead investigator Collins was on leave. But it continued:

It must be noted that a state's attorney's office may file criminal charges in a case regardless of a ruling by a coroner's jury that a death is accidental, if the investigation warrants such charges.

Finally, a change in state law that took effect in January 2007 gave Illinois coroners the option of bypassing the jury process and ruling on the manner of death independently, based upon their professional review of the evidence in a death investigation. This option has enabled coroners to remove a great deal of uncertainty from the process. Had this option been available in 2004, the ruling in this case would have been different.

So: It wasn't O'Neil's fault that the coroner's jury had misjudged the case. If there was anyone to blame, it was the jury, the investigating agency, the Illinois State Police, or the former state's attorney, Tomczak. *He'd* had doubts all along, O'Neil's statement suggested, and if it had been up to him, he would never have ruled the death an accident. Even if he had believed it was an accident, the state's attorney at the time,

Tomczak, had the power to prosecute a case, anyway. Now, since the law had been changed, a coroner like him could exercise his own judgment.

Well, coroners are still elected by popular vote in Illinois.

Two days after this, on November 9, the state's attorney for Will County and a representative from the Illinois State Police had a press conference.

20.
A Voice from the Grave

The Will County state's attorney—the prosecutor—was James W. Glasgow. Some thought Glasgow a colorful character. With his lean looks, long silver mane brushed back over his head, dapper dress, and flamboyant mustache, he might have been some Hollywood casting agent's choice to play a character like Wild Bill Hickok in his mature years, if Hickok had only survived his aces and eights in Deadwood. His image was perfect for a made-for-television trial, except for the fact that Illinois courts don't yet permit television cameras in the courtroom. But unlike some prosecutors, Glasgow liked to keep his own counsel. Except on very rare occasions, he kept his lips zipped, at least for the record. His taciturnity only added to his mystique among the news media.

Glasgow had a history in Will County, however. A Democrat, he had worked as an assistant prosecutor there from 1983 to 1986. Elected state's attorney in 1992, he was the boss until 2000, when he was unseated by Tomczak, a Republican. (Drew Peterson was also a Republican.) In 2004, Glasgow defeated Tomczak for reelection, and was sworn in for his third term in December of that year, eight months after Kitty Savio had been found drowned in her bathtub.

At least some of the blame for Tomczak's loss to Glasgow in November of 2004 lay with the Will County Sheriff's Department. This was the mess surrounding the Fox case—

not the cable network, but a man named Kevin Fox. As re-counted by Hosey in *Fatal Vows*, the problem began with the murder of Kevin Fox's three-year-old daughter, Riley. The crime was horrific—truly awful. On June 6, 2004, Kevin Fox discovered his toddler missing from the family home in the town of Wilmington, some miles south of Joliet. A huge search was conducted, and within a few hours, little Riley was found dead, floating in a small creek some distance from the house. She had been sexually abused, and duct tape had been wrapped around her mouth. The cause of death was drowning.

Five months later, in October 2004, Kevin Fox and his wife were taken to the Will County Sheriff's Department. Kevin Fox was interrogated. After fourteen hours, according to Hosey, he'd confessed: He'd killed his little daughter in an accident, then tried to cover it up by making it look like a sex crime by some unknown predator. Fox was arrested, and although he soon repudiated his confession as having been coerced, Tomczak charged him with murder, and promised to seek the death penalty. This came only a few weeks before the election in which Tomczak was seeking to retain his seat against the former incumbent, Glasgow, and there was talk that the prosecution of Fox, despite his recantation, was designed by Tomczak only to help his chances at the polls—to demonstrate to voters that he was on the job, foursquare against child murderers. Tomczak denied this political motivation, of course, but the timing of the charges probably hurt Tomczak more than they helped. Politics and crime indeed often go hand-in-hand.

In the voting, Glasgow prevailed to reclaim his old job. Meanwhile, Kevin Fox remained in jail. For some reason, the authorities did not immediately test DNA evidence that had been recovered from Riley's tiny body. Eventually, Fox's lawyer managed to have the DNA turned over to an inde-pendent laboratory for testing. The tests proved that the DNA belonged to someone other than Kevin Fox. Glasgow, by then reinstated in office, agreed to dismiss the charges against Fox, and he was released from jail. There was

controversy over Glasgow's decision, particularly in Will
County police circles, where officers pointed to Fox's con-
fession as proof of his guilt, despite his recantation, and the
DNA evidence.

Fox and his wife then sued the county for damages. In
December 2007, just as the news frenzy was at its peak over
Stacy Peterson's disappearance, Fox and his wife won a jury
award of $15.5 million against the county for violations of
Fox's civil rights. Will County continues to appeal the
award, but Glasgow's decision to "review" the death of Kitty
with an eye to possibly charging Peterson for her death was
seen by many as either a "gutsy" decision, given the lugubrious result of the Fox case, and suggested that Glasgow was
convinced of Peterson's complicity in Kitty's death, or alter-
natively, that it was an effort to placate cops who were still
angry over the Fox case, and at the same time embarrassed
by the insinuations that they had previously covered up for
Peterson. As noted, politics and crime are often familiar
bedpartners. In November 2008, after a year in which the
Stacy/Drew Peterson saga had dominated the cablewires
and the tabloids, Glasgow was elected to a fourth term. Some
suggested that Glasgow had all along intended to ride the
wave of Peterson ink to reelection, and that he saw the Bolingbrook cop as his reelection ticket.

Among those who saw politics in Glasgow's decision to
resurrect the Kitty case, of course, was Peterson's eventual
lawyer, Joel Brodsky. In Brodsky's view, in addition to pan-
dering to the Will County cops—always a potent political
force in any election—there was the bonus of all the national publicity for Glasgow. With Van Susteren and Nancy
Grace and Matt Lauer and Larry King—even Diane Sawyer—
watching, Glasgow had to realize that this could be his moment in the sun, at least in Brodsky's view. After this, the
sky might be the limit—who knew? A national legal talk
show? Van Susteren had done it. Nancy Grace had done it.
Higher political office? Even, maybe, a governorship? Illinois governors had stumbled before, and would again, as
Rod Blagojevich would soon demonstrate.

So it was apparent, at least to Brodsky, that Glasgow had a personal motive to stomp down hard on Drew Peterson, or even to cut some legal corners—as, some later claimed, Glasgow did.

On November 10, 2007, Glasgow announced that a court petition to exhume the remains of Kitty Peterson for a new autopsy had been filed by his office, and that a new investigation into the circumstances of her death would be undertaken.

After assuring the assembled news media that his office and the Illinois State Police were working hard to locate Stacy, Glasgow referred to the death of Kitty, and said that the reopening of Kitty's case was due to "new information" that had developed while investigating Stacy's disappearance. His remarks seemed to make the connection obvious—Stacy was missing because of what she might have known about her predecessor's drowning.

Glasgow said he'd looked at the photographs from the scene, and from the original autopsy. It looked to him, he said, that the wound on the back of the head would have bled profusely, yet probably had not caused Kitty to be unconscious. The blood residue in and around the tub seemed inconsistent with a scenario in which water might have drained from the tub over a period of hours. These facts suggested an alternative: Someone had murdered Kitty by first clubbing her on the rear of her head, then holding her head under water, then emptying the tub to get rid of any trace evidence. The killer would then have re-stopped the drain to make it look like an accident, overlooking the blood residue left *after* the tub had drained. The scene in the bathroom strongly suggested "staging" by a murderer, Glasgow said.

Of course, this notion raised other questions: How did the killer get her into the tub to begin with? While the tub was filling with water, if Kitty was not unconscious, wouldn't she have struggled, thereby possibly inflicting scrapes or cuts on her assailant? Her remains showed no such signs of a desperate defensive struggle, according to the original autopsy, although the bruising could suggest that a killer had held her down with his knees and one hand, while turning on the tap with the other, maybe thereby preventing any defensive scratches.

Well, maybe she was already *in* the tub when the killer surprised her—but would she really be taking a bath after 1 a.m.? And if so, how could the killer have gotten so close to her without her exiting the tub to see who it was? How could the killer have gotten inside the locked house and up to the bathroom and tub without Kitty being aware of it? (The locksmith called to the scene, of course, probably would have ruined any evidence of any intruder's lock-picking.) And could Peterson really have done this, when he supposedly had an alibi? Of course, his alibi witness, Stacy, was missing. Glasgow did not address any of these pertinent questions at this press conference.

Captain Carl Dobrich of the Illinois State Police then briefed the reporters on what was being done to locate Stacy. Somewhere between fifteen and twenty state police investigators were working full-time on the case, he said, and an analysis of the cell phone records of Stacy Peterson and Drew Peterson had been undertaken, with a view toward trying to determine where each spouse was during the critical hours of October 28. Searches had been conducted of those pinpointed areas, including inspections of nearby waterways.

That suggested that the state police weren't buying Peterson's runaway wife story. Why look in waterways for anything other than a corpse?

Meanwhile, Bychowski filed a police complaint against her next-door neighbor. She said that Peterson had begun shouting at her late one night, trying to get her to come over to his house. This unnerved Bychowski—her relationship with Peterson, once relatively cordial, had fallen into the deep freeze. Peterson later said he was only trying to get Bychowski to accept the urn of Stacy's sister's Tina's ashes; apparently he didn't want it in the 6 Pheasant Chase Court house another minute. It wasn't clear if Peterson had been drinking at the time. Bychowski said she'd decamped to a hotel to keep away from Peterson, and had checked in under a fake name.

But Peterson was not without defenders, among them his mother, Betty Morphey. After Peterson's father died some years earlier, Betty had married a family friend named Morphey, whose wife had also recently died. That made Mr. Morphey's son, Tom, an adult-acquired step-brother of Peterson. Tom Morphey was soon to become a central figure in the investigation, as will be seen.

In any event, in early November, Betty Morphey steadfastly defended her oldest child, Drew, even when badgered by Fox's Jamie Colby, a lawyer in her previous career.

"Betty, from the very beginning you've spoken out in your son's defense," Colby asked in a recorded telephone interview. "What are your thoughts today?" Colby was referring to Glasgow's announcement of the exhumation of Kitty's remains, and the broad implication that Peterson had just been promoted by Glasgow and Dobrich from "person of interest" to prime suspect.

"I still say he's innocent and he's been a wonderful son," Betty said. Colby asked how Betty's aged second husband, Tom Morphey's father, was handling all the furor.

"I'm just trying to keep him out of the way of all this, because at we, at our age, we don't need this. My son knows we're by his side and we're with him, and we know he's innocent. And that's why Drew has a lot of support, because he knows his mother thinks he's innocent, and knows he's innocent."

But a different tune was being sung by one of Peterson's old running mates in MANS. In a story published by the Chicago *Sun-Times* that same day, a retired former high-ranking ISP officer, Ronald Janota, claimed that Peterson had tipped off a major drug dealer to a "sting" investigation, and had told a "convicted killer" of the identity of another undercover drug cop. This seemed to be an echo of the deal gone bad with Bindy Rock more than twenty years earlier.

"Putting a fellow officer's life in jeopardy is unforgivable as far as I'm concerned," Janota told the newspaper. The paper contacted Peterson for his side of the story. Peterson said it wasn't true; he'd never divulged the name of another undercover officer, or ever divulged a covert "sting" operation.

By this point, Peterson had apparently decided that making himself scarce and not talking was doing nothing to abate the media circus, so he decided to join it.

The same day Glasgow promoted him to murder suspect, Peterson opened his garage door to find Geraldo Rivera waiting for him. Peterson again declined to go on camera, but gave Rivera an oral statement, because, Rivera claimed, Rivera was "a celebrity." Most reporters were pigs, Rivera said Peterson told him.

"I'm only letting you into my house because you're a celebrity," Rivera claimed Peterson told him.

"I just spent fifteen, twenty minutes with Sergeant Drew Peterson," Rivera afterward told his Fox audience. "He gave me an exclusive statement that I want to read for you. 'I feel I've been misquoted by the press, and the media has done nothing but harass my family and terrorize my children. . . . This entire ordeal has been the most traumatic experience of my life. As a result of this nightmare, I've lost over twenty-five pounds. The damage done by the media'—again, he's blaming the media," Rivera interjected, " 'I'm going to have to live with this, long after this is over.'

"He kind of cast himself in the role of rescuer to women from very dysfunctional backgrounds," Rivera added. "The tone the entire conversation was, Drew Peterson, victim, and again denying any criminal wrongdoing."

Rivera supplemented Peterson's statements with videotaped quotes from others involved in the drama, among them, Peterson's former friend, Mims.

"There's a lot of strange things going on with the case," Mims said, "and the more I find out about the details, I'm scared for what might happen to me. He called me and told me, 'So you switched sides on me, huh?' It was a brief phone

The house at 6 Pheasant Chase Court, Bolingbrook, Illinois, where Drew and Stacy Peterson lived with their two small children, and two of Peterson's children from his third marriage to Kathleen Savio Peterson, in October 2007 when Stacy Peterson vanished. *Carlton Smith*

A missing persons flyer distributed after Stacy vanished on October 28, 2007.

http://someoneismissing.com/ flyers/stacy-peterson.jpg

Cassandra Cales and her sister Stacy Peterson, posing in portions of Drew Peterson's police SWAT uniform, with weapons, probably in 2002.

Drew Peterson

The SpringHill Suites hotel in Bolingbrook, where Drew Peterson first met Stacy Cales in September of 2001.

Carlton Smith

The Bychowski family, the next-door neighbors of Drew and Stacy Peterson, became very close to Stacy Peterson. When Stacy vanished, the Bychowskis became convinced that Drew Peterson had murdered her.   *Carlton Smith*

The tarmac of Clow Airport, where Peterson kept an ultralight aircraft, and where Peterson claimed he had recovered Stacy's Pontiac Grand Prix on the night of her disappearance. Some in the news media speculated that Peterson used his ultralight to dispose of Stacy's body from the air.

Carlton Smith

Will County State's Attorney James Glasgow, who in 2007 re-opened the investigation into Kathleen Savio Peterson's drowning in a bathtub in 2004, an investigation which led to Peterson's arrest on murder charges four years later.

Will County State's Attorney's Office

Drew Peterson talks to the news media in May of 2008, after he was charged with a technical weapons violation. Peterson often talked to the news media between October of 2007 and May of 2009, much to the chagrin of defense lawyers.

Scott Olson / Getty Images

Joel Brodsky, Drew Peterson's defense attorney. Brodsky made numerous appearances on national television, arguing that his client was a victim of persecution by a politically ambitious prosecutor driven by the incessant publicity.

Courtesy of Joel Brodsky

Pastor Neil Schori, here with his wife (partially hidden) and daughter. Schori counseled Stacy Peterson over two years. After Stacy vanished, Schori said that Stacy had confided to him that Drew had no alibi for the night Kathleen Peterson died. *Neil Schori*

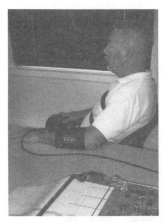

In May of 2008, a year before he was arrested but the subject of national publicity, Peterson took two lie detector tests at the behest of a Canadian author. He passed one, but showed deception on the second, according to the examiner.
Joel Brodsky

On May 7, 2009, after an indictment for murder by a special grand jury, Peterson was arrested by Illinois State Police within blocks of his house at 6 Pheasant Chase Court. An investigation into Stacy's disappearance continues.
John Smierciak/Getty Images

The Will County Courthouse, in Joliet, Illinois, where Peterson was scheduled to go on trial in the summer of 2010.
Carlton Smith

call, but I got a really eerie feeling from it. I think anybody [who] he feels is a threat to him should be concerned."

Kitty's remains were exhumed on November 13. A crane was brought in to lift the casket from the ground. A spokesman for Glasgow, Charles Pelkie, released a brief statement reporting that the coffin had been taken to the Will County morgue for a re-autopsy of the remains by an independent expert, Dr. Larry Blum. The results would not be made public, Pelkie said.

Later, Ric Mims would return to the Fox cablewires for Van Susteren. Mims told her that he had taken time away from his job to help the state police. He had been working with various journalists and investigators to get to the truth about his old pal, Drew Peterson. He consistently referred to "we" when he talked of the investigators, whether official or self-appointed. When Van Susteren asked him for something solid to demonstrate that Peterson had violent tendencies, Mims told of the hanging death of a teenager who had been the younger brother of a woman Mims said had been Peterson's girlfriend at the time he'd been married to Victoria back in the late 1980s or early 1990s. Mims thought the death of the teenager was suspicious.

Counting Gerry O'Neill, Kitty, and seemingly Stacy, that meant four deaths possibly connected to Drew Peterson. And Mims suggested that Peterson had crooks as pals—people who were capable of murder at Peterson's request. That was why, he told Van Susteren, he was hiding out.

And in the next day or so, Peterson's onetime stepdaughter, Lisa, came forward. Behind an electronically induced shadow, Lisa explained that her former stepfather had been intensely controlling of her mother, Victoria, Gerry O'Neill's sister. And, she said, in the years they'd lived with the Bolingbrook cop, he had occasionally beaten her with a belt.

Drew Peterson, it seemed, was not only a likely homicidal maniac, he was also a sadist, if not a pedophile. "Hinky," as Geraldo Rivera had declared.

All this, without hearing Peterson's side of the story. Hunkered down inside 6 Pheasant Chase Court, Peterson chafed at the way his life, or at least his public image, was being destroyed. He felt he had to do something—hit back, anyway. The media had measured him for the drop, had convicted him in the court of public opinion, and he hadn't even been legally charged with any crime. He wanted to sound off, fight back, expose the media for the incompetent, hypocritical moralists he was sure they were.

21.
Today

The next day, November 14, Peterson went live with Matt Lauer on the *Today* show on NBC. Lauer played a tape of Kitty's coffin being removed from the grave the day before.

Lauer told Peterson he'd been watching his face as the video played with "the image of your third wife's casket being taken out of the ground . . ." He wanted to know what was going through Peterson's mind. Peterson said it was "a shame" that Kitty's "resting place" had been disturbed "for something like this." There had already been an autopsy, he said, implying that there was no need for another one.

Did Peterson think there were no "mysterious circumstances" in Kitty's death? Lauer asked. Peterson said he understood "exactly why" the exhumation had been ordered. But he had no opinion on the development. Well, did Peterson think it was a waste of time?

"I don't know," Peterson said. "If there was anything that happened to her, you know, it should be found out."

Lauer turned to the media circus camped out in front of the 6 Pheasant Chase Court house. What did Peterson make of all the attention? How had it affected him and his family?

The constant presence of the news media in front of his house, as well as the ubiquitous updates on television, were nerve-wracking, Peterson indicated. Whenever the television broadcast a news report on the Petersons, he and his sons took the little children out of the room. They often had to "sneak" Thomas and Kristopher out of the house to go to school or other activities, just to keep them from being pestered by reporters' questions.

Lauer asked what Peterson had told the two little children about their mother's disappearance. Peterson said he had told Anthony and Lacy that their mother was "on a vacation."

Lauer asked about the search warrant, and the fact that the authorities had called him "a person of interest."

"You know all about these labels," Lauer said. "You know what this means."

He did, Peterson agreed.

But with the exhumation, the same authorities were now calling him "a suspect," Lauer noted. He asked why Peterson thought they'd changed their terminology.

Peterson said he was pretty sure the police had always considered him "a suspect."

"You know, the husband always did it," he said. It was just a term to show that the police were working on the case, he said.

Lauer said his information was that Stacy had asked for a divorce only two days before she disappeared. He quoted from an email Stacy had supposedly sent a week or so before to a friend.

"This is what it said," Lauer told Peterson. "Quote, 'As I mature with age, I'm finding that the relationship I'm in is controlling, manipulative and somewhat abusive. If you could keep me in your prayers, I could use some wisdom, protection and strength.' What do you think she meant by that?"

Lauer did not say who the email had been sent to, or how it had come into the possession of NBC.

Peterson shook his head. "I don't think [those are] her words," he said. "That doesn't sound like a thing that she would say. And that vocabulary is certainly out of line for her. So I think this was fabricated, as a lot of things have been throughout this case, and this is a made-up email."

Lauer played a tape showing a Cales family relative asserting that Stacy had warned her family that if she vanished, it meant something bad had happened to her, and that they would need to search for her. Why would Stacy say such a thing? Lauer asked.

Peterson said he had no idea.

Lauer asked Peterson to describe his marriage with Stacy.

Here Peterson seemed to fumble with words, and when they finally came out, it was as if he was describing something from a book. In the beginning, he said, his relationship with Stacy was "very romantic." But after Stacy's half-sister, Tina, passed away, "[Stacy] took a serious downslide, of her emotions . . . And ever since her sister died, we actually had her go to a psychiatrist. And she was on medication, mood medication." After Tina's death, Peterson added, every day "was basically an emotional roller coaster. Every day."

Lauer pressed Peterson: Was the marriage "volatile? Was it ever violent?"

Peterson said he didn't "believe it was ever violent."

Lauer seized on Peterson's weasel wording.

"You'd either know if it was violent or not violent," Lauer pointed out.

They'd had arguments, Peterson admitted. And once Stacy had thrown a frozen steak at him, but he'd walked away.

"Did you ever hit *her*?"

"Never."

"Never raised a hand to her?"

"Never raised a hand to her," Peterson said. He recalled an incident where he and others had tried to throw Stacy into the backyard pool, and Stacy "came up swinging." But it was just horseplay, Peterson said.

What about Peterson's claims that Stacy had told him she was seeing another man? Did Peterson believe that at that very moment, Stacy was with someone else?

"She never told me she was seeing another man," Peterson said. Then he appeared to backtrack. "She—well, maybe she did. But I believe she's with somebody else right now."

Lauer pressed again. Did or did not Stacy specifically tell him she was seeing someone else?

That wasn't exactly how Stacy had put it to him, Peterson said.

Did Peterson actually believe that Stacy was alive and well, and that she had run off with someone else? That's what he believed, Peterson agreed.

Peterson had claimed from the very beginning that Stacy "was a good mom," Lauer pointed out. Why would a "good mom" of two small children leave with another man and never call her children to tell them where she was, or that she was all right?

Peterson he didn't know, he had no answer for that. Lauer's skepticism was apparent.

Lauer asked if Peterson was cooperating with the police in their two investigations.

He'd given a statement, "a full account," to police on the day the search warrant was served, Peterson indicated. But since that time, lawyers had advised him to answer no more questions from the police.

Well, Lauer asked, why wasn't Peterson out participating in the searches for Stacy?

No, he hadn't joined in the searching, Peterson admitted, for two reasons: first, because he'd become such a media magnet that he'd be a distraction to the searchers. And second, because he didn't believe Stacy was really missing. "She's just gone," he said. "She's where she wants to be."

Lauer veered back into the subject of Kitty's death in the bathtub in 2004. After sketchily and not quite accurately describing Mitchell's autopsy findings, Lauer referred to Glasgow's assertions that the death scene appeared to be a murder staged to look like an accident. Did Peterson at the time think it was an accident?

Peterson told of the circumstances of the discovery of Kitty's body—how it had been discovered in the tub by Mary Pontarelli and Steve Carcerano. He was the one who had asked the neighbors to go inside the house while he waited on the porch. He hadn't wanted to go inside the house, he said.

Why not? Lauer asked.

Peterson explained that Kitty had accused him of stealing things from the 342 Pheasant Chase Drive house before.

Lauer pointed out that Peterson was a police officer.

"That was Kathy," Peterson explained. "That was Kathy."

Peterson hadn't actually answered Lauer's question—at the time Kitty's body was discovered, did he think it was an accidental drowning?

Lauer turned to another subject. Was it true that Peterson stood to inherit a million dollars from a life insurance policy on Kitty?

No, Peterson indicated, but the two boys did. The money was in a trust account for their benefit, not his.

Lauer asked Peterson to describe his marriage with Kitty.

Kitty was an emotional person, Peterson said, who had come from "an abusive home life, growing up." It sounded almost like a reply of Peterson's description of his marriage to Stacy, first "romantic," then "emotional." Kitty was very competitive with him, Peterson added, meaning argumentative.

Lauer took note of the similarities in Peterson's description of his last two wives, especially Peterson's use of the term "emotional," and "troubled" backgrounds. He wanted to know why Peterson was attracted to them.

Both Kitty and Stacy were "very beautiful," Peterson said. And at first, he and Kitty had had a wonderful marriage, "a lot of fun. Very beautiful woman."

Lauer got to the heart of the matter. "Can you look me straight in the eye and tell me that you had nothing to do with the death of your third wife, Kathy, or the disappearance of your fourth wife, Stacy?"

"I can look right in your eye and say I had nothing to do with either of those incidences."

Lauer told Peterson that he seemed "extraordinarily calm and collected." If it were him, Lauer said, facing "possible indictment as early as today or tomorrow . . . I think I'd be a little more, I don't know, rattled."

Peterson shook his head. He wasn't afraid of being charged with a crime, he said. He was afraid of the news media. "And

I've been hounded by the media, and the media's what's causing my aggravation, or me being upset, with life and living today."

At this point, Lauer took a commercial break. Just why he thought Peterson was close to being indicted was curious. For what? All the evidence about Stacy was ephemeral—second- or third-hand anecdotes, mostly, from relatives or friends. Hard evidence of a crime—such as a body—was entirely lacking. And as for Kitty's death, the re-autopsy had only just been completed, and if there was clear evidence of a crime in her death, it certainly wasn't obvious at the *first* autopsy. Otherwise, Peterson would have been charged with a crime in 2004.

But Lauer, with his use of the word "indictment," somehow knew something that had not yet been reported: State's Attorney Glasgow had resolved to convene a special grand jury to investigate the cases of Peterson's wives. Even so, an indictment of Peterson was hardly imminent. As it happened, the special grand jury of 16 people would meet on most Wednesdays for the next 18 months before any indictment was voted. Clearly, the case of the Peterson wives was not as simple as Lauer's comment seemed to imply. But by November 14, 2007, Peterson was well-established as the new national O.J. Simpson.

Lauer returned from the break with more questions—and commentary—for Peterson.

Didn't Peterson understand why people were suspicious of him, given that Stacy had reportedly demanded a divorce just two days before she vanished?

He understood, Peterson said. But Stacy frequently threatened divorce, he said. "However, Stacy—I'm not trying to be funny here—but Stacy would ask me for a divorce after her sister died, on a regular basis. I'm not trying to be funny. And it was based on her menstrual cycle."

Lauer seemed momentarily taken aback by this, but plunged on.

"So—so, when Stacy asked you for a divorce on October 26th, it didn't anger you? You weren't upset by it?"

No, Peterson said. Every time Stacy got upset, she talked about divorce.

What did Peterson have to say, when people claimed that because he'd been a cop, that he would know how to get away with murder?

Peterson said he had no way of responding to such talk.

Lauer tried the same question again, more obliquely:

"As someone who does know the system and who's understood for years what it takes to piece together a case, to bring together evidence, how does it feel to have the weight of that system now turned and focused on you?"

"It's very frightening, very frightening," Peterson said.

Lauer asked what Peterson was most frightened of.

Legal fees to defend himself, Peterson said. He'd been told it could cost up to $250,000 to defend himself if he were charged with murder. "So, basically," he added, "I'm reaching out to attorneys of America for help. If anybody would like to take my case and help me out here, please call. Let me know what you can do for me. Help me out."

"If you were me," Lauer said, "or if you were the average citizen on the street, who's read about this case and seen it on TV, would you think you're guilty, that you had some involvement in this?"

"Based on the media coverage, I'm as guilty as they come." Peterson suggested that the intense news media attention might drive the authorities to act, even in the absence of a provable case.

Lauer asked Peterson if he could offer anything to him that "might prove your innocence." Lauer was now sounding like both the judge and the jury.

No, Peterson said. Whatever was going to happen, would happen, he said.

Lauer pointed out that a lot of lawyers would have advised Peterson not to make public statements, as he was doing on *Today*. Peterson agreed—that was the conventional wisdom.

So why had Peterson agreed to the interview?

He was doing it "to get the media . . . off my back. Get them off my family's back. That's all I'm asking. And I'm here today in an attempt to basically let them see my face: Here I am, please get away from my house and leave my family alone."

Did Peterson think that was going to work?

"I'm begging that it does. Or if it turns up the heat, then I made a mistake coming here."

Was he worried that if he was charged and convicted, he might spend the rest of his life in prison, or even get the death penalty?

Yes, Peterson said. And while it was a frightening prospect, "my family's provided for, my kids will be okay. They're with my brother and sister-in-law and my son. And I can go in peace, if that happens."

If there was one thing Peterson could say about himself, what would it be?

"What they're seeing is not me," Peterson said. "I'm— I've been a jokester all my life. And it's just like, now that they're seeing this serious person in deep trouble, and this isn't me. 'Me' is a guy playing jokes on people and kidding around and trying to have fun with life and living."

What would he say to Stacy, if she happened to be watching?

"Come home," Peterson said. "Tell people where you are. And that's all I can say."

This interview represented Peterson's initial emergence from the cocoon of non-commentary on his situation. From this point forward, he would engage with the news reporters on a regular basis, often sarcastically, usually sardonically, occasionally with wit. As he put it later, when you're engaged in a media war, you have to use the media to fight back. It was 180 degrees away from what almost every criminal defense lawyer in America tells their client: Sit down and shut up, go to a secure undisclosed location, because nothing good can come from making public statements when you're the accused. But Peterson just couldn't hold himself in any longer. It had taken only a little over two weeks for him to jump out of the cake.

Watching this performance back in Chicago was a rather well-known criminal defense lawyer, Joel Brodsky. He saw in Peterson a client who was sure to continue to garner substantial media attention, especially since he so steadfastly denied culpability. A high-profile client meant a higher profile for Brodsky—more media appearances, and an opportunity to demonstrate his legal legerdemain on a national stage. And then, too, there was the money: Had Peterson just offered to pay someone $250,000 to defend him? That's what it sounded like. Within a matter of days, Brodsky had reached an understanding with the villain of the hour—he'd take the case, Brodsky said.

The same day Peterson showed his face and used his voice with Matt Lauer, the Savio family filed legal papers asking that the probate case of Kitty's estate be reopened for the purpose of removing Peterson and his uncle, Carroll, from control of its assets. A struggle over money was about to begin—again.

22.
Can I Get a Witness?

If anything, Peterson's duet with Lauer only stoked the national media interest in the made-for-television saga of the lives and wives of Drew Petersons. His plea to them—back off!—only generated more of what the media craved: conflict, and better yet, confrontation. Now it wasn't just Peterson versus his wives; it was Peterson versus The Public, but the public garbed as newspeople, brandishing microphones and cameras and notepads. It was as if O.J. had challenged them, or more aptly, Gary Hart, fooling around on the *Monkey Business* with his girlfriend, a quarter-century earlier: *Go ahead, follow me!* And the media took up the challenge. *People want to know!*

The day after appearing on the *Today* show, Peterson was once again the focus of tabloid television, this time on Nancy Grace's *Headline News* program. Sitting in for Grace was former Washington, D.C., police investigator Mike Brooks, usually billed as the cable channel's law enforcement expert.

"Tonight: After weeks of hiding out and lashing out at the media, it seems Drew Peterson just can't stop talking," Brooks opened. "The veteran police sergeant continues his media blitz, still denying he had anything to do with his third wife's mysterious death or his fourth wife's disappearance. He says twenty-three-year-old Stacy Peterson left on her own, and now says he's angry with her for creating this media circus. And with a second autopsy under way of wife number three, more witnesses were reportedly called before a grand jury."

Brooks pulled in Jon Lieberman, a correspondent for the program *America's Most Wanted*, and told the audience that Peterson had been talking to Lieberman, too.

What did Peterson have to say to *America's Most Wanted*?

Lieberman said he'd been "hammering away" at Peterson, telling him that he thought Peterson should be out searching for Stacy, if he was really innocent.

Brooks agreed. He asked Lieberman what Peterson had said to this.

Lieberman said that Peterson had told him he was mad at Stacy for all the attention that had been focused on him and the kids—a "circus," as Lieberman claimed Peterson described it. He'd asked Peterson if he wanted Stacy back. Peterson told Lieberman that was "questionable." Lieberman thought Peterson meant having Stacey back as his wife. But Peterson said he hoped that Stacey was "alive and well." Lieberman then asked Peterson if Stacy *was* "alive and well," and Peterson said that he hoped she was.

Brooks was clearly skeptical of Peterson's honesty as to this question. He asked Lieberman about Peterson's demeanor.

Peterson was "calm . . . cool . . . collected," Lieberman said, and expressed amazement at Peterson's behavior. "He wasn't rattled at all," Lieberman told Brooks. "He said he was frustrated by the fact that our host, John Walsh, had gone on some shows . . . and basically convicted him." Peterson told him, Lieberman added, that he was upset that he'd already been found guilty by the news media. He insisted that he'd had nothing to do with Stacy's disappearance, or Kitty's drowning. Lieberman said he thought Peterson's emotional detachment was "eerie."

Brooks referred to the interview on the *Today* show with Matt Lauer, and played a segment of the interview for his audience. Following the clip, Brooks brought in a psychologist, psychoanalyst Bethany Marshall of Los Angeles, and asked what she thought of Peterson's demeanor.

Marshall said she was amazed at Peterson's demeanor

while being interviewed by Lauer. She critiqued his body language during the interview, claiming that his posture seemed to demonstrate both arrogance and indifference. She thought the way Peterson was sitting demonstrated that he was a "sociopathic" personality.

Marshall observed that during the interview with Lauer, Peterson had barely mentioned his children, beyond observing that if anything happened to him, the children would be provided for. To Marshall, Peterson's interview with Lauer showed "it's all about him." Peterson had, Marshall opined, a "stalker-type mentality." She considered him a dominator, "literally on top of his wife." Peterson's lack of details to Lauer as to who Stacy might have run off with seemed to show he was lying, she said.

The capper, for Marshall, was Lauer's last inquiry: Did Peterson have anything to say to Stacy, in case she might be watching? Peterson's pleas for her to "come home," which Marshall thought was delivered with a laugh by Peterson, seemed to show he was "indifferent" to his young wife's fate, or aware that there was no way she was still alive.

"You know," Brooks went on, "we talked yesterday with one of Kathleen Savio['s]—wife number three—with one of her relatives, who said that he was extremely violent towards Kathleen Savio. And yesterday, also on the *Today* show, he says—Matt Lauer said, 'Did you ever hit her?' Peterson said, 'Never, never hit her, never raised a hand to her.' And then he goes on to say, 'I don't believe our relationship was ever violent. There were a few incidents where Stacy and I would have verbal confrontations, and I'd be in her face and she hated being cornered. And one time she hit me in the head with a frozen steak.' "

Brooks seemed to be commingling Kathy's claims of violence—unproven—with what Peterson had told Lauer about his relationship with *Stacy*, suggesting that to Brooks, it was all part of the package that was Peterson: Kathy/Kitty was the same as Stacy, in Brooks' on-air formulation. In short, Brooks' formulation mashed together the facts of Kitty's claims with Stacy's disappearance.

Brooks invited Marshall to comment. Marshall thought—as far as she could parse Brooks' commingling of Kitty and Stacy—that it only showed habitual marital abuse. "He's on top of the woman all the time," she said, reiterating her theme of malevolent male dominance. Peterson's assertion to Lauer that Stacy was hormonally emotional, Marshall thought, justified in Peterson's mind his attempts to dominate: "He says, 'Oh, kind of out of control, aren't you, little missy?'" Here it seemed quite likely that Marshall was projecting her own imagination into a domestic relationship she really knew nothing about, and using her own experience to color the participants, and assign them their roles. Marshall pointed to Peterson's remarks about Stacy's "period" as evidence that Peterson at heart believed women were born emotionally unstable, that it came with their physiology. Peterson had a "lack of insight," Marshall opined, as to the true nature of the problem, which "seemed to fit the profile of the abuser." Peterson, she said, wanted to blame the victim for his own misdeeds.

Having induced Marshall to psychoanalyze Peterson from an armchair 2,000 miles away, based on fragments broadcast on television, Brooks brought in a "psychological profiler," Pat Brown. He asked Brown what she thought.

Brown thought that Peterson had attributed Stacy's emotionality to her menstrual cycle as a means of rationalizing his increasing inability to control her as she had gotten older. Peterson had dominated Stacy when she was seventeen, but once she'd become a mother, "more of a woman," Stacy "started fighting back." This made Peterson feel that he was losing control—impotent, Brown seemed to suggest.

Brooks asked if Marshall agreed with Brown. She did, Marshall said, but she also thought it showed a lack of "insight" on Peterson's part as to the nature of Stacy's anger at her husband. If Stacy was always threatening to divorce him, Marshall said, it was "because she really doesn't want to be with him." In his interview with Lauer, Peterson had completely glossed over his own actions, she noted.

Brooks took a call from someone watching the program who wanted to know if the reason Peterson seemed so calm while on the Lauer show was because he'd gotten someone else to "knock these wives off."

Brooks asked Lieberman if that scenario had come up with the investigators.

Yes, Lieberman said. He said his television show had "sources inside the investigation" who were thinking about that. The cops wanted to know who Peterson had met with and talked to in the days preceding Stacy's disappearance, he said.

This caught Brooks' focus. There was a grand jury now, he noted, and various relatives and friends of Drew Peterson had been called as witnesses. What had Lieberman heard about the grand jury? Brooks' segue suggested that Drew's brother, Paul Peterson, and other Bolingbrook officers might have information about Drew's possible "help," which might be why they had been called to testify before the special grand jury.

On this, Lieberman had something to offer. The special grand jury, he said, wanted to know who on the inside of the Bolingbrook Police Department might have talked to Peterson after Kitty was found dead in the bathtub. Lieberman's remark suggested what everyone was thinking: There had been a police cover-up.

The circumstances of Kitty's demise had raised a lot of questions, especially after Stacy's disappearance, Lieberman noted. So the investigators wanted the special grand jury to hear from people who had been involved in the investigation into Kitty's death. "Did Bolingbrook try and sweep this under the rug?" Lieberman asked. Peterson's reputation as a lothario also figured into the mix, Lieberman said. Brooks found this "interesting," which, judging by Brooks' countenance, was another word for suspicious.

After another call from the audience, Brooks moved on.

"Let's uncage the lawyers," he said. Brooks introduced Richard Herman, a defense attorney from New York, and Renee Rockwell from Atlanta. If Peterson was his client, Brooks asked Herman, what would he tell him?

Peterson should shut up, Herman said. He should lock himself inside his house and stay away from the news media.

Marshall's comments—her assessment that Peterson was a "sociopathic" personality—demonstrated that much. Anything Peterson said was going to be taken badly, as Marshall had just shown, which was why any competent defense attorney would tell his client to zip his lips. There was nothing Peterson could gain for his side of the story by talking. Everything he said only made his situation worse.

Had Peterson helped himself by talking to Matt Lauer?

"Mike, he's absolutely worse off," Herman said. He thought Glasgow was trying to "make a name for himself," to get reelected. He thought Glasgow intended to indict Peterson, whatever the evidence, for the political benefits. The *Today* show interview would be used by Glasgow at trial, and it would be bad for Peterson. He thought it was nuts of Peterson to have done the interview.

Brooks said he agreed with Herman, forgetting momentarily that scores of media people had been hounding Peterson for two weeks to say something. Brooks turned to Renee Rockwell. Why in the world had Peterson gone on national television, in her opinion?

Rockwell suggested that Peterson was angling for a defense attorney who wanted to take a high-profile case. Some lawyers, she said, would "line up" for such a chance, even do the case for free, if it generated enough air-time. But Peterson was flirting with disaster when he agreed to public interviews. Statements he made to the media were absolutely fair game in any trial. It wasn't the same as making statements to the legal authorities. Peterson had claimed he'd never "been violent" with his wife in the interview with Lauer. All the prosecution had to do was play the tape, then produce evidence that Peterson had lied.

"Those words will come back to haunt him, Mike," Rockwell said. When the media interviews someone, they have no Miranda rights—the right to remain silent, to consult a lawyer before answering any questions. It is what it is. Peterson needed to shut up and make himself scarce, Rockwell agreed.

After a brief discussion of the 2004 autopsy on Kathleen,

and what might be found in the re-autopsy, Brooks veered back to the two defense experts. He wanted to know whether Peterson was likely to be indicted for murder.

Peterson should not be indicted, Herman said, because there was no real evidence against him.

Brooks was incredulous. "Oh, Richard! Come on!" he exclaimed. "What do you mean, there's no case in either one of these?"

Herman insisted that there was no indictable evidence against Peterson. Even though everything Peterson had said to Lauer on the *Today* show would be admissible, it didn't come close to evidence that he'd murdered anyone. Rockwell agreed with Herman. There was simply no evidence against Peterson, no matter what was said in the news media.

Brooks clearly was doubtful about this. Rockwell suggested that the case against Peterson was so thin that the best thing he could hope for was to be indicted by the special grand jury. Once indicted, she said, the authorities would have only one chance to convict Peterson, and if they failed after a trial, he'd be home-free. So it would be in Peterson's best interest to make the authorities try him sooner rather than later, and an indictment would play into his hands.

Brooks asked Herman how long he thought the grand jury's inquiry was going to last.

Herman thought that, as a special grand jury, charged with investigating, the panel could last for six months, or even more than a year. He agreed with Rockwell that it would be crazy to vote an indictment on television time—that is, within the next few days. The whole idea of the new autopsy, he thought, was ridiculous. There was almost nothing the new pathologist, after the exhumation of Kitty, could find that wouldn't have already been documented by Dr. Mitchell. The whole thing, he thought, was nothing more than a public relations exercise by the state's attorney, Glasgow, and the Illinois State Police.

"What's going on now, this exhumation of the body, is an absolute disgrace," Herman said. Any competent pathologist would admit that there was nothing new to be found.

"This is just done for the public, to win votes. That's what's being done now."

Brooks was taken aback by Herman's suggestion that the new Peterson investigation was politically motivated. He looked to Lieberman to offer a counter-opinion.

Any suggestion that the exhumation and re-autopsy of Kitty was nothing more than a political gambit by Glasgow was itself ridiculous, Lieberman riposted. People had to look at the larger picture: it wasn't just the re-autopsy that was important, but the context of Kitty's death, when taken in conjunction with Stacy's disappearance. Together, the death and disappearance suggested criminal culpability on Peterson's part.

Brooks agreed. "And Richard—Richard and Renee, can you say *timeline*? Doesn't add up here, folks." Brooks' observation wasn't exactly clear—why the "timeline" didn't "add up"—but he was apparently under the impression that Kitty's claims of violence from Peterson were followed immediately by her death, which of course was not the case. Or perhaps he meant Stacy's disappearance, followed by her ominous silence. Either way, it was apparent that Brooks' grasp on "the timeline" was less than perfect.

"But can you say Scott Peterson?" Brooks quipped.

Everyone laughed.

The next morning, the *Chicago Tribune* had an interview with Vicki, Peterson's second ex-wife. In an excellent piece of reporting by Erika Slife, Vicki described Peterson as controlling, often verbally abusive. At one point, she said, Peterson told her he could kill her and make it look like an accident. This was so close to what Kitty had later claimed Peterson had told *her* that it either showed Peterson had a penchant for making that particular threat, or—possibly— that Kitty had borrowed the phrase from her predecessor, in her letter to Fragale. But at least Vicki had some corroboration: She said she'd told friends on the Bolingbrook police force of Peterson's threat, "So they would know he said these things to me." That meant there were possible witnesses to such a statement prior to Kitty's death, even if they could only refer to Vicki, not Kitty. This would give Vicki's hearsay evidence reliability, if it ever came into dispute.

Peterson would occasionally hit her, but never hard enough to cause her to get medical treatment, Vicki said. The violence was just infrequent enough to be least expected, she added. "It was mind games, it was head games."

All the publicity about her former husband left her unsure what to think, she added. One part of her doubted that Peterson would commit murder, while another part told her he was capable of getting away with it if he ever did.

"He has the experience, the knowledge, the means, and the mind to do that," she said, her voice trailing off. "That's all I've thought about. . . . I'm still working through it, I'll be honest."

Peterson was a charmer, Vicki remembered. But there also seemed to be a Mr. Hyde aspect to his personality. "The thing with Drew Peterson, and I'm sure if [Kitty and Stacy] were here to comment, they would say the same thing—when it was good, it was wonderful, it was great. But when it was bad, it was really bad."

When Peterson was at his best, she said, he was ebullient, "just oozing confidence." When they'd first met, in a bar, "he wanted to dance with me and buy my girlfriends drinks. And he set his eyes on me and it was like he was going to get me. He couldn't get me to move in with him fast enough."

Peterson always saw himself as the knight in shining armor, Vicki noted. "He thought he took me away to a better life. He definitely felt that way. It's ironic. In his eyes, he did believe that." This seemed to echo what Peterson himself had told first Rivera, then Lauer, about "rescuing" Kitty and Stacy. Somehow, being seen as the hero was vital to Peterson's sense of himself, in Vicki's view.

"I believe that man had a disease to his ego. He's a legend in his own mind. . . . He really led a double life. But what fed his ego was his line of work, how he could deceive people. When he'd come home, he'd be the exact opposite." (What Vicki meant by this seemingly contradictory remark wasn't clear.) "He could do it and he could do it with no problems."

But as time went on, she said, Peterson's duplicity at work as a narc began to infect the way he saw everything. Eventually he came to believe that Vicki was cheating on him—again echoing a theme he'd raised in connection with Stacy's disappearance.

"We had bugs in our house," Vicki said. "He put a microphone in our kitchen and taped our conversations. He was cheating so much he wanted to make sure I wasn't. His whole thing with us [was] that, 'I need to know my family is safe at home and you're not going to be doing anything you shouldn't be doing'—and that enabled him to do whatever he wanted."

Slife reported no remarks from Vicki about Suds Pub, or her brother, Gerry, shot to death on Chicago's South Side in 1994.

That same evening, Greta Van Susteren interviewed Baden again. Baden had observed the re-autopsy of Dr. Blum, and then examined the remains himself, at the request of the Savio family a day or so later.

Baden noted that Kitty was still wearing her jewelry when she was found in the tub—the Savios told him she usually removed it before bathing, which suggested that she did not go into the bathtub of her own accord. With the re-autopsy, Baden said, X-rays were taken. No broken bones were discovered.

In his opinion, Baden told Van Susteren, the manner of Kitty's death was homicide: there was no doubt, "to a reasonable degree of medical certainty." That should have been obvious during the first autopsy, he said. The bruises had been fresh at the time of the first examination. Baden had inspected the bruises under a microscope, and concluded that they were inflicted about the time of death.

He theorized that a killer had pushed Kitty's head down under the water, not letting her up until she was dead.

23.
Ratings Honey

Three days later, on November 19, Peterson returned to *Today,* this time with Joel Brodsky, who had contacted Peterson after the first show, and as Renee Rockwell had predicted, offered his legal services to the embattled, by-now-retired cop, whether for "free" wasn't entirely clear. While still in New York, Peterson was also interviewed and photographed by *People* magazine, which made arrangements to follow Peterson back to Bolingbrook, so photographers could snap him in the backyard of the by-now infamous 6 Pheasant Chase Court. Over two weeks, Peterson had been transformed from a nonentity into a national celebrity.

In the new interview, Lauer tried to get Peterson to react to Baden's opinion, that Kitty had definitely been murdered. But Peterson sat silent as Brodsky fielded the questions from Lauer.

Baden, Brodsky said, had already made up his mind before even attending Blum's re-autopsy.

"Dr. Baden, with all due respect to him, is a renowned pathologist, but he had a pre-existing opinion before he did the autopsy," Brodsky said, referring to the interview Baden had given Van Susteren in early November. "His conclusion was a self-fulfilling prophecy."

Lauer and Brodsky fenced with each other about questions Brodsky would allow Peterson to answer. "Mr. Peterson, are you upset to learn that she may have been murdered?" Lauer asked.

What sort of a question was that? Did Lauer really expect Peterson to say "No, I'm not upset"? The question wasn't intended to develop any information other than a television image of Peterson reacting to the provocative question. Surely Lauer didn't expect Peterson to break into tears and sobs and admit that he'd killed his third wife, as if Perry Mason had confronted him on the witness stand. So the question was loaded, intended only to mousetrap Peterson between extremes of emotion, in order to expose him as a fake. Well, it was television.

"Yes, I am upset to hear something like that," Peterson said, in a measured response. "Very much so." But it hardly seemed that way—score one for Lauer.

As for Baden, Brodsky said that Baden's earlier statement that people "don't drown in bathtubs" simply wasn't supported by the facts. "We do disagree with his finding," Brodsky said. "The first autopsy, from what I understand, was very thorough. They concluded it was an accident."

Lauer complained that Brodsky seemed to be intent on keeping Peterson from directly answering any questions.

"It appears now that I'm going to be walking a fine line between what you want to tell me, Mr. Brodsky, and what Mr. Peterson is allowed to tell me," he said. He asked Peterson about the *Chicago Tribune* story featuring Vicki a few days earlier. It seemed clear now, Peterson said, that Vicki had some animosity toward him—why else would she have said what she said? But it wasn't until he read her remarks in the newspaper that he was aware of it. "I thought we were friends," he told Lauer.

Lauer asked if he'd really told Vicki that he "could kill her and make it look like an accident," but Brodsky told Peterson not to either affirm or deny the claim.

"People [who] are divorced are always making accusations and comments about each other," Brodsky told Lauer. "This is simply a comment by someone who went through a divorce with Mr. Peterson." Brodsky knew that if Peterson denied ever saying something like that to Vicki, the state could use that at trial, then call Vicki as a witness to rebut the denial. That was one of the dangers of a potential defendant going public, as Herman and Rockwell had pointed out a few nights earlier on the Nancy Grace show.

Lauer continued his effort to get an emotional rise out of Peterson.

"Are you worried about her, Mr. Peterson?" Lauer was referring to Stacy.

"Of course," Peterson said. "Your wife leaves, and I have kids at home, you are very much worried about her." The distancing—from the ordinary "I" to "you"—didn't help Peterson at all. An innocent person might have said something like, "Of course, I'm frantic, I'm worried sick! I can't sleep at night—who knows where she might be, or if she's in trouble? For all I know, some maniac might have convinced her to run away with him. Maybe even someone who wants to get back at me by harming her." But Peterson's laconic, pro forma response suggested he wasn't worried at all.

"Although you think she is with another man, are you worried that she may never come back to be a mother to these children?" Lauer's producers wanted to hit the "mom" and "children" angle again and again—they knew their demographic well.

"Yes, I am. . . . Kids need a mom . . . Basically, I'd like to have her publicly show herself now, and clear all of this up."

Peterson returned to Bolingbrook after the second *Today* show to find, if anything, an even larger gaggle of newspeople camped out in front of his house. If he'd thought his appearance on national broadcast television would convince the media circus to fold up its tent and decamp to another town, another story, he was wrong. Dead wrong.

But at least he wasn't hiding out any longer. He popped up on several cable and broadcast channels, always begging the reporters to leave him alone.

"It's mind-boggling," Peterson told one reporter. "You

know, it's just like people are looking at me under a magnifying glass. And it's very upsetting. I mean, what I had for breakfast is a big—is newsworthy."

And:

"Please go home. Thanksgiving's in the next couple days. Please go home. Please leave me alone. Please don't get involved in my . . ." Peterson's voice trailed off as he turned away.

But the more he tried to shoo the media flies away, the thicker they swarmed. His very demeanor made him ratings honey. That same morning, November 19, Diane Sawyer had his first wife, Carol, as a guest. From once interviewing Richard Nixon after his fall to interviewing the first of four wives of a suburban police sergeant was quite a come-down, for Sawyer. It wasn't Sawyer or even Carol, though; it was a measurement of how low the media could go in an era when ratings dollars called the tune. She asked Carol if she'd seen any signs of "controlling behavior"—a somewhat elastic term, but one that had become shorthand for almost any male marital suspect after O.J. Simpson in the 1990s and early 2000s—and Carol said she had not. What she didn't like about Drew, Carol said, was that he habitually cheated on her.

Well, in a way, that could be construed as "controlling behavior"—a form of humiliating a spouse. Until Carol said "enough." But Peterson hadn't drowned her in a bathtub, or caused her to vanish.

Brooks' earlier *Headline News* show, substituting for Nancy Grace, seemed so successful that his producers apparently decided to do it again.

"Well, Drew Peterson is again saying he wants the media to leave him alone," Brooks said that same night, November 19, 2007. "He doesn't want them camped outside of his house anymore. He wants them to go away. But it seems like he hasn't met a camera that he hasn't [fallen] in love with. He was back on the *Today* show for the second time. Let's take a listen."

(For some reason, the phrase "let's take a listen" crept

into almost all cable anchors' vocabulary about this time, signifying they were about to replay previously recorded material, although why the redundant word "take" was necessary wasn't clear, when "let's listen" already fit the bill. Soon it ranked at the top of the anchors' hit parade, right along with "facts on the ground," "boots on the ground," "absolutely," and "right you are," as network audio/video transitional clichés by 2007.)

Brooks and his cohorts "took a listen" to Peterson on *Today*, Round Two. When the clip from the tape was played, Brooks brought in another psychologist, a psychotherapist named Robi Ludwig, the author of *Till Death Do Us Part*, a book about spousal abuse.

Brooks asked Ludwig what she made of Peterson's body language during his second tour with Lauer.

Ludwig said she thought Peterson's demeanor "very bizarre." He didn't seem to have any empathy, Ludwig said. She thought Peterson seemed "a little annoyed and angry," as if he resented being asked questions, as if he considered himself the victim, because his wife had left him. Ludwig said that based on Peterson's demeanor, she believed that Stacy had left, and that was why Peterson was angry. Ludwig seemed not to have considered the possibility that Peterson was being taciturn on the advice of his lawyer, Brodsky.

"So I think, in his mind, he feels that she left him, he's unloved, and therefore, that's what happened. He's somehow justified. Of course, I don't want to say that he's guilty, but you know, this is a very dangerous person, somebody who's angry, feels left, and that's very often what happens with controlling husbands. They very often get violent when they feel that they're losing their wives. And instead of losing them, they take the ultimate in control, and they basically eliminate their wives."

Well, this was interesting: Ludwig was suggesting that Peterson truly believed that Stacy was having an affair with someone else, and that he might have killed her—not to shut her up about Kitty—but out of rage at being abandoned. Of course, this was the problem with trying to psychologically assess anyone from across a continent, and from only a few excerpts of video-taped conversation, made while under the hot lights of television. It was far too easy to project one's own beliefs and prejudices onto the image. Peterson was being deemed guilty on the basis of the way he seemed, not actual evidence, as Richard Herman had tried to point out a few days before. But the tide was in flood and rapidly washing away the presumption of innocence.

Brooks also called once more on Lieberman, of *America's Most Wanted*, who had previously claimed to have "sources" inside the nascent investigation, although on that same day, investigators from the ISP had insisted that they were doing their job, that they weren't rushing their conclusions to satisfy television, and would keep their own counsel, until they had a real case. "This is not a television story. This will not be resolved quickly. An investigation like this takes time," someone from the ISP asserted, in an unattributed quote in one of the newspapers.

Brooks asked Lieberman if he'd heard anything that suggested the state police were culling closed circuit television recordings from banks, convenience stores or other such places in an effort to establish Stacy's whereabouts on October 28.

Lieberman said the investigators were doing exactly that, although they were trying to keep their efforts "close to the vest." Lieberman said he could, however, reveal that the special grand jury was still meeting, and that certain pieces of evidence would be provided.

This statement from Lieberman suggested that the police investigators had in fact collected video evidence of Stacy's whereabouts (or lack of it) in the days before and after October 28. Lieberman said the police were keeping this endeavor secret. But, he said, the investigators were very interested in checking out the timeline of the events, at least as it had been told to them by Peterson. To that end, the ubiquitous video cameras might be very useful.

Then Lieberman disclosed some astonishing information: His outfit had "confirmed," as he put it, that Peterson had appeared before the special grand jury, and had then asserted his privilege not to testify against himself under the Fifth Amendment.

This was a truly startling piece of news—that Peterson had been called as a witness before Glasgow's special grand jury, and that he had declined to testify. Ordinarily, targets of a grand jury aren't called as witnesses, and usually, if they are, it's not until a grand jury has completed an investigation, and even then, usually, only at the target's own request. Had Peterson really demanded to be heard? And if so, once before the jury, why would he claim a Fifth Amendment privilege? Why demand to be heard, then clam up? It made no sense.

Lieberman threw this bit of Fifth Amendment incendiary news out over the cablewires as if it was a hard fact, but without any effort to establish his report's reliability. Moreover, witnesses before grand juries were supposed to be secret, and so, supposedly, was their testimony. So, if Lieberman was right, there had to be a leak, which would be a violation of the law. But Lieberman gave no provenance for his "scoop"—the *Headline News* viewers just had to take his word for it.

Brooks was amazed, and said so—not at the lack of provenance for Lieberman's "inside information," but that Peterson had supposedly declined to testify.

"So he took the Fifth during the grand jury. That's amazing," Brooks said. Lieberman said that *America's Most Wanted*'s sources had "confirmed" this information.

"You know, right now, I want to uncage the attorneys," Brooks said, referring to them as if they were wild, slavering beasts. In the New York City cage was Alex Sanchez and Lauren Lake, both defense attorneys.

What did Sanchez think of Lieberman's information about Peterson and the Fifth Amendment? Brooks asked.

Sanchez said he was flabbergasted to hear Lieberman's report about the special grand jury. He wanted to know how that factoid had emerged. Any grand jury proceeding was supposed to be secret, Sanchez said. If Lieberman's information was accurate, that meant someone had to be leaking, in violation of the law. In his view, that meant that someone in authority was already bollixing up any possible case against Peterson by committing potential prosecutorial misconduct. Sanchez' commentary buttressed Herman's contention from a few nights before, that someone had a political agenda, if indeed Lieberman had "sources" leaking grand jury information.

Brooks passed over this apparent violation of the law, and Sanchez' suggestion for what it might mean for the legal adequacy of any eventual prosecution of Peterson, at least as to potential prosecutorial misconduct. He went to Lake to see what she had to say.

Peterson had "lawyered up now," Brooks said, using the police vernacular for when a person avails himself of his rights. To a cop, or even a former cop, only a guilty person would consult a lawyer; that is, "lawyer up." Unless they were a cop themselves, of course. He wanted to know what Lake thought that meant. Brooks seemed to be trying to induce Lake to say that Peterson was the prime suspect in one or two murders. He slipped over the reality: whether innocent or guilty, anytime someone is labeled a suspect, as the state police had Peterson, and anytime someone is summoned to testify before a grand jury—if Lieberman was right—he'd be an idiot not to "lawyer up."

"Absolutely," Lake said, falling back on the transitional word *du jour*, the primary utility of which was to provide a pause to think before saying anything substantive, almost as a shield. Then: any person in Peterson's situation *had* to have a lawyer, Lake said.

But, Lake added, Peterson and any lawyer who was advising him had messed things up. Peterson needed to clam up at this point, Lake said. "All of these appearances and playing up to the camera and photo shoots, I'm not liking it at all," Lake said. "And what I really don't like about it is that Mr. Peterson's not coming off as a very lovable character. And so the more we get to know him, unfortunately, the more negative commentary we have about his personality, and the way he seems to come across."

Brooks went back to Sanchez, and asked if he agreed with Lake.

Yes, Sanchez said, Peterson had "buried himself" with his public remarks. Sanchez wasn't sure he could ever be resurrected. Peterson's remark to Lauer about Stacy's menstrual cycle only showed him to be an insensitive oaf, and ignorant as well.

"I mean, these are very offensive statements," Sanchez said. The best thing for Peterson to do at this point, Sanchez said, was to hide out, but not before putting out a statement—through a lawyer—saying that he was "very concerned about the whereabouts of his wife."

Lake wanted to chime in, again taking off from Peterson's interviews with Lauer. When Peterson had said that he didn't "mean to be funny" about Stacy's menstrual cycle and her demands for divorce, that was a disaster for Peterson's image, Lake said.

"[When Peterson] said, 'This is hilarious.' What's hilarious? What is hilarious about your wife missing? 'This isn't how I planned to spend my retirement.' Mr. Peterson, go somewhere and sit down!"

(Actually, what Peterson said was, "I don't mean to be funny." He'd never said the situation was "hilarious." Nor, does it appear, did Peterson ever say he hadn't planned to spend his retirement as a news media piñata. It appears that Lake was paraphrasing second- and third-hand reports to make her point, which was nevertheless still valid—Peterson should clam up.)

Brooks said he agreed with both defense lawyers. He said he thought Peterson should shut himself inside his house, and say no more. Brooks said he didn't think Peterson was getting very effective legal advice.

Sanchez agreed. No experienced lawyer would allow Peterson to spout off the way he had, Sanchez said. Peterson was out of his depth in dealing with the carnivores of the news media. "He doesn't know what it's like to speak on television and to be interviewed by reporters. . . . He needs to stop."

"And on the *Today* show, they'd asked him a question, [and] he looked to his attorney, like, 'Can I answer this?'" Brooks said.

This remark by Brooks was truly vapid—having just excoriated Peterson for *not* taking legal advice and not clamming up, he now excoriated him once more—for *taking* legal advice and clamming up. On the other hand, if Peterson had barricaded himself inside 6 Pheasant Chase Court, Brooks (and others) would have accused him of hiding something. It only proved that once one was in the media crosshairs, one under suspicion was damned no matter what they did, said, or did *not* say. And, perhaps, it showed that Brooks had finally gone over to the dark side—ratings counted more to him than his former lawman's responsibility for fairness, or at least objectivity. In short, Brooks, in his cablevision persona, had seemingly flushed the U.S. Constitution down the toilet, or certainly Constitution 101 from the police academy.

With his mindset, revealed by his commentary over the week of November 14 to November 19, 2007, Brooks would have fit right in with the vigilantes of San Francisco, California, or Montana of the 1850s and 1860s. *Hang 'im!* Or so it seemed at the time. At least it was popular, if not constitutional. Yes, Peterson might have been a dog, even a murderer, but he had a right to a fair trial, which Brooks seemed not to understand, or at least care very much about. Like most lynchers, Brooks had cloaked himself in the most popular red-white-and-blue prejudices, and then took his money to the bank.

Over the next week or so, there was more of this, much more, and not just on CNN or Fox. The airwaves, cable wires, and public prints were all filled by snippets from psychologists, pathologists, lawyers, armchair investigators, a few psychics, self-proclaimed "profilers," mixed with recorded shorts and occasional live interviews with real people who knew, or thought they knew, something of what was going on, with one to six degrees of separation.

For a while in late November and early December of 2007, it seemed as though it was all Peterson, all the time. Had the news media had as much intense curiosity about Osama bin Laden in the months before September 11, 2001, perhaps today we would be living in an altogether different world.

On the same evening that Brooks had teed off on Peterson, his competitor Van Susteren had Baden on her show again. Only a few days after he'd finished his own autopsy at the request of the Savios, Baden once more reiterated his earlier opinion: Kitty Savio had been murdered, not drowned accidentally. Baden suggested that the lack of rigor mortis and the degree of lividity (that is, the subsidence of blood to the lowest parts of a dead body via gravity) showed that the death had occurred "at least thirty hours" before the body's discovery in the tub, by Carcerano and the Pontarellis.

If Baden was correct about "at least thirty hours"—time of death is always an iffy proposition, depending on room temperature and other variables, as his own testimony in the Spector case only a few months before suggested—that also indicated that Kitty Savio was dead by 7 a.m. on Sunday, February 29, 2004. In other words, Kitty, according to Baden, had died within the six- or seven-hour alibi period Stacy Peterson had provided for Drew Peterson during the 2004 Illinois State Police investigation. That is, between 1 a.m. and 8 a.m. that same early Sunday morning, February 29, 2004.

And of course, Stacy was now a missing person.

24.
On the Media Couch

"You're being harassed by the media," one of the TV gaggle camped out in the Pheasant Chase Court cul-de-sac asked Peterson in late November of 2007. "Why are you talking to us? I mean, why are you—what is the point of going on TV with Matt Lauer last week, and also doing several interviews today?"

"That was up to my attorney."

"I mean, what—well, then, what is . . ." Sometimes television reporters can be particularly inarticulate, knowing that they have an all-seeing camera in back of them.

"You're going to have to get with him for his thoughts and feelings on his—why he wants to talk to the media," Peterson said.

"But why—but originally, you didn't have that attorney last week."

"Right."

"So what point are you trying to get across by talking to us?"

"Leave me alone." That *was* the point, Peterson seemed to be saying—just leave him alone.

"Drew, anything else you'd like to say about, you know, your feelings as Stacy's husband? Three weeks now she's been missing. As a husband whose wife is missing—granted, you said, you know, she left you for another man. But what are you *feeling*, that it's still [the] woman you were married to, the mother of your two youngest children?"

"Right. I'm still in love with Stacy, and I miss her."

Could anything be worse than being considered wife-killer, pedophile, crooked cop, and cuckold, all rolled into one? With a next-door neighbor hiding out under a fake name, convinced you murdered her friend, your twenty-three-year-old wife? With four preadult children, including two preschoolers, wondering what's going on? With the television people jamming your suburban cul-de-sac with their satellite trucks, salivating for your imminent arrest, O.J. Simpson–style, pining for the picture? With Greta Van Susteren, Nancy Grace and her cohorts, Larry King, Matt Lauer, Diane Sawyer—even Diane Sawyer!—in hot pursuit, dredging up parts of your past you'd rather not remember? How would you like it?

How could things turn upside down so quickly? That was certainly how Drew Peterson felt in the last week of November 2007, as he became the latest Cable Age Bluebeard, the man who supposedly used, abused and then murdered two wives. Yes, he was a nasty, selfish randy dog—he would readily admit as much a year later. But did that mean he was a murderer? These were two different things. Just because he was one didn't mean he was the other. It certainly didn't prove it legally, although it devastated Peterson in the larger court, that of public opinion. Peterson was portrayed by various armchair experts as a showboat, a psychopath, a camera hog, a narcissist, a liar, a cheater, even a "scumbag."

As the rest of the last week of November ensued, at least one person came to his defense: his mother, Betty Morphey, then seventy-nine. Asked what she would say to Stacy, if she was around, Betty pulled no punches.

"I would tell her I'm ashamed of her, for putting the family through this," Betty told the *Sun-Times*. "She knows where she is. . . . I could swear on a Bible that he would never hurt anyone at any time," she said of her son. "I'm proud he's my son and I feel so bad he's got to go through all this, because of her. She was just too young. . . . All of this is not necessary. . . . She didn't have to walk out and leave everybody stranded and not knowing what to do. All she has to do is call and say she's fine." Clearly, Betty believed Peterson when he said his fourth wife had left him for someone else, taking her "favorite bikini" with her.

On November 20, two days before Thanksgiving, Brooks was at it again, this time with a psychologist from Texas, William July.

"Mike, this is exactly what I'm talking about in *Behavior of Interest*," July's recent book. Going on camera to weigh in on Peterson gave authors a chance to hawk their own wares. "We're looking at one or two things here. Either he is a narcissistic personality and he can't help but to go and get in front of the cameras—it reminds me of O.J., because he's always in trouble. And this guy is doing the same thing. He's got to stay in front of the cameras. Or the other alternative is . . . he is trying to—because he knows what he's doing, he's a former detective and everything, maybe he's playing to all of us, and he's trying to put forth an image of innocence by doing the things that an innocent person would do, which is to be forthright and forthcoming. But when we watch him, we see narcissistic behavior."

Brooks called on Pat Brown, the "profiler," once more, who was pushing her own book, *Killing for Sport*.

"Pat, what do you think about this guy—what this guy's behavior over the last week?"

"Well, first of all, I think action speaks louder than words, and we know he is a liar, because he says he doesn't like the media, but he does love the media," Brown offered. "So that we know, right up front. And I think it's real interesting what his mum says." (Brown's use of the word "mum," rather than "mom" or "mother," identified her as British, perhaps someone not well attuned to American cultural paradigms, which somewhat undercut her expertise as an expert "profiler," *Killing for Sport* notwithstanding.)

"She says she's ashamed of Stacy," Brown continued. "And if I were in her position, I would be ashamed of raising a son like that, a lying, cheating adulterer, scumbag-of-a-son like that. And I can tell you if it was my son, there would be one less plate at the Thanksgiving table. But this is the kind of mother that will raise a son like this, kind of like a psychopath from a narcissist, in my point of view."

From another point of view, though, Brown possibly only hoped to use *Headline News* to sell more copies of her book, *Killing for Sport*. Her excess of language seemed to suggest as much—"scumbag," indeed. It was hard not to feel sympathy for "this kind of mother," a "narcissist," meaning Betty Morphey, after Brown's intemperate attack. Truly, live television often brings out the worst in people: venal vendors, or even narcissistic authors.

Then, in the final week of the month, nearly thirty days after Stacy Peterson vanished, a new report surfaced: the talk about the "blue barrel."

Tracing the origin of the "blue barrel" tale is, much like the story of Stacy Peterson's disappearance, an exercise in frustration. There is some suggestion that fragments of the story had been rumored for several weeks prior to late November, but based on an analysis of the transcripts archived by ACandyRose.com, an Internet website that compiled many Peterson news media reports, it appears that the first public mention of the "barrel" tale came on Fox by Geraldo Rivera.

On November 24, without citing any source, Rivera reported that "a neighbor" (unnamed by Rivera) had told "law enforcement" (again unnamed) that Peterson and another man had been seen putting a blue container into Peterson's Denali around the time of Stacy's disappearance. Rivera followed this up with another blind quote, this one to the effect that Cassandra had once observed a blue barrel of swimming pool chlorine in the Peterson garage.

It didn't take very long after these reports for a theory to form: Peterson had dumped the chlorine from the barrel into the backyard swimming pool, then put Stacy's dead body into the empty chlorine barrel, moved the barrel into the rear of his Denali with the help of another person, then drove off with the barrel holding Stacy's body to get rid of the corpse.

Rivera didn't say where any of this information came from, but by saying that the information had been provided to "law enforcement" festooned it with legitimacy. Very soon the pack was on the scent of the other man, the one who supposedly had helped put the "blue barrel," as it was soon referred to, into the back of the Peterson SUV.

Within a matter of days, the name floated to the surface: Drew's putative helper was none other than Tom Morphey, his stepbrother by way of his mother Betty's remarriage.

Now Betty Morphey had twice the worrries.

25.

The Blue Barrel Polka

The origin and reliability—the provenance—of the Morphey connection to this part of the Peterson wives' tale remains obscure, at least to the public, years after its emergence in the media in late November of 2007. The news transcripts compiled by ACandyRose.com suggest that the tale of the blue barrel was first publicly linked to Peterson's stepbrother on November 27 on CNN's *Headline News*, in a report by Mary Frances Bragiel, a Chicago radio reporter.

Jane Velez-Mitchell, subbing for Nancy Grace, asked Bragiel for the latest dish.

"Mary, what can you tell us specifically about these new bombshells involving a possible blue barrel, and a possible accomplice?" Both CNN and Fox News were always citing "bombshells," as if the Peterson story was some sort of war zone, and where "boots on the ground" like Bragiel were, in some perverted media cliché, combat correspondents.

"Well, the blue barrel story has been out there since this investigation began," Bragiel said, "which is why Illinois State Police investigators have been focusing all their time on the water. In terms of this accomplice, Illinois State Police will only say that they're looking at a person who may have helped Drew Peterson, and sources tell me that it is a family member through marriage who was seen with him, regarding this body, and that that family member tried to commit suicide three days after Stacy Peterson went missing."

(Actually, the supposed suicide attempt was the day after the disappearance, according to later reports.)

"And this family member, just to make sure I understand this theory correctly, was spotted, allegedly, by some neighbor moving a blue barrel, allegedly, with Drew Peterson?" Velez-Mitchell asked. (Clearly, some of CNN's lawyers had cautioned Velez-Mitchell and others in the network to tread carefully as to Peterson's possible guilt. If Peterson wasn't charged and convicted, the legal consequences for the network could be very, very expensive, allegedly.)

"That's correct. Of course, Drew Peterson's attorney denies all of it, and questions the investigation by Illinois State Police, which he claims all these stories are being—all these stories are being made up, as a result of this investigation." Bragiel's grammar was somewhat off the reservation, but still communicated Brodsky's point—all the publicity so far had resulted in a slew of wild tales that nevertheless had to be delved into by the state police.

"Well, you know," Velez-Mitchell said, "we absolutely want to stress that Drew Peterson has not been charged with anything. He deserves the presumption of innocence. CNN cannot independently confirm these published reports. And of course, we always invite Drew Peterson or his attorney to appear on the show to tell their side of the story. In fact, we tried to contact his attorney today and were unable to reach him."

By the following evening, Tom Morphey's actual name had surfaced. As pieced together by Fox's Fuhrman and others, it appeared that Peterson had supposedly called Morphey, and asked him to meet him at a nearby donut shop sometime on the evening of October 28, the day Stacy disappeared. At first the details of this encounter were sketchy, but as the next week unfolded, it appeared that the police were working on the theory that Peterson had given Morphey his own cell phone to hold. Then Peterson had told Morphey to wait for him at the donut shop for some minutes, and if the Peterson cell phone rang, he was not to answer it.

Some minutes later, the cell phone did ring. Morphey, according to the theory, obeyed Peterson's instructions, and let it ring unanswered, but noted that the call had come from Stacy. At some point thereafter, Peterson reappeared at the donut shop, whereupon Morphey informed him that Stacy had called. The theory of the police was that Peterson himself had made the call to his own cell phone, using Stacy's cell phone to establish an alibi for himself. Peterson, the theory went, obviously knew that the call would be traced to the relaying cell phone tower, and hoped to use the ruse to show that Stacy was alive and well on the evening of October 28, and some distance away from Peterson, as both cell phones would indicate. That story would stand up, as long as Morphey didn't tell anyone the truth, of course.

Then, according to the media scuttlebutt, Peterson had asked Morphey to help him with a small job: they drove to the 6 Pheasant Chase Court house, where Morphey supposedly helped Peterson remove a blue barrel from the Peterson bedroom to the rear of Peterson's Denali. Just why there would be a barrel of any hue in the Peterson bedroom wasn't explained by any of the media reports—such a thing would obviously be out of the ordinary for bedroom décor, and the implication that it was used to transport a dead body was obvious, but uncommented on.

After this, again supposedly, Peterson gave Morphey some money and told him to go home. Then, according to the unfolding media theory, Peterson alone drove the blue barrel to some deserted location, likely a river or canal, and dumped the barrel containing Stacy's body, weighted down by Peterson's scuba-diving weights, which were said to be missing from the Peterson house.

The next day, Morphey was hospitalized, after attempting—again allegedly—to commit suicide.

The tale neatly wrapped things up: It accounted for Peterson's absence when Cassandra first telephoned him on the evening of October 28, when Kris had said his father was out looking for Stacy. It accounted for the calls from Stacy's cell phone to Peterson around 9 p.m. that night. It accounted for the unnamed neighbor who claimed to have seen Peterson and another man load a blue barrel into the rear of the Denali on the night of October 28. And if Morphey had really tried to commit suicide the day after Stacy's disappearance, didn't that indicate at least the possibility of a guilty conscience?

As Mark Fuhrman put it on Greta Van Susteren's show *On the Record* on November 27, it all seemed to fit.

"Morphey's statements are crisp with truth, and there is no reason for him to come forward," Fuhrman opined, although why there was no reason for Morphey to "come forward" wasn't particularly obvious. "Peterson is very hesitant with the timeline, and Morphey fills the timeline right in. Peterson picks Morphey up at a park, so there had to be a phone call right there. Peterson takes Morphey to a coffee shop and leaves him with a cell phone. A phone call comes in, is not answered, and the display shows 'Stacy.' There is a seven to ten p.m. window here. I don't know how that's all filled in. Morphey claims he went into an upstairs bedroom and helped him move a sealed, one-hundred-twenty-pound container that was warm to the touch, and put it into the Denali. There were blue plastic scrapings on the tailgate of the Denali. The suicide attempt is not accidental, if he shares with a friend and his wife of what he thinks he's helped Peterson to do."

The biggest problem with this seemingly logical analysis was that it didn't come directly from Morphey himself. He'd been incommunicado since the day after Stacy vanished, first with his hospitalization, and then later as a supposed material witness held in protective custody by the police. So how did Fuhrman and others learn of Morphey's "claims," as even Fuhrman referred to them?

It soon appeared that a friend of Morphey, one Walter Martineck, first spilled the beans, and apparently to both the *Chicago Tribune* and *Sun-Times*, which published stories about the tale on November 29. Both newspapers cited unnamed police sources to seemingly confirm Martineck's version, which supposedly came directly to Martineck from Morphey. By this point the "blue barrel" had been transformed into some sort of blue rectangular container. But it was still "warm to the touch" on the night of October 28, according to the two newspapers.

That night, the talking heads examined the story with their usual blend of outrage, humor and conjecture.

"I'm Jane Velez-Mitchell, in for Nancy Grace. A flurry of major new developments [at least they weren't bombshells] in the case of Stacy Peterson, who simply vanished into thin air on October 28. Did a relative unwittingly help dispose of her remains while they were still warm to the touch? Are all these shocking new leads true? And if they are, what should police be doing about them? For the very latest, we go straight out to CNN correspondent Keith Oppenheim, who is in Chicago. Keith, what is the very latest?" The front-loading of the cablecast with provocative, unanswered questions was pure tabloid-style. *Is Elvis Alive on Venus?*

Despite the boffo intro, Oppenheim, it appeared, had little new to offer, other than what had been reported in the Chicago newspapers. The police, he said, were being "very tight-lipped." So Oppenheim drew upon the newspaper reports, specifically the story that a relative of Peterson might have helped him remove a container of some sort from the 6 Pheasant Chase Court house on the night Stacy disappeared. Along with the transported container story, Oppenheim said, the papers were also reporting that the relative had told others that he was afraid he had helped Peterson dispose of Stacy's body. Then, Oppenheim added, the following day that unnamed relative had tried to commit suicide, and the day after that, Peterson had visited him in the hospital—at least according to the newspapers.

Velez-Mitchell then provided the usual caveat to this sort of unattributed information: the cable channel couldn't confirm what the newspapers had reported, that some of the information was "fourth-hand," and that Peterson's lawyer, Brodsky, had dismissed the reports as unfounded "rumors," and that in any case, the unnamed relative had "serious psychological issues." Nevertheless, Velez-Mitchell called the newspaper reports "a major break in the case" that was being "reported widely." (Velez-Mitchell seemed to confuse actual information with "a major break," from the mere fact that it had been "reported widely." Just because it was being "reported widely" didn't mean it was accurate.)

Velez-Mitchell turned to Mike Brooks, the channel's expert on law enforcement. Wouldn't it be likely that if someone needed help to put a container in a vehicle, he or she would also need help to take it out? Didn't that mean that the relative, whoever he was, would have information as to where the body was?

Brooks agreed, seemingly, but pointed out that the body could have been moved again, later. Brooks seemed to ignore the evident reality that putting a heavy container *into* a vehicle is much harder than removing it—gravity helps, after all. Brooks made it seem as simple as A-B-C, which, of course, it wasn't—a loader didn't have to be an unloader, so maybe Morphey had no idea of where the body was left, if in fact the supposed container held Stacy's body. The whole idea was stupid—it revealed nothing more than Velez-Mitchell's desire to inculpate Peterson, and Brooks' own slavish desire to validate Velez-Mitchell as a supposed law enforcement "expert." Journalism, Cronkite-style, this was not.

Meanwhile, Brooks said, the FBI was on the case. And that was good—the FBI had many resources, among them polygraph experts. Brooks noted that Peterson had, in a recent interview, indicated a willingness to take a polygraph test. So the FBI should offer him one, Brooks said. They should also give one to the relative, Brooks said, identifying the relative as Peterson's step-brother, but not using Morphey's name. Even though polygraphs weren't admissible as evidence in court, they were still useful in an investigation, Brooks said.

Velez-Mitchell said she thought the relative should be summoned "immediately" before the special grand jury. Then she had a second thought—if the relative (Morphey) did have psychological problems, as Brodsky had contended, would he be a reliable witness? She asked two defense lawyers, Mark Eiglarsh and Renee Rockwell, for their opinion.

Rockwell zeroed in on Brooks' suggestion that Peterson be given a polygraph. That wasn't going to happen, ever, Rockwell said. Any competent defense lawyer would never let it happen. If Brooks was talking about the relative, there were other problems with that, she said.

Velez-Mitchell was still focused on the special grand jury, however, not Brooks' suggestion about lie detector tests. She thought the relative should be called to testify so that the authorities could see if there was anything to the tale that had been reported in the newspapers.

Rockwell seemed to agree. "Absolutely," she said. But then she contradicted herself. The relative shouldn't do anything, or testify anywhere, unless he had his own legal counsel. If the relative did know something, he needed a lawyer to negotiate immunity for him. It was always possible, she said, that if the story of the container was true, the relative could be criminally liable. "So he needs to retain counsel, get an immunity agreement, and go and tell it like it is," Rockwell concluded.

What did Eiglarsh think?

A former prosecutor in Florida, Eiglarsh said he agreed with Rockwell, at least as far as the relative's need to retain a lawyer. But it was always possible that the relative had committed no crime in helping Peterson move a container, if one had actually existed. If the relative had helped move a container without knowing what was in it, he had no criminal liability.

Velez-Mitchell lassoed another talking head: Kathy Chaney, a reporter for *The Chicago Defender*. There were other unconfirmed reports, Velez-Mitchell said, that the relative was in fear, and that he'd been admitted for some sort of treatment. What did Chaney know?

"Yes, he is," Chaney said, not specifying which, or both: fear or treatment. Brodsky had reacted to the report about the container by claiming that the relative had spent previous periods in mental hospitals. Chaney segued from Brodsky's assertion to the relative without making this clear. The relative, she indicated, was "keeping mum" because he wasn't sure if he'd helped Peterson dispose of "Kathleen's body—I'm sorry, Stacy's body," Chaney amended. But the relative was in fear, which was why he had not come forward to be interviewed by the news media, "because he's scared." Just how Chaney knew Morphey's mental state—"he's scared"—she did not make clear, but given that Morphey was then incommunicado, a rational analyst had to think that Chaney was just guessing, or projecting. Or maybe Chaney was buying what some unnamed police sources were claiming about Morphey's fear.

Velez-Mitchell wanted to know whether the relative had been interviewed by the police.

Yes, Chaney said—the investigators had spoken to the relative.

Velez-Mitchell turned back to Brooks. Did Brooks think the relative had anything to fear from Peterson at this point?

Not really, Brooks said—the ISP and the FBI would have the situation well in hand.

Velez-Mitchell said she had the impression that Peterson was actually enjoying his turn in the news media crosshairs. She noted that someone in the media had loaned Peterson a video camera, which he'd used to video-tape the media video-taping *him.*

What did Bethany Marshall, the psychoanalyst, make of that behavior? Velez-Mitchell asked. She noted that Marshall was the author of *Deal Breakers: When to Work Out a Relationship and When to Walk Away*, which Velez-Mitchell thought should be retitled to "When to *Run* Away."

Everyone on the show laughed.

Peterson, Marshall said, seemed to be enjoying himself, all right. To Marshall, that suggested that Peterson was an exhibitionist. (Of course, even Peterson would admit to that.) Marshall thought Peterson was having "the time of his life" by being in the camera lenses. But Marshall said she was "struck" by Peterson's demeanor—he didn't seemed to be stressed out over his situation, at least as he was being portrayed by the news media in the sidewalk interviews he continued giving. It reminded Marshall of O.J. Simpson with his account, *If I Did It*. Peterson, she indicated, had no remorse, and didn't seem to care about upsetting the families of Kitty and Stacy. She thought Peterson seemed "triumphant."

Velez-Mitchell suggested that might mean that Peterson would stick around for the finale—not flee—because he enjoyed the limelight so much.

"He's having way too good of a time," Marshall agreed.

"Oh, my gosh," Velez-Mitchell said. "You can't make this stuff up."

There were a few problems with the "blue barrel" tale, however, and even Velez-Mitchell, who seemed fairly convinced that Peterson was a likely killer, still observed the niceties of innocence until proven guilty, probably because of the worries raised by the CNN slander lawyers. Most of these problems had to do with inconsistencies in the tale.

For one: if the container was "still warm to the touch" after 9 p.m. on the evening of October 28, didn't that indicate that a body placed inside it could be only recently deceased? If Stacy had been murdered that morning, as the prevailing theory held, why would the container still have been "warm to the touch" so many hours later? Did that mean Stacy had been killed, not around 11 a.m., as the prevailing theory held, but in the evening?

If it really *was* Stacy's body in the container, and it was "warm to the touch," where had she been between 11 a.m. and 9 p.m.?

Second, the calls from Stacy's cell phone to Drew Peterson that had occurred around 9 p.m. included one that had lasted at least four minutes. If Morphey hadn't answered Drew's phone, how was that possible? None of the calls should have registered even one minute, let alone four. Of course, Peterson could have left a voice mail message using Stacy's phone lasting that long, then later erased it from his phone before throwing away Stacy's phone. But in that case, might there be telephone company records still extant that reflected what was said on a voice mail message? It wasn't clear, so there were some rough edges to the tale that would have to be smoothed out for it to stand up as truly "bombshell" type evidence.

And the third problem was, it was all hearsay, the account of one man with a supposed history of mental problems, hospitalized after a suicide attempt, an account related to a second man, Martineck, who in turn related it to the news media, then supposedly "confirmed" by a possible leak from investigators. As far as the media was concerned, this was dangerous territory—double hearsay, at the least. It was a far, far cry from "hard evidence," as Sue Doman would soon ask for.

Peterson, caught on camera that afternoon, steadfastly denied the "blue barrel" tale, saying, "I have no idea what anybody's talking about . . ."

What about the report that the container was "warm to the touch"?

"No," Peterson said.

"He says he believes that he helped you dispose of your wife's body," the reporter persisted. "Can you at least respond to that?"

"No."

"Not at all?"

"No response. Talk to my lawyer. I got nothing to say about it."

"No truth to it whatsoever?"

"None. Nobody helped me with anything . . ."

That was how things went when you were in the news: if you said anything at all, you were called an exhibitionist. If you said nothing but "talk to my lawyer," you were badgered, because on television, at least, the picture *was* the story, even when it signified nothing. Walter Cronkite knew that much, even if he didn't approve of it. If only Peterson had screamed at the reporter or taken a swing at her . . . hey, that would have meant some serious face time, just what a news career needed . . .

26.
The Clergyman

There was one more thing in the newspaper that day that was only briefly touched on, but it was an assertion that was just as ominous as the "blue barrel" tale, at least for Peterson. This was an unattributed, unsourced report in a *Sun-Times* gossip column by Michael Sneed that, in the days before her disappearance, Stacy had been talking with an unnamed "clergyman," and that she may have told the clergyman that Peterson had killed Kitty, and had made it look like an accident.

STACY TOLD CLERGYMAN DREW KILLED EX, the newspaper headlined, in its inimitable tabloid style.

"A source close to the investigation tells Sneed the 23-year-old, who had been pregnant and living with Peterson when Savio was found dead in an empty bathtub in 2004, also told two other people close to her about her husband's statements regarding Savio's demise," Sneed reported, referring to himself in the third person. Sneed wrote that an unnamed source had told him that Stacy had told Peterson she wanted him to move out of 6 Pheasant Chase Court by Wednesday of the following week—Halloween, as it happened. The source told Sneed that investigators were sure that Stacy had died the same day she'd told Peterson this—on Sunday, October 28.

"All we need now is the body," Sneed said the source told him. He said the source told him that experts were searching a canal near Lockport, based on the location of cell phone calls made and received on the night of October 28. (Lockport is about five miles south of Bolingbrook, and fronted by the Illinois Sanitary and Ship Canal, one of the locations searched by the ISP. A Lockport cell phone tower would have put Stacy's cell phone fifteen or twenty minutes away from the supposed donut shop where Peterson had allegedly given his own cell phone to Morphey.)

Sneed said his source sketched in a possible timeline for the evening of October 28: Peterson had met with Morphey at the donut shop about 7 p.m., and had supposedly given him his cell phone. Then Peterson drove to a location near the home of one of Stacy's old boyfriends, Scott Rosetto, and placed a call on Stacy's phone to his own, held by Morphey back at the donut shop. The source said police believed that this was part of an attempt by Peterson to make it seem like Stacy had run off with Rosetto.

If so, this was pretty lame for a supposedly shrewd, veteran cop: wouldn't Peterson have known that once the police checked with Rosetto, they would realize that Stacy hadn't run off with him, or that he had a provable alibi? Pointing to an obviously uninvolved "suspect" on Peterson's part was almost the same as admitting that he himself was responsible. Was Peterson really that stupid? Or was this just the investigators' attempt to make the theory fit the facts, however badly? Sneed didn't address these caveats to his source's information.

Afterward, Peterson and Morphey removed "a blue plastic barrel," "feeling warm," from the 6 Pheasant Chase Court house, according to Sneed's source.

"Peterson's attorney, Joel Brodsky, claimed Morphey's story makes no sense, and described him as a man with psychological issues," Sneed added.

"There never was a blue barrel; there never was any carrying objects out," Sneed said Brodsky told him.

And that was it: astoundingly, after beginning with a blockbuster claiming that Stacy had told people, including a clergyman, that Peterson had killed Kitty, Sneed never returned to his "scoop," or offered a single word of attempted corroboration. Who the hell was the supposed "clergyman"?

That night, Velez-Mitchell asked Sue Doman what she made of Sneed's blind quote about the mysterious "clergyman."

"It sounds so familiar because that's what my sister had always told me that he [Peterson] would do," Susan said. "But as far as her talking to clergymen, I don't know, I don't know that." Well, how could Sue Doman know what Stacy might have said to a clergyman? At the time Stacy vanished, she was still the enemy, "the young girl" who had taken Peterson away from Kitty, in Doman's mind, so Stacy was hardly likely to have told the Savios about any conversations with a minister. Sometimes the cases of Kitty and Stacy seemed to get confused, at least in the presentations by the talking heads on cable TV.

"Have police talked to you? Because one of the things that's sort of striking about all this," Velez-Mitchell said, "is that it's all coming from 'sources,' some of them 'police sources,' who are talking to Chicago newspapers, and obviously those guys develop relationships over the years, but at this point—do you think the police should hold a news conference and sort of set the record straight, with all of these stories, wild stories, flying around?" Velez-Mitchell was clearly leery of putting too much emphasis on the fragment from the gossip column, unsigned and unattributed as it was. She was trying to use Sue Doman as a stalking horse, to induce her to demand that the police publicly address the issues raised in Sneed's report. But Sue wouldn't oblige.

"I have been in contact, pretty much every day, with the police," Sue said. "They're pretty much tight-lipped right now. I think they're going to need more evidence, hard evidence . . ."

Until they had more to talk about than rumors and un-named sources, she said, she didn't think the police would have anything to say on blue barrels or mystery ministers alike.

* * *

But meanwhile, over on Fox, Mark Fuhrman was on the case. That same night, Fuhrman told Greta Van Susteren that he'd identified the "clergyman," and the church, and had confirmed that the man had been in contact with the police investigators. And, Fuhrman added, he'd spoken to Morphey's pal, Martineck, who claimed that Morphey had told him that he'd helped carry a "tote bag" warm to the touch out of the Peterson house on the evening of October 28.

The following night, Van Susteren aired a tape of an interview she had conducted with Brodsky the night before, after Fuhrman's report, to discuss the latest twist.

"Good evening, Joel," Van Susteren said.

"Good evening."

"Joel, have you spoken to your client, Drew Peterson, today?"

"Yes, I've spoken to him briefly this morning."

"How's he doing?"

Peterson was doing as well as anyone might expect, given all the media focus, Brodsky told Van Susteren. But his client kept wondering what the next news cycle might bring.

That was a perfect lead-in for Van Susteren, who now asked about the Sneed column in the Chicago *Sun-Times*, about the unnamed reverend and Stacy's supposed assertion that Drew had murdered Kitty. Van Susteren tried to entice Brodsky to comment on Sneed's report by acknowledging that the reverend's version of Stacy's supposed statement "could never be used against him, because it's a hearsay statement," as Van Susteren put it. As a general proposition, hearsay statements—unsworn, out-of-court statements, as Stacy's supposed remarks to the unnamed reverend would be—are not admissible in any trial. (Van Susteren was underestimating prosecutor Glasgow's resourcefulness, as we shall see.)

But while acknowledging that the supposed statements of the reverend—probably double or even triple hearsay—couldn't be admitted in court, Van Susteren was anxious to hear what Peterson's lawyer, Brodsky, had to say about them. Was Brodsky rattled?

No, Brodsky said. His client was "totally amazed, and in disbelief." That the statements attributed to Stacy had come from some unnamed "clergyman," he added, and had been published in a newspaper's "gossip column," doubly served to undercut their validity. Peterson wasn't worried at all—people were making crazy statements all over the place, given the notoriety of the case.

Then Van Susteren dropped her bomb: "Well, you know what? Let me tell you something that's probably going to make the hair stand up on the back of your neck . . . we've actually found the source. Mark Fuhrman has spoken to the person directly, and that person has confirmed the content of the conversation to us. So, it's not so fanciful." But, she added, she still didn't think the clergyman had admissible evidence against Peterson. Still, didn't it give Brodsky pause for concern as to his client's veracity? "Apparently, the clergyman's going to say that Stacy said that," Van Susteren told Brodsky.

Brodsky fumbled a bit for a response. He found the closest port of refuge—attacking the unnamed clergyman for failure to honor the confidentiality of the penitent privilege. He thought that was a "little bit disturbing." And, he added, rallying, the supposed violation of confidentiality tended to undercut the credibility of the supposed clergyman. Brodsky seemed caught by surprise in Van Susteren's mousetrap, particularly the notion that Fox had already identified the clergyman; his fumbling response suggested that Brodsky might be conceding there could be something to the tale, and that he himself had known nothing about it.

In short, Van Susteren had caught Peterson's lawyer with his pants down. If Brodsky had known this before, why wouldn't he have had a more effective counter-punch—such as, "Oh yes, we know all about that, and we can show that someone is making up tales to get attention from the media—I can assure you, it never happened." The lack of an effective response to Van Susteren's sally suggested that the cable network knew more about the case than Peterson's attorney, never an enviable place for any defense lawyer to be.

Brodsky fell back to another rhetorical rampart. As Van Susteren had just said, Brodsky agreed, even if such a clergyman existed, and even if the clergyman were to claim under oath that Stacy had told him that Drew had killed Kitty, it would be inadmissible in any trial of Drew Peterson. The double hearsay—perhaps even triple hearsay—nature of the statement made it inherently unreliable. No court would accept it under the existing rules of evidence. And, he counterattacked, the alleged "clergyman's" credibility would be subject to severe attack, given his supposed violation of the priest-penitent privilege.

But Van Susteren wasn't talking about the vagaries of the courtroom law, but the law in the court of public opinion— "the practical matter," as she put it, in Fox's own courtroom of the cablewaves. Peterson and Brodsky were in the unhappy position of having to say the supposed clergyman was lying, after already claiming that his own step-brother was lying. Two supposed liars were one too many, Van Susteren was suggesting.

Brodsky seemed to be relieved to get off the subject of the supposed clergyman. He was happy to talk about Peterson's step-brother, Morphey.

"Yes. Well, the stepbrother—there's two things about the stepbrother," Brodsky told Van Susteren. "One that I just saw this evening was, now the stepbrother's story seems to be a tote bag taken out of the house. It started as a fifty-five gallon, blue barrel drum. Then it became a rectangular container, and now it's changed to a tote bag. The—it's morphing. It's—it's—I think what they call it, *Transformers*. It's incredible the way the story keeps changing." Or even Morphey-ing.

Morphey, Brodsky said, was suffering from various psychological ailments, and had tried to kill himself on earlier occasions: "There's no question that he is a very disturbed person." If Morphey was credible as a witness, why hadn't Glasgow brought him before the special grand jury to testify? Morphey had memory lapses, Brodsky added. He was simply not a credible witness.

Van Susteren asked Brodsky if Peterson had had any contact with Morphey on Sunday, October 28, the day Stacy had vanished.

"Absolutely not," Brodsky said.

Wow, this was unequivocal—either Peterson was lying, or Morphey via Martineck was lying. Van Susteren pressed Brodsky. Peterson had never seen Morphey, or picked him up in a park, or had taken him to a coffee or donut shop, or had given him a cell phone to hold, Brodsky said.

And it could be proved, Brodsky added—all the police had to do was recover the video surveillance from all the nearby coffee or donut shops—almost all had them—to prove that Drew Peterson had never met with his step-brother, Tom Morphey, on the day in question. The lack of any such video tape, he said, would prove that the Morphey story had no credibility.

Well, Van Susteren pressed on, was it true that Peterson had visited his step-brother in the hospital after Morphey had tried to kill himself with an overdose, a few days after Stacy had vanished? That was true, Brodsky admitted. Peterson felt sorry for Morphey—his life had been filled with difficulties, and Peterson only wanted to support him. But, Brodsky added, Morphey's many difficulties only undercut the credibility of his supposed story, double hearsay as it was through Martineck. Multiple suicide attempts showed that Morphey could never be a reliable witness.

Van Susteren asked if Peterson was cooperating with the investigators.

No, Brodsky said. Peterson had already given the authorities a comprehensive statement, and there was no need for him to elaborate. "They have their statement and he's sticking by it," Brodsky said.

Van Susteren asked Brodsky to clarify what happened on Sunday night, October 28, and explain what Peterson was doing when Cassandra Cales had come by the house, and had noticed both vehicles gone, and then returned sometime later. There was no confusion, Brodsky said—both vehicles were at the house. Then Brodsky went on the offensive, pointing out that Cassandra had reported Stacy missing at 4 a.m., which he thought was a strange time to report a missing person.

This was definitely an attempt by Brodsky to obfuscate the facts, since the record showed clearly that Cassandra had tried repeatedly to report Stacy missing hours earlier. But Brodsky used the ISP missing report time of 4 a.m. to suggest that either Stacy and/or Cassandra were out in the local bars until the early hours of the morning. He ignored Cassandra's attempts to report Stacy missing to Downer's Grove or Bolingbrook earlier.

"Four o'clock in the morning seems to me a very strange time to be reporting somebody missing," Brodsky said. "I don't know, was she [Cassandra] waiting for the bars to close? Maybe she knows something more about Stacy's habits than she's saying."

His side had hired professional consultants, Brodsky said, among them Dr. Cyril Wecht, the Allegheny County, Pennsylvania, medical examiner. Brodsky contended that Wecht had concluded that Dr. Mitchell's original autopsy report was sound, that Kitty had died of an accidental drowning. This only seemed to show that medical evidence could be shaded in favor of whoever was paying the fees, whether Will County, a TV network like Fox, or Peterson.

Van Susteren asked Brodsky if he'd had any preliminary discussions with Glasgow. Not a one, Brodsky said. But of course, Peterson hadn't yet been charged with any crime, although he certainly was the prime suspect. Brodsky said he thought that was unusual. But Brodsky said he still trusted Glasgow not to charge his client.

"As far as my belief as to whether or not my client is going to be charged, as I sit here today, I still do not see one piece of admissible evidence against my client. There's not one thing that they could bring into a court of law . . ."

But having evidence was one thing, Van Susteren said, and being charged was another. "That's a different question," she said. "Do you think he's going to be charged?" Van Susteren was edging around the politics of the case—even if there were no "hard evidence," as Sue Doman had referred to it, would Glasgow charge Peterson anyway, for the political advantage of doing so?

"No, I don't," Brodsky said. He did not think that Peterson would ever be charged with murder. "And that's because Jim Glasgow, Mr. Glasgow, the state's attorney in Will County, is a good lawyer. He's a fine prosecutor. And he is not going to walk into a courtroom on a murder—on whatever type of charge he may choose to bring—when he doesn't have evidence to support it."

Well, there was nothing in the canons of ethics that prevented a lawyer from stroking the ego of the opposition, even if they never returned your calls.

Given that Fox News had been leading the charge against Peterson almost from the outset of Stacy's disappearance, Van Susteren had to be grateful that Brodsky had agreed to be interviewed: fair and balanced, as Fox likes to say of itself— we report, you decide. At least with Brodsky answering Van Susteren's questions, the network could say it had tried to get the other side of the story. Van Susteren wanted Brodsky to admit her outfit was fair:

"For some reason, I love asking you this question," Van Susteren said. "I don't know why. But have I treated you fairly tonight?"

"Of course you have, Greta. Of course you have."

It seemed that Brodsky and Van Susteren had kissed and made up after their early November feuding.

27.
Backtalk

Over the ensuing week, all the usual players popped up in all the usual venues—Van Susteren, Velez-Mitchell, Brooks, Larry King, the local television channels. Comparisons were made between the two Petersons—that is, Scott and Drew. Psychologists and profilers assessed Drew Peterson as a psychopath, a narcissist, a manipulator, a controller of women, and likely a wife-beater. A former girlfriend from the early 1980s popped up, claiming Peterson had once shoved her over a coffee table. More pathologists chimed in, marveling that the 2004 autopsy of Kitty could have reported her death an accident, while former prosecutors wondered why Dr. Mitchell had been seemingly blind to the bruises on her body. It appeared that few of the talking heads had actually read Mitchell's original autopsy report, which seemed to indicate that at least some of the bruising had occurred some hours or even days before death, despite Baden's assertions.

For most former prosecutors invited to pontificate on the tube, the bruising and the death and the reports of domestic disturbances were all part of the same immediate sequence of events, proof positive of murder. Most of the former law-enforcement contingent on the airwaves and cablewires did not acknowledge the fact that there was little documented record of domestic violence between Kitty and Peterson; instead, only Kitty and Drew's alternating claims of non-violent custodial interference, and even these were over a period of years, not the days immediately preceding Kitty's death in the bathtub. The same was true for Stacy and Peterson—no documented record of spousal violence.

But the mere claims of domestic disturbances, the bruising, and the stories of controlling behavior all melded into a portrait that shouted Peterson's guilt. It walked like a duck, quacked like one, so . . .

These ongoing media reports, many of them videotaped and then replayed from channel to channel, made for a cacophony of voices sounding and resounding the same themes—the replay effect added to the din, the sense of a growing consensus of people in the know, even if they only represented the same few snippets used over and over again. "Let's take a listen," the anchors said, again and again, and played and replayed parts of something that had already been aired elsewhere.

And as the repeatedly re-reprised furor rose, inevitably some stranger tales emerged and hopped aboard the rumor conveyor belt. One involved a trucker or truckers who swore they'd seen Peterson and another man at a truck stop. The pair had asked the trucker(s) to deliver a barrel to some distant location, where the pair would then reclaim it. It took a few days to determine that the tale was literally fabulous— that is, invented.

To be fair and balanced, Brodsky was given opportunities to rebut the consensus, but even then, he was often baited with provocative statements. On November 29, for example, even as tongues were still wagging about Morphey, the "blue barrel," and the still-unnamed clergyman, a reporter for Chicago's NBC affiliate, Dick Johnson, twitted Brodsky with Sneed's "scoop." What did Brodsky have to say about *that*?

"This one is strange," Brodsky said, "in that we have an unnamed, unauthorized source breaking this supposedly devastating news to a gossip columnist about an unnamed clergyman being told about a murder by a person who is missing. It's just very strange. It doesn't seem to make logical sense that it would occur this way." If there was anything real to the story, Brodsky wondered, why hadn't the clergyman said anything to the police at the time? And why would the police leak it to a "gossip columnist"? Was it possible that Sneed's source was none other than the clergyman himself, trying to drum up a little notoriety, not unlike the fabulous truckers?

"Where there's smoke, there's fire," Johnson riposted, "and there's a lot of smoke in this case, sir."

" 'Smoke' is not evidence," Brodsky said. "The only piece of evidence that has been identified so far has been this Thomas Morphey, who has some very serious psychiatric and alcoholic problems."

"I don't believe he's been accused of being delusional and making up stories such as this," Johnson argued.

"I don't know, *we* don't know why he's been hospitalized," Brodsky persisted. "He may be schizophrenic, I'm just speculating here, as I've asked other people not to do. I suppose one of the reasons he's been hospitalized is because of schizophrenia, which means you live in a little bit of a fantasy world . . . I don't know."

"Your client is reacting to leaks by videotaping the media," Johnson prompted.

"I have to take a little bit of credit for that, it was my idea," Brodsky said.

The next night, Fox gumshoe Fuhrman was on the scent once more. He'd gone to a Bolingbrook Krispy Kreme donut shop. There he queried the manager: Had the ISP come by to see if Peterson and Morphey had been in the shop the night Stacy vanished? The manager told Fuhrman that the ISP had collected the names of workers at the donut shop, but then left. Fuhrman induced the manager to find a surveillance videotape of the night in question. The grainy tape showed two fuzzy male figures in the donut shop for about two hours. One of the men left for some period of time, whether to go to the bathroom or drive some distance away to make a fake cell phone call was anyone's guess. Neither man could be identified as Peterson or Morphey, and the time coding of the tape wasn't clear. In fact, it wasn't even clear that this was the right donut shop, and since Brodsky had denied Peterson had met with his step-brother at all on October 28, the two men could have been anyone. How many donut shops in Bolingbrook had been visited by two blurry men on the evening of October 28? Fuhrman said he'd suggested to the ISP that they get the videotape from the donut shop for enhanced analysis.

The night after that, Brodsky was on Larry King. After King invited other guests to compare the two Petersons, Scott and Drew, he turned to Brodsky.

"Joel Brodsky, as the attorney for Drew Peterson, one of the problems in a case like this where so much attention is given, is there's almost a presumption of guilt, right?" King asked.

"Yes," Brodsky said. "And it goes counter to the American justice system. I find that this trial by rumor and speculation and innuendo, is disturbing, it really is."

"And what do you do about it as a lawyer?"

"Well, as a lawyer, in analyzing what I have been hearing all over . . . the one conclusion I come to and my colleagues come to, is that there isn't one shred of evidence that is admissible in a court of law that's been brought forth—not one. And that leads to the conclusion that what we're left with is to try this man by innuendo and rumor, and matters that took place over a quarter-century ago, and that's really unfair." Brodsky was referring to the story told by the woman who had just claimed that Peterson had shoved her over a coffee table in the early 1980s.

"What does he tell you? Does he say he's innocent?"

"Absolutely. I mean, so many things differ from what you hear in the media."

King played a videotaped interview of Morphey's friend Walter Martineck, the person who had first told Morphey's tale—no one else, except possibly the police, had actually talked to Morphey himself.

"His eyes were sunken in the back of his head," Martineck described Morphey in the videotaped interview. "He took me by my shoulders and told me I can't say anything, and he just told me that he thinks he helped dispose of Stacy's body."

"Why did he think that he had done that?" a reporter asked Martineck.

"Because when he helped Drew, that's what he told me, when he had helped Drew take something out of the house, it was warm to the touch."

King turned again to Brodsky.

"All right, Joel, I would imagine as a good lawyer, you would have asked Drew about that?"

"Well, absolutely. And it did not occur. Thomas Morphey is a very troubled individual. In looking at his past, he has multiple psychiatric admissions, he has multiple DUI convictions. His wife, by the way, Tom Morphey's wife, vanished ten, twelve years ago without a trace." Brodsky was attempting to draw a behavioral parallel with Stacy—sometimes women abandoned their husbands and families, and it didn't prove that they'd been murdered.

"So when you look at this individual," Brodsky went on, "you really have to wonder how credible of a witness he is. And the fact that he may have [said] something that a neighbor [Martineck] repeated doesn't make him any more credible. He's just a troubled individual. And his story doesn't seem to make sense, because we're talking—people talk about moving a barrel, and then the barrel becomes a tub and then the tub becomes a tote bag. In fact, the state's attorney in Will County has so much trouble [with] his testimony that they haven't taken him before the grand jury, because of what has been reported about his memory lapses . . ."

"I got you," King said. "Will Drew take a lie detector test?"

"No. I belong to an organization called the National Association of Criminal Defense Lawyers, and they commissioned a study that appeared in their magazine about a year ago, and it talked about the statistical reliability of lie detector tests. And the conclusion they came to was that a lie detector test is about as statistically reliable as flipping a coin. So if you ask him to take a lie detector test, you might as well ask him to flip a coin—it's just as reliable. So no, he won't take a lie detector test."

A bump further up on the cable table, on the *Headline News* brand, Jane Velez-Mitchell was weighing in again, this time with a "family lawyer," Susan Moss, and Daniel Horowitz, a criminal defense attorney. Velez-Mitchell soon focused attention on the story of the clergyman.

"And according to these reports, which we cannot independently confirm, this clergyman made a judgment call on his own to not say anything about it and not consult with members of his church about what to do. So he did nothing," Velez-Mitchell said. "Did he fail morally? In other words, does she [sic] have [a] moral obligation to protect secrets or prevent crimes? Let's start with you, Dan Horowitz."

"His obligation to protect secrets is greater than any other obligation," Horowitz said. "There has to be someplace that's sacred, and that's in the confessional, or at least in the religious context. But I say that legally, his decision not to go forward—because I guess he believed he had that choice—supports the defense. He judged this woman who he knew very, very well—he judged that she really was *not* in such great danger that he would break the privacy to protect her." In other words, the clergyman apparently did not take the supposed statement from Stacy all that seriously, Horowitz implied. Otherwise, if the clergyman felt that Stacy was in danger of being killed, he would have contacted the police.

"But she's missing, he was wrong," Velez-Mitchell said.

"No, she left, maybe, maybe she left," Horowitz said. "That's ridiculous. Look, you're judging that she's dead. Maybe she left because she *thought* she was in danger, or didn't like him. We don't know."

"You think she's in the Caribbean right now with twenty-five thousand dollars and a bikini?" Velez-Mitchell was incredulous. She turned to her other guest. "Susan Moss, take it away."

"You want to convict him now, on the air?" Horowitz interjected.

"Absolutely not," Moss said, responding to Velez-

Mitchell's remark about the money, the Caribbean, and the bikini, and ignoring Horowitz's protest. "*Absolutely* not, and it also [has been] reported that she told him [the clergyman] that Drew might have made some confessions about his third wife. And that makes a lot of sense. Remember that autopsy showed that she had seven independent bruises. So what happened was, allegedly, this woman went in the tub, hit herself around seven different times, including a huge gash, and then was somehow able to pull the plug, because as we all know, she died with wet hair in a bathtub with no water. This makes no sense."

"Okay, what about motive?" Velez-Mitchell asked, hopping from Kitty onto Stacy, but not making the transition clear. "Is the possibility, as you said, Susan, the papers are saying that she [Stacy] told the clergyman, a clergyman and two other friends, that her husband had revealed to her that he had killed his third wife, Kathleen Savio; would that be a motive to get rid of her, since she knew the truth?" Velez-Mitchell had a penchant for frontloading softball questions to selected guests who shared her bias.

"It's not only a motive," Moss agreed, "but there's also the same modus operandi with these two women. Apparently there are accidents or somehow unexplained disappearances. One we *know* is a death and one, I think, soon we'll find a body, and also know *it's* a death." Moss seemed to be confused between motive and modus operandi—they weren't at all the same thing—a death by drowning was vastly different than an unexplained disappearance.

A week after this, in November, Peterson gave another interview, this one to the *Chicago Tribune*. If anything, Peterson was even more antic than in the past—the sardonic side of his personality somehow just didn't come across well in print or on camera, not when much of the context went on the cutting-room floor. In this interview, Peterson talked of becoming "a celebrity." As edited, it looked as though he was bragging, not gigging the media with his sarcasm. And when Peterson complained he would no longer be able to get "a date," his critics rushed to take him seriously, missing the wry commentary completely. Once again, Peterson's own personality had betrayed him.

That night, on the Nancy Grace program, Jane Velez-Mitchell roped in Brodsky to explain his client once more.

"And while we have you right there," Velez-Mitchell told Brodsky, "I've got to ask you about some of your client's latest comments, which are getting so much play. And I have to just recap them. He says, 'I'm a celebrity now. I'd rather be a celebrity for good.' [A celebrity for good deeds, as opposed to being a murder suspect; not someone permanently in the public eye, Peterson meant. By wrenching the remark out of its context with biased editing, Velez-Mitchell twisted the meaning by 180 degrees. Well, that was show biz.]

"But he considers himself a celebrity," Velez-Mitchell continued. "He says, 'I'm not going to get another date.' And he also said at one point, 'Despite what you may have heard, I'm *not* going to be on the cover of *Playgirl*.' What is he thinking, to be making these comments? Because he's upset that his former cop buddies aren't talking to him, you think?" Velez-Mitchell had used the edited sentences to show Peterson in the worst possible light. It wasn't journalism, but vigilantism, driven by advertising ratings.

"Well, I think, to some extent, he's playing with the media," Brodsky told Velez-Mitchell, displaying remarkable forbearance to Velez-Mitchell's provocation. "I mean, that's—Drew's personality is—he's messing with you guys. You know, every time he goes to the mail [box], to take his mail out, you know, there's fifteen cameras on him. And he just—he's just messing with you. That's the long and the short of it. So that's what it is."

"Well, what do you tell him to do? Because everybody's been hollering, you know, 'Stop talking, Drew, doesn't your attorney tell you to stop talking?' What do you tell him?"

"You're right, his attorney *does* tell him to stop talking, every single day. But, you know, it's hard when you go to the mailbox and you're surrounded by twenty cameras, or you're trying to back your car out of the driveway and they stick cameras in your face and a microphone in your face. It's kind of hard not to say something. We're trying to, you know, give him things to say, but it's difficult . . . especially for Drew. I mean, his personality is that he wants to say something. He wants to get a rise out of [people] sometimes, and that's what he wants to do."

This was probably Brodsky at his most honest—it described exactly what he had to contend with in representing Drew Peterson.

And later on the same show:

"Let me ask you a question, because he feels that the media has conducted a witch hunt, and I think you've even been quoted as saying something similar to that," Velez-Mitchell told Brodsky. "When you see him behaving like this, do you understand why he is portrayed the way he is in the media?"

"Well, it's like feeding—what we call feeding the beast, to some extent," Brodsky said. "You have to understand [that] what's going on . . . in front of his house, is absolutely unprecedented. I cannot think of any other person who's been held in siege for a month and [his] house turning basically [into] a bunker, you know, and the media just—they can—they—the police will not, or cannot [prevent it]—I think it's, they will not [force] the media to get away, from the front of his house. Three o'clock in the morning, the generators come on. They wake everybody up. They're—it's unreal. And what he's doing, to some extent, is a reaction to that, I'm sure—in fact, I know this for a fact: If the media wasn't out in front of his house to the extent it [is], and they were down the block in a parking lot, and we were doing, you know, [a] kind of controlled—controlled situation, you'd see a totally different person.

"You'd see—you wouldn't get these types of wisecracks. It would just—it would be a different situation. So to some extent, he is a victim of the—of the media attention." Peterson was reacting to being in the spotlight, Brodsky meant, in his own inimitable fashion—he was psychologically compelled to engage, and lash back.

"Oh, but you know what?" Velez-Mitchell interjected. "I

don't necessarily buy that, because *I'm* in the media. I've been on those stakeouts. And you know, it's never pleasant, but it is—it's part of our system. Just like there are police, we are an important part of the entire picture." (Just how television cameras parked in front of someone's house, firing up their generators at three in the morning, wrecking the peace of the neighborhood, contributed to the public's "important" understanding of the process of justice wasn't made clear by Velez-Mitchell. Being there wasn't the same as being fair—an obnoxious presence did little to give the public the objective facts, but it did add to ratings.)

"And I've been on stakeouts," she continued. "I've covered the Michael Jackson case, the Robert Blake case, the O.J. Simpson case. They were always media circuses . . ."

"Right." Brodsky nodded, agreeing that these other cases *were* all media circuses.

". . . wherever we went," Velez-Mitchell concluded.

"But did you ever have it out in front of a single family home in a small suburb . . .

"Yes!"

"Not with Michael—for this period of time? Not with Blake, where he lived in a mansion, or with Michael Jackson, where he lived in a compound. But I mean, right on the front lawn of the house for weeks and weeks and weeks [with] hundreds of hundreds of media personnel?"

"Let's bring the attorneys back," Velez-Mitchell moved on. "Richard Herman and Christine Grillo, he's making a point that, obviously, he feels very strongly about. Do you think this is an excuse for [Peterson's] behavior, Richard?"

"Joel, there's nothing you can do to help him right now in the public eye," Herman said. "Everything he does, he does wrong. If he was out searching for the body, he would be criticized for *that*."

"That's true," Brodsky said.

"He's got to go. You've got to wire his jaw shut, take him out of Dodge, hide him away somewhere and get rid of him for a while. And you've got to stop talking about the case and let it take its course, because you're not doing him any good, and he's killing himself in the public eye."

"Well, I've got to disagree with part of that," Brodsky said, meaning Herman's advice for him to clam up. "I would certainly like to see, you know, Drew be quiet. There's no question about it. I *do* advise him to stop many of his comments. But as far as my getting out there—you know, we have to respond to certain things. For example, this truck driver, you know, the truck-stop thing, where it turns out that, we come out and show that the truck driver that said he was . . . meeting Drew was, in fact, in Louisiana at the time. Or the mistakes that Dr. Baden made in his statements about the autopsy. We have to get out there and get our message out that a lot of—there's a lot of misinformation being broadcast, and I'm trying to, you know, hold back the tide and get at least some of our story out there, that there's a lot of misinformation. That's my purpose in coming on."

Velez-Mitchell asked Grillo, a former prosecutor, what she thought about Brodsky and Peterson being so public.

"No, Joel, just—what I'm thinking is, wouldn't—isn't it better—isn't he attracting it even more? His responses almost warrant them jumping on him even more, that if you—I understand and I do agree that, yes, some things need to be addressed, but need to be addressed appropriately. He's acting so inappropriately time in and time out, again and again, giving—almost feeding that media, that they want to be out there, they want to keep questioning him because he's making it more of a circus. He's not saying anything that's going to help him. So wouldn't it be in his best interest, and you as his attorney, to really—yes, to address those things like the truck drivers, and then go out, get your paper, come back in. Don't come out with a video camera. Don't make it worse."

That was probably good advice from Grillo, but it would soon be overtaken by another sensational event: The clergyman had decided to go public.

28.

The Reverend

"Last week," Van Susteren opened her show on December 11, "we told you about a report involving Stacy Peterson's pastor, that Stacy told him Sergeant Peterson admitted to murdering wife number three, Kathleen Savio. Is it true? Did she say that? Well, now you will hear from the pastor himself. We sat down with Pastor Neil Schori earlier."

Van Susteren's director cued up a videotape. Van Susteren had handled the interview herself the day before. On camera, Schori appeared very young, slightly heavy-set, with dark hair, and very earnest, as befitted a youth minister affiliated with an evangelical church. The lingering question for other ministers was: Why was Schori agreeing to tell what Stacy had supposedly told him, and on national TV? Wasn't the clergy-congregant privilege sacrosanct? Why would Schori transgress it? Or was Schori actually acting on Stacy's instructions, following her disappearance? The entire situation was murky. Schori's own credibility would soon come into question, at least from Peterson's lawyers. Was Schori an unwitting part of Stacy's "plan" to take the kids and maybe the money and run, while leaving Peterson holding the bag over Kitty's death?

How long had he known Stacy Peterson? Van Susteren asked Schori.

Around two years, Schori said. She had attended his church sporadically. That put Schori's first encounter with

Stacy sometime in the fall of 2005, about 18 months after Kitty's death. So, if Stacy had been troubled by her story to the ISP as to Drew's alibi in March of 2004, it hadn't bothered her for more than a year.

Or perhaps, if she had lied then, had she subsequently feared the consequences as a possible accessory after the fact? What was her intent in supposedly telling Schori that her husband had confessed to murdering his third wife? These were important questions. Van Susteren eased into the situation. Had Drew Peterson also attended the church? she asked. Peterson would attend occasionally, but less frequently than Stacy, Schori said.

Van Susteren tried to assess how well Schori had known Stacy. Had he ever met privately with her?

From time to time, Schori said, he'd met with Stacy to discuss her situation—younger wife, with two small children, married to an older man who had already been married three times to other women. Still, there was little that was unusual in his meetings with Stacy, he said—just ordinary issues of life.

What did Schori make of Stacy?

Schori said he thought Stacy was "very sweet," focused very much on her children. She talked about the kids a lot, Schori said.

What about Drew Peterson?

Peterson was more reserved than Stacy. Nice enough, but someone who kept his feelings to himself.

How would Schori characterize the Peterson marriage? Schori said that it seemed normal enough to him, although he thought there were also "deeper issues." Van Susteren did not ask what those issues might have been.

Did Schori think the marriage had a future?

Any marriage had its ups and downs, Schori told Van Susteren. Whether it worked or not depended on whether the partners were willing to make changes, to adapt to each others' needs. That didn't satisfy Van Susteren. She wanted to know whether Peterson and his young wife seemed willing to make adjustments.

Sometimes, Schori said. But he still saw reason for "deep concern."

Again Susteren did not probe further as to what Schori's "deep concern" might have been, just as she failed to ask about the "deeper issues." What was Schori trying to suggest?

Van Susteren asked if a time came when Stacy had asked to meet with him alone. Now she was moving to the heart of the question—had Stacy told Schori something about Drew and Kitty?

Stacy had called him in August of 2007, Schori said— about two months before she vanished.

Schori had been at the church at the time, he said. It had been some time since he had last spoken with Stacy. She'd told him she had "some stuff" to talk with him about.

They met at a coffee shop in Bolingbrook. Schori said he hung back, waiting for Stacy to say what was on her mind.

After some innocuous preliminaries, Stacy talked about her marriage with Peterson. On the surface, it seemed like old ground, to Schori. But something told him that Stacy had something specific she wanted to tell him.

Schori gently told her that if she wanted to confide in him, she could.

"And then she blurted out the reason," he told Van Susteren. "She said, 'He did it.'"

Van Susteren seemed taken aback.

"Just like that?" she asked.

Yes, Schori said, that's how it was: an abrupt statement. Whether it was a simple accusation on Stacy's part, or an admission of her own part in what happened afterward, was hard to determine from Schori's description.

Van Susteren wanted to be sure of what Schori meant. She asked whether Schori knew what Stacy was talking about.

He thought he knew, Schori told Van Susteren, but he wanted "clarification," so he asked Stacy to be more specific. Although talk had been rife in the community about Peterson's possible involvement in Kitty's drowning, Schori told Van Susteren, he'd never discussed this with Stacy before. But he knew instinctively that she was talking about Kitty's death. He'd asked Stacy what she meant when she'd said, "He did it."

"And she said, 'He killed Kathleen,'" Schori told Van Susteren.

What did Schori do then?

He'd asked Stacy for details, Schori told Van Susteren, and Stacy had told him things about the night Kitty died. He didn't want to share these details, Schori said. But, he said, he had been amazed at Stacy's story. He'd asked her what he should do—should he tell someone? Had she told anyone else what she'd told him?

She'd never said anything about this to anyone else, Schori said Stacy had told him.

Why, then, had she told Schori? Van Susteren asked.

Schori said he'd been wondering about that ever since that day in the coffee shop. He thought Stacy felt compelled to share the information with him as someone she could trust. But he really didn't know why Stacy had passed this on to him.

Van Susteren wanted to know how Schori had determined that Stacy's story had any validity.

Stacy had "specific information," Schori said once more. Van Susteren asked him to recount these. Schori said Stacy knew that Drew hadn't been in the 6 Pheasant Chase Court house the night that Kitty had died. Then, afterward, Stacy had discussed this with Peterson, according to Schori.

Had Peterson actually told Stacy he'd killed Kitty?

No, Schori said.

Well, Van Susteren said, wasn't it possible that Stacy was just guessing, or that Peterson might have suggested he was involved in Kitty's death to impress her, or even scare her?

It was more than that, Schori said. Stacy had told him details of that night that he didn't want to share on national TV.

But Van Susteren persisted.

If Stacy knew or believed that Drew had killed Kitty, why did she stay married to him after knowing this? Van Susteren wanted to know.

Schori said he didn't know, but guessed that Stacy was afraid of Drew.

Well, Van Susteren asked, had Stacy ever told him she was afraid of her husband?

She had, Schori said.

Had she told Schori she intended to leave Peterson?

No, Schori said.

Had Stacy told Schori why Drew had murdered Kitty?

No, Schori said.

Had she talked to the police?

Yes, Schori said—but she'd never told the investigators what she knew.

Had Stacy told him why she hadn't told the police back in 2004?

No, Schori said. He said he believed that Stacy had kept her mouth shut because she was afraid of Peterson.

But beneath this was a deeper question: If Stacy had lied to the police, was her reluctance to come forward later the result of fear at being charged as an accessory in Kitty's death? Did her supposed delay in telling what she knew somehow enmesh her in a conspiracy? But Van Susteren did not follow this up, and at that point she took a break, promising more from Schori later.

"So what did you do?" Van Susteren asked, when the videotape resumed. "I mean, it's a rather awkward situation. You're in a coffee shop and she tells you that her husband murdered wife number three."

He wasn't sure what to do, Schori admitted. He thought that Stacy only wanted to clear her conscience, not have him immediately ring up the police and tell them what she'd told him. So he'd done nothing, Schori admitted.

In this, it's possible, perhaps even likely, that Schori had misread Stacy's intention in telling him the story. Had Stacy expected that Schori would call someone in authority, relay the message, while keeping her name out of it? Was this Phase One of Stacy's plan to dump Drew and take the children off to sunnier climes? Dd Schori misread her signal?

Or was it that Schori didn't really believe her—that he thought Stacy's story was an imaginative justification for her marital problems with her husband?

All of these questions were doubtless coursing through Van Susteren's mind at this point. After all, it's not every day that someone goes on national television and accuses, albeit by proxy, another person of being a murderer. How valid was Schori's story? Schori said he thought Stacy only wanted to use him as a "sounding board."

And at this point, Van Susteren missed a golden opportunity to ask the "sounding board" what advice he'd given to Stacy. If Schori had really believed that Stacy had incriminating information about Kitty's death, had he suggested any alternative for his counselee? Say, for instance, imparting the information to a lawyer, if not the police? What, in fact, was the proper role of a clergyman in such a situation?

Van Susteren asked Schori if Stacy had intended to provide her information to the police.

Schori said he didn't think so.

Van Susteren seemed a bit flummoxed by what she was hearing. If she had the story straight, Schori was saying that Stacy had told him, in August, two months before she vanished, that she had information implicating her husband in his third wife's death. But she didn't want to tell anyone other than Schori. And she hadn't told Schori to tell anyone else. Then why tell Schori in the first place? What had Stacy intended?

Van Susteren went back to the beginning. Had Stacy really told Schori that Drew had actually confessed to killing Kitty? Did she provide any details?

Yes, Schori said.

Like what?

Schori hedged, saying he wasn't sure he should provide any specifics.

Van Susteren pressed. How could anyone be sure that whatever tale Stacy had told Schori wasn't some attempt on Stacy's part to get Drew in trouble? How could anyone be sure it wasn't some sort of fantasy on Stacy's part—an attempt by a woman to get even with a man in a troubled marriage? People said all sorts of things when they were mad at their spouse, Van Susteren noted.

Schori agreed, but said that Stacy had told him things that made him believe she knew what she was talking about. For one thing, he said, when Stacy had asked Peterson where he'd been that night, Peterson had told her, "You know where I was."

Van Susteren asked Schori how soon this was "after the murder?"

It was the morning after, Schori said, apparently meaning the morning after Kitty's body was discovered, not the morning after the death, which would have been nearly 36 hours earlier. After all, Kitty's body wasn't discovered until the evening of March 1, 2004.

If Peterson had really said this to Stacy on Sunday morning, February 29, that truly would have been a confession, since at that point no one supposedly knew Kitty was dead. This illustrated one of the difficulties of hearsay evidence. Without the full context of the supposed conversation between Stacy and Drew, or knowledge of when it actually took place, it wasn't possible to know for sure what either participant was actually referring to. Schori's recollection of what he claimed Stacy had said to him in the coffee shop in August 2007, more than two years after Kitty had died, might well have been incomplete, or misunderstood.

Was that all Peterson had said about it? Van Susteren asked.

That was all he wanted to say about Peterson, Schori said.

Well, had Schori spoken to Peterson since Stacy disappeared?

He had not, Schori said.

Had he spoken to Peterson after Stacy had told him the story in the coffee shop?

Yes, Schori said. Peterson had called him at the church shortly after his conversation with Stacy, and suggested that they get together. It was clear, Schori said, that Peterson knew that Stacy had just talked with him. How Peterson knew this wasn't clear—had Peterson been shadowing his wife, as

Sharon Bychowski had suggested was his wont, or had Stacy herself told Peterson that she'd told Schori the whole story?

Van Susteren asked if Schori had met with Peterson after getting this telephone call. No, Schori said.

Did Schori think Peterson knew what Stacy had told him?

Schori said he wasn't sure, but it was apparent that the thought had crossed his mind. He "sort of backed out of" meeting with Peterson, Schori said.

Van Susteren commented that Schori must have felt nervous about meeting with Peterson after just hearing from Stacy that Peterson had murdered Kitty, with the inference that Peterson then knew what Stacy had just told him.

"Oh, my gosh. Sure," Schori said.

Van Susteren asked Schori if he thought Stacy was still alive.

He hoped so, Schori said. But he didn't think so.

29.

No Answer

Reverend Schori's interview with Van Susteren seemed, on the surface, to clinch the deal: If Schori was on the level, Stacy had had evidence that her husband, Drew Peterson, had at least implied, if not outright confessed, that he had murdered Kitty. But Schori's account raised other questions. First and foremost, why had Stacy supposedly provided an alibi for Drew when she was first interviewed by the state police back in March of 2004?

Second, apart from the issue of the reliability of Schori's memory of his August 2007 encounter with Stacy, was Stacy's account to *him* reliable? And even if it was, was Peterson's supposed assertion—"You know where I was"—anything more than just idle talk on Peterson's part to somehow impress his young wife with all his supposed power, an attempt to bolster his mystique, however fraudulently?

And, if Stacy had believed that she had critical information about the night Kitty died, and failed to provide it when asked by police, would she be, legally, an accomplice to Peterson, an accessory after the fact, if indeed Peterson *had* murdered Kitty? Was one reason that she was afraid, at least as Schori had described her, due to the possibility of being prosecuted herself?

There's also the vital question of why Stacy would have selected Schori, a relative stranger, to confide in, rather than her sisters Cassandra or Tina, or even Sharon Bychowski, along with the long delay between the event of Kitty's death in 2004 and August 2007. Anyone examining the hearsay statement of Schori—purporting to represent the words of someone who wasn't now available to confirm or deny his account—had to wonder whether these statements by Stacy weren't part of some sort of plan to inculpate her husband as step one in a divorce campaign intended to, first, put her husband behind bars, and next, get control of all the assets, including the older boys' million-dollar trust. After all, Stacy had told her aunt that she had "a plan" to leave Peterson and take all the children with her, including Thomas and Kris. Putting Peterson in the soup this way might be one way to bring this off.

Certainly a competent defense lawyer would have raised these questions, had Peterson been charged with Kitty's death based on Stacy's alleged account to the Reverend Schori; that is, of Peterson's whereabouts on the night Kitty died. Stacy's possible motive in making such an allegation would have been fair game for any defense lawyer—maybe she wanted the older boys, and their million-dollar trust account.

On the other hand, this was a gate that swung both ways: Even if he hadn't killed Kitty, Peterson might have had a motive to kill *Stacy*, if she'd told him she was ready to say he had killed Kitty, and that she'd already prepared this ground by telling Schori, and that she intended to say the same to Kitty's former lawyer, Harry Smith, as well. After all, Stacy supposedly had an appointment to meet Harry Smith the week she vanished.

This was the fundamental problem with hearsay evidence—it was inherently unreliable because of so many possible interpretations, and fraught with inadvertent omissions, since it came from third parties. The vagaries of hearsay's significance usually made it inadmissible in any legal proceeding. It was difficult, maybe impossible, to know what someone intended when they'd said something to someone else. This was why hearsay wasn't normally allowed, under the rules of evidence.

Or so Van Susteren, a lawyer, believed, as apparently did Reverend Schori.

It would turn out that Van Susteren, and all the other lawyers on the airwaves and cable wires were wrong about this, although it would take a future act of the Illinois state legislature to contradict them.

Two nights later, on December 13, 2007, Mark Fuhrman tried to fill in some of these possible gaps while appearing on Van Susteren's show.

"Tonight: former LAPD homicide detective Mark Fuhrman has picked up on a clue, a clue that the rest of us missed," Van Susteren announced. "Now, this could be a very damning piece of evidence in the investigation into how Sergeant Peterson's wife number three died in the bathtub, and who did it. Former LAPD homicide detective Mark joins us live in Chicago. All right, Mark. You picked up on a clue that the rest of us missed. What is it?"

He had a source, Fuhrman said, that Stacy had told Schori at their August meeting in the coffee shop that Drew had *not* been at home the night Kitty died. That in fact, wondering where he was, she'd made numerous cell phone calls to his cell phone, none of which were answered. If this was accurate, that meant Stacy had lied to the police about Peterson's alibi.

But there was more: Fuhrman said that although the ISP had claimed at Kitty's 2004 inquest that they were obtaining the relevant telephone records, it appeared to Fuhrman that they'd never bothered with the records for Stacy and Drew.

The ISP, Fuhrman said, had told the coroner's jury that they didn't believe that the telephone records—unspecified at the inquest, but probably those of Kitty and Maniaci— would change anything, even though they hadn't been received by the time of the inquest. Fuhrman meant that the state police agent Hardy had told the coroner's jury investigating Kitty's death in May of 2004 that the ISP did not believe that the telephone records would contradict anything already established in their investigation. Nothing was said at the inquest about the phone records of Drew and Stacy.

That got Fuhrman thinking. He went to the Will County courthouse, and asked to see the records for search warrants. He knew that Stacy and Drew each had Nextel cell phones, which ordinarily kept records of calls for five years. That meant that had the ISP looked in 2004 for records of Drew and Stacy's phones, they would have been able to recover them. Fuhrman found that no search warrants had been issued in 2004 for those records.

In a situation like the death of Kitty, Fuhrman went on, it should have been easy to get a warrant for those records within a matter of days. When he'd been with the LAPD, he added, his department had often gotten them within hours, because the records were computerized.

And there was still more: as far as he could determine, the special grand jury investigating Peterson had not, to that day, asked to see the records.

Fuhrman had put his detective's magnifying glass on a glaring omission in the 2004 ISP investigation into Kitty's drowning, and even of the current special grand jury investigation.

"We can make this conclusion absolutely," Fuhrman continued. "There was not *one* search warrant written." That meant either that ISP agent Hardy had been misinformed by others, or that he'd misinformed the coroner's jury. Either way, despite the testimony at the coroner's inquest, no effort had been made to obtain *all* the relevant telephone records.

Had the ISP in 2004 obtained the records of Stacy's cell phone, it would have showed unanswered calls by Stacy to Drew's telephone on the night in question—that is, if Stacy had told the truth to Schori in August of 2007. If the ISP had had this information, they could have broken Stacy's alibi for Drew, Fuhrman suggested.

And once Drew's alibi was broken, Fuhrman said, Stacy would have had "two choices." She could be implicated as an accessory in a possible murder, or she could have chosen to "tell the truth. If she had [told] the truth, Drew's alibi goes south, the investigation [of the death of Kitty] is not an accident, it's a homicide, and Stacy [would] still be with us."

In other words, if Stacy had told the police about the supposed unanswered telephone calls she'd made to Drew in the early morning hours of March 1, she might still be alive, and Peterson would be in prison.

Van Susteren gave kudos to Fuhrman. She admitted that she'd missed the significance of the inquest testimony about the telephone records. Fuhrman had done "extraordinarily good work." She quoted Hardy from the transcript of the coroner's inquest. " 'The only thing we're waiting for now is some phone records, to find out if certain phone calls were made when they said they were made.' "

But Hardy's testimony seemingly related only to Kitty's telephone call to Maniaci around 1 a.m. in the morning of March 1, 2004, not to any calls from Stacy to Peterson that night, or even Peterson to Kitty, even perhaps one attempting to persuade her to let him into the house at 392 Pheasant Chase Drive. And in light of Fuhrman's discovery, it appeared that no telephone records were actually ever collected from any of the parties—not Kitty, not Maniaci, not Stacy, and not Drew.

At best, Van Susteren said, this was sloppy work by the ISP in 2004, and maybe even so far in the present investigation. Fuhrman agreed—anytime a homicide detective gets an alibi from "a girlfriend, a wife or a mother," it had to be corroborated, since those were the categories of witnesses most likely to lie.

The ISP still had time to get the 2004 phone records of Stacy and Drew, Van Susteren noted.

Fuhrman agreed, and said he hoped the ISP was tuned in.

Fuhrman did not identify his source by name, but inadvertently gave him away when he told his audience that no search warrants for Stacy's 2004 cell phone records had ever been obtained, even to that day, and also by his suggestion that the grand jury investigating the two cases demand the records, which in turn indicated that the grand jury hadn't yet seen them.

Clearly, Fuhrman's source was not with the police or the grand jury or the prosecutor. Most likely it was the Reverend Schori himself. And where would Schori have obtained this information? From Stacy's account to him in August.

But Fuhrman's point was still valid, regardless of the source: if indeed the telephone records showed that Peterson had not answered calls from Stacy on his cell phone between 1 a.m. and 8 a.m. on Sunday, February 29, 2004, he would have some explaining to do. The fact that the ISP apparently did not bother obtaining Stacy's cell phone records for the time of Kitty's death in 2004, when Stacy apparently was Drew's alibi, was indeed "sloppy," as Van Susteren put it.

Or maybe politically corrupt.

If Fuhrman's report about the absence of phone calls was true, this was actual evidence, not simply more character innuendo, which had dominated the whole story from the outset. It suggested that Peterson had lied about being home with Stacy the night Kitty died in the tub. And it also suggested that *Stacy* had lied, if she in fact had been his alibi. Further, it suggested that Stacy might have been an accessory after the fact in Kitty's murder, if that's what it was. A dark portrait of the Peterson-Stacy marriage was thus limned: that Peterson and Stacy were locked together in a conspiracy of silence, each able to implicate the other, until death did one of them part.

30.
A Wrongful Death

Over the ensuing winter, the media finally began to back off, at least a bit, from the Peterson saga. Rather than leading the Van Susteren and Nancy Grace shows on an almost nightly basis, it receded into "updates"—only side dishes of the broadcasts, rather than the main course. Other crimes and other sensations got top billing. The news media trucks and their generators and satellite dishes, which had so annoyed the neighbors on the Pheasant Chase Court cul-de-sac, packed up and departed, but promised to return when something finally happened.

Still, the disappearance of Stacy Peterson was hardly forgotten, at least in Bolingbrook. Throughout the late fall and during much of the early winter, volunteers organized in part by Sharon Bychowski combed nearby woods and waterways for Stacy's body. The searches seemed haphazard, based on little more than gut instincts of the searchers as to where Stacy's body might have been left, if indeed she was dead. Some thought that the blue barrel might have been dumped in the Chicago Sanitary and Ship Canal, which tied Lake Michigan to the Mississippi River drainage system. The canal was so murky and polluted that the chance of finding a single barrel containing a body was almost nil.

Bychowski, along with Cassandra, seemed to be one of the prime movers in keeping Stacy's disappearance from fading away. She helped organize a website, FindStacyPeterson.com, which solicited the public for funds to help finance further searches. (Peterson organized his own competing website, justicefordrew.com, and similarly asked for donations; whether any came in is uncertain.) Eventually the "findstacy" money was used to help purchase a boat, which was to be used by the volunteer searchers to scour various local bodies of water for Stacy's body. By the dead of winter, the boat lay unused on its trailer in the Bychowski driveway, next door to the Peterson house. Meanwhile, the Bychowski front lawn had turned into a shrine of sorts to Stacy: signs, angels, and other memorials to mark her disappearance from the house next door. Vigils were held; at one, according to Bychowski, Peterson's attorney Brodsky appeared, and made some sort of threat to "torch" the findstacypeterson.com boat. Brodsky denied it, and said Bychowski had gotten carried away with her role as one of the initiators of the "findstacy" movement.

Yet another strange thing happened in December 2007: someone broke into a state police vehicle in a Joliet parking garage and made off with a number of confidential reports on the Peterson investigation, at least one of them identifying an important witness. The extent of the theft, and who did it, remained a mystery, although Glasgow's office was later to point out that the confidential witness was later contacted by Fox News, just as the Peterson case was reaching a climax, much to the witness's discomfiture and even alarm.

On February 13, 2008, a lawyer representing the Savio family filed a petition to reopen Kitty's estate. Attorney Martin Glink, of Arlington Heights, citing the prospect of a wrongful death suit against Drew Peterson for the death of Kitty, asked for the removal of Peterson's uncle, James Carroll, as executor of the estate.

Among other things, Glink alleged that no notice was given to the Savios at the time in 2006 that Kitty's estate was discharged from the probate court. A wrongful death lawsuit against Peterson represented a new potential asset for the estate, Glink said, and this warranted the estate's reopening, and the removal of Carroll.

"[A] wrongful death cause of action against Drew Peterson would be a newly discovered asset of the estate or an unsettled portion of the estate of Kathleen Savio . . . since such action would be based on facts unknown during the pendency of the estate," Glink wrote, "arising only after two 'second' autopsies of Kathleen Savio were done."

Glink cited Baden's statements to Van Susteren the previous November that Kitty's death was not an accident, but a murder, as well as Schori's statements to Van Susteren as to Peterson's culpability, as grounds for a potential wrongful death lawsuit against Peterson.

As Peterson's uncle, Glink went on, Carroll "would be in a direct conflict of interest as to the proposed wrongful death action . . . he may also have committed waste or mismanagement of the estate . . . and failed to file an adequate inventory . . . and was incapable of suitably discharging his duties" as executor. When Carroll fired Harry Smith as Kitty's divorce lawyer after her death, he had in essence gutted Kitty's divorce claims against her former husband, even though those claims survived her, legally speaking, Glink asserted. This claim would be an asset for Thomas and Kris, as well as Eric and Stephen, as beneficiaries of Kitty, and therefore ought not to be under the control of Drew's uncle. Carroll, the Savio lawyer concluded, should be ordered to show cause as to why he should be allowed to continue as the estate's executor in the face of these allegations.

One week later, on February 21, 2008, the results of Dr. Blum's "re-autopsy" of Kitty's by-now re-interred remains were announced by prosecutor Glasgow's office: Kitty had been murdered, Dr. Blum concluded.

"Dr. Blum's forensic report renders his expert opinion that this is a homicide," Glasgow said in a press release issued by his office. "We have been investigating this as a murder since reopening the case in November of last year. We now have a scientific basis to formally and publicly classify it as such." The report of the re-autopsy would not be released, Glasgow's office said. However, the office provided a quote from Dr. Blum's conclusion:

"It is my opinion based on my education, training, experience and personal observations, and to a reasonable degree of medical and scientific certainty, compelling evidence exists to support the conclusions that the cause of death of Kathleen Savio was drowning and further, that the manner of death was homicide."

Van Susteren wasted little time in spreading the news.

"This is a Fox News Alert," she said, opening her *On the Record* show of February 21, 2008. "Well, it was homicide. The death of Sergeant Drew Peterson's wife number three, Kathleen Savio, has officially been ruled a homicide. The state's attorney's office in Illinois made the official announcement just a short time ago . . ."

Van Susteren's producer had already dialed up Baden, so he could say *I told you so* over the telephone.

Van Susteren pointed out that one of her program's producers had obtained the original 2004 autopsy report shortly after Stacy's disappearance, and that even then, the Fox people believed Kitty's death had been a murder, not an accident.

"That's right," Baden agreed. "And because you made a fuss about it and all that, the coroner [O'Neil], same coroner, went back and had an official exhumation done by Dr. Blum." Blum's autopsy was the one that counted, legally, Baden said. His own was for—what, exactly? Baden did not say, but his periodic presence on Van Susteren's show seemed to demonstrate at least one possible motive—publicity for his private pathology business. Baden was a celebrity expert, for fun and profit.

But, Van Susteren pointed out, a pathologist, whether Baden or Blum, didn't necessarily say who the culprit was. That wasn't the job of a pathologist, was it? she asked.

Baden agreed—a pathologist was only supposed to determine the cause and manner of someone's death. "We don't know *who* did it," Baden said. But a good pathologist ought to be able to provide information that could narrow things down. For instance, he said, a competent autopsy ought to be able to determine the approximate time of death, and that could be very useful information. If, for instance, someone claimed to have an alibi for the time of death, he or she might be off the hook, assuming the alibi could be proved. But if the time of death conflicted with the alibi, they might be back in the mix as a possible perpetrator. That's why a careful autopsy was critical.

In Kitty's case, the lividity—the settling of the body's blood to the lowest point in the body due to gravity, and the extent of rigor mortis, the stiffening of the body's muscles after death—"would indicate that she was dead for a good thirty-six hours," Baden said. He admitted that any re-autopsy by itself couldn't shed much light on what happened. "But by reading over what the medical examiner and the doctor did at the time, the people who came in, various police officers, [and] made statements as to the color of the body and the stiffness of the body," it was still possible to arrive at a fairly accurate time of death, Baden indicated.

Baden seemed to be trying to steer Van Susteren toward the underlying reason for Blum's official conclusion, with which he agreed, and had, for months. Van Susteren seemed to miss Baden's signal. She asked him what he would say to a prosecutor, if he'd been the official pathologist.

Baden backed up. There was no question that Kitty had been murdered, Baden told her. He didn't think anyone would dispute that.

"The issue is, whodunnit?" he said. "Now, just because it's a homicide doesn't mean the husband did it. But if the husband doesn't have a good alibi for the time that the death occurred, that becomes an issue."

Van Susteren was still at sea.

"And of course, that's a challenge," Van Susteren said, "because we can't determine . . . we can't narrow the window, except for, probably, the weekend."

Nope, Baden said. The re-autopsies *could* narrow the time of death down to when the murder had actually happened. The biological evidence, Baden said, seemed to show it had to have happened thirty-six hours before Kitty was found dead in the bathtub on Monday evening, March 1. The evidence from the first autopsy, as well as information from those who had been at the scene, seemed to show that Kitty had died more than a day before her body was found—up to thirty-six hours earlier, Baden said; around midnight on February 29.

The light dawned on Van Susteren. "Oh, I got it. I see," she said.

"So that at the time of the coroner's inquest, the original one three years earlier, it was thought that he had a good alibi, the husband," Baden added. From this, it appeared that Baden believed that Stacy's alibi for Drew applied to Sunday night, not early Sunday morning. And who knows? Maybe no one from the ISP had ever asked Stacy about the night before the trip to Shedd Aquarium.

"And some material has come out," Baden said. "The police investigation has indicated, in talking to people, that Stacy had said that [at] the time the death may have occurred, her husband was not in bed. And she went down and found him . . ."

"And made a phone call and things like that," Van Susteren added, referring to Fuhrman's "scoop."

". . . doing laundry and was dressed in black or something," Baden ran on. "So all those things are the things that are going to be important to the [state's] attorney." If Kitty had died sometime between Sunday morning and Monday evening, there was no question that Drew had solid alibis. But if she had died between 1 a.m. and 8 a.m. Sunday morning, as the biological evidence seemed to suggest, according to Baden, Stacy Peterson seemed to be her roué husband's only alibi.

Baden's concluding remark was interesting: it appeared that someone involved in the investigation had told him more information about Peterson's whereabouts on the night Kitty died, again according to Stacy, possibly via Schori—that Peterson was in the 6 Pheasant Chase Court laundry room, dressed in black, when Stacy finally saw him on the night she'd supposedly made the unanswered calls to Drew's cell phone, early Sunday morning, February 29, 2004— Leap Day.

With an official finding of homicide for Kitty's death, Glasgow now had a formal legal basis to justify a criminal prosecution of someone, and there was little doubt by anyone in Will County, or for that matter, anyone in most of North America, that Drew Peterson was the someone Glasgow had in mind. A formal homicide finding was good, at least for Glasgow, as well as Glink and the Savios, who could now pursue their wrongful death claim against Peterson. But by itself, it wasn't enough.

The stark reality was, outside of Morphey—and who knew how reliable his evidence might be?—the state's attorney had precious little evidence to link Drew Peterson to any murder, whether Kitty's or Stacy's, if indeed she was dead, and not actually sunning herself in ignorant bliss on some isolated Caribbean beach. Glasgow's main problem was that there was no substantial forensic evidence tying Peterson to any crime. If there had ever been hairs, mud, fibers, paint scrapings, DNA or similar trace evidence from 392 Pheasant Chase Drive, it had long been lost. Peterson—and Stacy—of course had cleaned up Kitty's house shortly after her death.

No, all the evidence against Peterson was circumstantial at best, and tenuous at worst. So much relied on secondhand statements—the hearsay of Schori being a prime example— and, as Van Susteren and the other legal talking heads kept saying, it wasn't admissible evidence in a trial. Everything that Kitty had said about her former husband was hearsay, whether to her sisters, her neighbors, her lawyer Harry Smith, Walter Jacobson of Chicago's Fox affiliate, the police, or even the assistant state's attorney, Fragale, assuming that she had ever read Kitty's plaintive letter of 2002. Everything that Stacy had told Cassandra or Sharon Bychowski, or Reverend Schori, or anyone else, before she disappeared, was likewise hearsay, and similarly inadmissible.

So that meant Drew Peterson could get away with murder, if he did it?

Not so fast, Glasgow thought. Maybe there was a way around the hearsay prohibition. For one thing, Glasgow knew that hearsay that one person intended to kill another *was* admissible when it came to proving that someone had killed another person in order to collect an inheritance, or life insurance. True, it was a narrow exception, and it required other, harder evidence to show that a murder had actually occurred, but at least hearsay could be adduced to demonstrate such a motive, and therefore evidence, as to the likely culprit. So maybe, just maybe, there might be a way to get this they-said-that-she-said material before a jury. And besides this, there was another long-recognized exception to the hearsay ban: If someone was murdered to prevent their testimony at a legal proceeding, and if there was evidence that the person accused had a motive for doing the deed, that too was admissible.

On April 15, 2008, Glasgow's press office announced that the state's attorney intended to work with Illinois State Senator A. J. Wilhelmi to draft legislation "that would eliminate the incentive for criminals . . . to kill, threaten or bribe witnesses to prevent them from testifying at trial."

The proposed new law was widely seen as Glasgow's attempt to get hearsay evidence admitted against Drew Peterson in the death of Kitty Peterson, and in the disappearance of Stacy Peterson. Naturally, the media soon dubbed the legislation "Drew's Law," despite protestations by Glasgow that it wasn't directed at any individual.

"Under the proposed legislation, criminal defendants could no longer profit at trial from their illegal activities by claiming that the statements from witnesses they silenced are hearsay," the press release from Glasgow's office recounted. "The proposed Senate bill borrows from a federal rule that has assisted prosecutors in pursuing organized crime and drug cartel cases involving criminals who killed, threatened or bribed witnesses to silence them."

Meanwhile, after a hearing, a Will County judge agreed

with Glink and the Savios—the wrongful death lawsuit against Peterson for Kitty's death was a new asset for the estate, and Peterson's uncle, James Carroll, did have a conflict of interest. The judge removed Carroll as executor of Kitty's estate, and appointed Kitty's brother and sister in his stead.

In late April of 2008, Glasgow, accompanied by State Senator Wilhelmi, went to Washington, D.C., to observe oral arguments at the U.S. Supreme Court in the case of *Giles v. California*. That case threatened to knock the pins out from under the Glasgow-Wilhelmi legislation before it even got drafted. Glasgow wanted to listen very carefully to the arguments before the high court. Surely, he thought, there had to be some wiggle room—if Giles prevailed, potential murder defendants would be encouraged to knock off potential witnesses against them, left and right. No potential witness in a murder case would ever be safe.

31.

"Drew's Law"

The Giles case was rather peculiar—it was one of the few Supreme Court cases over the past decade in which the conservative majority of the court stood up for a criminal defendant's rights. In some limited ways, the Giles case seemed almost identical to the Peterson situation: A man had been accused of murder based on what his girlfriend told others he had threatened to do. And from the way the majority of the Supreme Court saw *Giles*, basing a conviction on such hearsay was unconstitutional. Under the Sixth Amendment, anyone accused of a crime has a right to confront and cross-examine his or her accuser. Of course, one can't confront a witness who is dead—cross-examination is entirely ineffective at that point.

In the case before the Supreme Court, a man named Dwayne Giles had shot to death his former girlfriend, Brenda Avie, in 2002. Giles claimed he'd fired in self-defense, but prosecutors produced statements Avie had previously made to a police officer claiming that Giles had threatened to kill her if he ever caught her cheating on him. The earlier statements of Brenda Avie to the police, although hearsay, were admitted into evidence under a section of California state law that allowed admission of such nonconfrontable, out-of-court statements when the person who made the statements was unavailable to testify, and the statements were deemed "trustworthy" by the court. With the statements in, Giles was convicted of Avie's murder.

Subsequently, in 2004, the U.S. Supreme Court, in *Crawford v. Washington*, held that the admission of unconfrontable out-of-court statements to police and others was unconstitutional, in that it ran contrary to the Constitution's Sixth Amendment guarantee of a defendant's right to cross-examine witnesses against them. Then, four years later in 2008, looking at the Giles case, the Supreme Court applied its previous reasoning in *Crawford*, and held that Brenda Avie's premurder, unconfronted statements to police about Giles's threats should not have been admitted in Giles's trial. They sent the case back to California for a new trial.

In applying the Crawford standard to Giles, however, Justice Antonin Scalia found there were narrow exceptions to the confrontation requirement, based on English common law. One was a so-called "dying declaration," in which a person on his or her deathbed was presumed to speak the truth, even though hearsay. That obviously did not apply in Kitty's case; whatever she might have said just before dying, no one was around to hear it, except her killer, if indeed she was murdered. But a second exception was when, as under the federal rule of evidence, as Glasgow had already noted, the accused murderer had committed the crime with the fundamental intent of preventing the dead witness from testifying against him in other matters, such as in a racketeering case, for example.

Well, Glasgow thought—wasn't that exception exactly the situation with Drew Peterson and Kitty Peterson? Kitty Peterson's hearsay couldn't be accepted by a court to show that Peterson had murdered her to prevent her from testifying that he had murdered her—that was a bootstrapping absurdity, since the supposed statements had occurred before her death. But Kitty *was* scheduled to testify against her former husband in the property settlement phase of their split-divorce case in April of 2004. Then, fortuitously for Drew Peterson, Kitty Peterson had been found dead in her bathtub just one month before that penultimate hearing. Now, with an official finding from Dr. Blum that Kitty had been murdered, Glasgow thought he could use the hearsay from Kitty to show that Drew had killed her to prevent her from testifying at the divorce settlement hearing, in order to keep all the marital community assets for himself. Thus, under this reasoning, Peterson had murdered Kitty with the intent to prevent her testimony, and Scalia's exception to *Giles* was met. Or so Glasgow believed.

The Supreme Court issued its decision in *Giles* in late June of 2008. By then, Glasgow and Wilhelmi had already written their proposed legislation. In "Hearsay exception for intentional murder of a witness," the proposed new law established:

> (a) A statement is not rendered inadmissible by the hearsay rule if it is offered against a party that has killed the declarant . . . intending to procure the unavailability of the declarant as a witness in a criminal or civil proceeding.

The "declarant" meant the witness—in other words, Kitty or Stacy. Kitty would have been a witness in a civil proceeding, the divorce case, while Stacy might have been a witness in a criminal proceeding, the trial of Drew for the murder of Kitty. Therefore, under the proposed Glasgow/Wilhelmi law, hearsay from either Kitty or Stacy, or from them through others like Schori, would be admissible as evidence.

> (b) While intent to procure the unavailability of the witness is a necessary element for the introduction of the statements, it need not be the sole motivation behind the murder which procured the unavailability of the declarant as a witness.

As this was written, while intent to prevent testimony of a witness had to be proven for admission of the statements, it didn't have to be the only motive for murder.

(c) The murder of the declarant may, but need not, be the subject of the trial at which the statement is being offered. If the murder of the declarant is not the subject of the trial at which the statement is being offered, the murder need not have ever been prosecuted.

This section appeared to qualify Stacy's hearsay, because, unless her body was recovered, there might not ever be a prosecution for her murder—that is, if she *had* been murdered.

(d) The proponent of the statements shall give the adverse party reasonable written notice of its intention to offer the statements and the substance of the particulars of each statement of the declarant. For purposes of this Section, identifying the location of the statements in tendered discovery shall be sufficient to satisfy the substance of the particulars of the statement.

All Glasgow had to do under this part was simply give the location of the hearsay statement in the mound of paper evidence that would be provided by the prosecutor after a person was charged. That left it up to the defense to figure out when, where, and to whom the statement might have been made.

(e) The admissibility of the statements shall be determined by the court at a pretrial hearing. At the hearing, the proponent of the statement bears the burden of establishing 3 criteria by a preponderance of the evidence . . .

This part was even worse for the defense. "A preponderance of the evidence" meant nothing more than a 51 percent likelihood that the statement was true, far short of "beyond a reasonable doubt."

The law called for a judge to decide, out of the presence of a jury, by the "preponderance," that first, the declarant had been murdered by the accused, and for the purpose of preventing the testimony; second, that the timeliness, content and circumstances of the hearsay were sufficient to establish the statements' reliability; and third, that "the interests of justice will best be served by the admission of the statement into evidence."

The judge was required to make separate findings for each of the three determinations. Although the law did not state so specifically, it appeared that the judge had to make affirmative decisions "by a preponderance" for all three of the criteria. It would finally be up to a jury to decide whether the hearsay statements thus allowed in were sufficiently reliable to permit a conviction beyond reasonable doubt. But most defense attorneys were aghast—permitting jurors to consider "he-said-that-she-said" information in the absence of cross-examination of the original declarant was to them tantamount to allowing the basest rumor into the courtroom.

The Glasgow-Wilhelmi law sailed through the Illinois legislature, and was approved by an overwhelming vote in August of 2008. By then, of course, every legislator in Springfield had heard of Drew Peterson and his wives.

But also by then, Peterson was again in counterattack mode. He wanted people to know the real Drew, not the media monster. So he agreed to sit down with Derek Armstrong to give his side of the story. Eventually Armstrong persuaded Peterson to submit to two polygraph examinations, which would generate some peculiar and possibly suggestive results.

32.

Armstrong

Armstrong arrived in northern Illinois in mid-May, even as Glasgow and Wilhelmi were drafting their law, and Scalia was finding the exception in *Giles* that they would use. A Canadian journalist, novelist, and self-proclaimed private investigator, Armstrong's idea was to prepare a book about the media celebrity that Peterson had become. While he appeared to want to strive diligently to be "fair and objective" (to hijack Fox News' own claim), any fair reading of *Drew Peterson Exposed* suggests that Armstrong allowed himself to be overwhelmed by Peterson's personality. Armstrong claimed to have spent many hours interviewing Peterson; regrettably, he seems to have spent comparatively little time getting any other side of the story. At no point, in fact, does Armstrong indicate that he ever interviewed Sharon Bychowski or any of the Cales or Savios. Instead, he seems to have relied almost exclusively on Peterson's generally negative characterization of his neighbor and in-laws. So in essence, *Drew Peterson Exposed* might actually have been titled *Drew Peterson Masked*.

As already noted, Armstrong's take on the Suds Pub aspect of Peterson's second and third marriages is somewhat at variance with the facts, doubtless because Armstrong relied almost exclusively on Peterson's own version of the events, rather than the public record. That the fate of the pub was central to the divorce contention between Kitty and

Drew is undeniable, particularly in light of the records available in both the divorce and probate files, not to mention Harry Smith's suspicions, even long after Kitty's death, that Drew had pulled something sneaky with the money from the pub.

Likewise, Armstrong's description of the drug sting gone sour with Bindy Rock is all Peterson—in Peterson's own view, he was the victim of political persecution by Will County officials and the village of Bolingbrook. There's no indication in Armstrong's account that he ever consulted the existing public records on that imbroglio.

After regaling Armstrong with his stories of serving in the military police, and his days as a long-haired, undercover narc, Peterson seemed to take pride in his infidelity as a husband. It was almost as if Peterson wanted Armstrong to believe he was a champion cocksman, irresistible to women. Peterson seemed caught between two self-images—on one hand, the fabulous lover, and on the other, the doting, patient father and husband. All his wives but the first, Peterson told Armstrong, had emotional problems, while he was the pillar they relied upon.

By far the most interesting aspect of Armstrong's encounters with Peterson, however, are the two lie detector tests. Armstrong writes that he kept pressing Peterson to submit to the tests—one for Stacy's disappearance, a second for Kitty's death—but that Peterson seemed reluctant, as was Joel Brodsky.

But eventually, on May 18, 2008, Peterson allowed himself to be wired up by an independent polygrapher, Lee McCord, but not before signing some sort of release to hold Brodsky harmless from any legal malpractice liability. All questions on that date concerned Stacy's disappearance.

By now, from television dramas if not reality TV, most people are aware of what's involved in a polygraph test. The subject is asked to sit in a chair. A band across the chest measures the rate and depth of respiration. Other devices record heart rate, blood pressure and "galvanic skin response," a measurement of electrical conductivity of the skin, which is thought to correspond to emotion: in other words, sweat. All of the polygraph's measurements are based on physiological responses to stress, the so-called "fight or flight" instinct when confronted by a threatening situation. Under the theory of the polygraph, before someone lies, the body instinctively activates itself to prepare for fight or flight—deception makes us do it, whether we want to or not.

There have been suggestions by some psychologists that certain personality types, usually those termed "sociopathic," have the ability to "beat" polygraph tests. Certainly some sociopaths have a highly developed capacity to lie without displaying the usual physiological signs of deception. But most professional polygraphers contend that an expert polygrapher can, in fact, unmask even a sociopath. While acknowledging that giving a "lie detector test" is more of an art than a science, they say that the validity of the test depends most on the polygrapher's skill in asking the questions, interpreting the results, then narrowing the field of inquiry by follow-up questions. Even the most inveterate sociopath can neither run nor hide when strapped in the hot seat. Or so say those who believe in the value of polygraphs.

In any case, the pros say, a truly effective polygraph examination involves three phases: the interview stage, in which the examiner attempts to establish rapport with the subject, explains the test procedure, and goes over the mutually agreed-upon questions; the instrumentation phase, in which the subject is connected to the machine and the questions are asked; and the interrogation phase, which follows the analysis of the instrumentation phase results.

As far as can be determined from Peterson's tests, the examinations he took only involved the first two phases. The omission of the third interrogation phase, the polygraph professionals contend, made at least the first of the two tests taken by Peterson invalid.

"The [usual] exam is given three possible scores," notes a prominent law enforcement polygraph examiner not involved with any Illinois police agency, who, in an interview for this book, was asked to review Armstrong's description in *Drew Peterson Exposed* of the polygraphs taken by Drew Peterson, on the condition of anonymity.

The inevitable results are, according to this polygrapher:

"DI (Deception Indicated), NDI (No Deception Indicated), or Inconclusive.

"If the score is NDI, the exam is over and the subject has passed. If Inconclusive, you may explore with the subject why he might be inconclusive and whether or not to try it again with a different set of questions. However, if the exam is graded as DI, then the examiner should begin to interrogate the subject to find out why" he might have been deceptive.

"These basics pertain to a proper police polygraph. When it is being done privately and for a defense attorney, there is never an interrogation phase. There is no danger of any contradictory statements or statements against interest ever being used against the subject and there is no chance of a confession, once the test is done. So defense exams like these are really only two-thirds of an exam, which makes them useless."

The May 18, 2008 exam had six "relevant" questions:

"On Sunday, October 28, 2007, did you last see your wife Stacy in your home before going to bed after coming home from work?"

According to Armstrong, Peterson answered "yes" to this question. McCord judged the answer deceptive.

"Did you have any involvement in the physical removal of your wife Stacy from your home on Sunday, October 28, 2007?"

Peterson answered "no," and McCord judged this not deceptive.

"Did you in any way physically harm your wife Stacy during the time she disappeared?"

"No." Again, there was no deception, according to McCord.

"Do you know the whereabouts of your wife Stacy?"

Peterson answered no. McCord found this deceptive.

"Did you receive a phone call from your wife Stacy on

the evening of October 28, 2007, telling you that she was leaving you?"

Peterson answered yes. McCord found that deceptive.

"Did your wife call you on Sunday, October 28, 2007, and tell you that if you wanted the car, it was parked at the Clow Airport?"

Peterson answered yes. McCord found no deception.

What did these results mean? It's impossible to know for sure—this is why a police polygrapher would have followed up with the "interrogation" phase. What did it mean that Peterson had supposedly lied about last seeing Stacy in the marital bed early Sunday morning? Or not knowing the whereabouts of Stacy?

Why hadn't Peterson seen her? Where was she when he *did* last see her? Did Peterson's answer to the fourth question, couched as it was in the present tense, mean that he knew where she was *right then*? A police interrogator would have pushed Peterson to answer these imponderables in an interrogation phase.

What did it mean that Peterson had supposedly lied about getting a telephone call from Stacy on Sunday night? That there was no such call from Stacy, exactly as Fuhrman, among others, had suggested? And what about the statement that Stacy had called about the car? Did that mean Stacy had called *earlier* than 9 p.m.? Where had she been when she made *that* call?

Putting all the answers together—assuming that McCord's examination was accurate within its limits—suggested that Peterson knew what had happened to Stacy, even if he hadn't *personally* done anything to harm her. The answers opened the possibility, at least, that someone else had harmed Stacy, and if Peterson knew her present whereabouts, then he knew who, where, and how.

One week later, Peterson took another polygraph test administered by McCord, this one concerning Kitty. This time there were four relevant questions:

"Did you see your ex-wife Kathy alive at any time after you picked up the kids from her house on Friday, February 27, 2004? Did you have any type of contact with your ex-wife Kathy after you picked up the kids from her house on Friday, February 27, 2004? Did you have any involvement in the death of your ex-wife Kathy in 2004? Were you present at the time of your ex-wife Kathy's death?"

Peterson answered "no" to all four questions. McCord found no deception.

So here was a puzzle: If Peterson had showed no deception to all the questions on both tests, a cynic dubious of polygraph tests might well argue that he had "beaten" the machine—like a sociopath. But the fact that he had displayed the physiological indicators of deception on three of the questions from the Stacy test seemed to somehow validate the no-deception answers on the Kitty test. If the two tests could be believed, Peterson had "no involvement" in Kitty's death, but knew more than he was saying about Stacy's disappearance.

But what if Peterson had deliberately been deceptive on three of the Stacy questions as part of a plan to convince Armstrong, and anyone else, that the results from the Kitty test were valid? Was this possible?

The experts weren't entirely sure. What they did know was that, without an interrogation phase on the Stacy test, the results of both tests were meaningless.

33.
Nabbed

Throughout the remainder of 2008 and into the first half of 2009, the Will County special grand jury continued to convene, looking into the death of Kitty, the disappearance of Stacy, and, it appears, the disappearance of another Will County woman, Lisa Stebic, who had also been the subject of considerable news media attention in the Chicago area. The jury met on Wednesdays, in Joliet, supported by Glasgow's office and the efforts of several dozen ISP agents, backed by experts from the FBI. If the initial investigation into Kitty's death had been cursory, the new probe was akin to an all-points dragnet. All the insinuations on nationwide television in the fall of 2007 that the ISP had covered up for Peterson in his third wife's 2004 bathtub drowning only made the ISP more determined to leave no pebble unturned.

In November of 2008, the normal one-year term of the special grand jury was extended for six more months. That meant, under the law, that the jury had to reach a decision on who, if anyone, to indict in Kitty's death by mid-May of 2009. Otherwise, their service would be wasted, and Glasgow would have to start over with another grand jury.

Peterson rarely appeared in the news media during this time. When he did, he seemed philosophical about his possible fate. While he admitted that he was worried that he might be charged with the crime of murder of one or both of his last two wives, he knew there was little he could do to affect the jury's decision. It was up to the fates, or at any rate, Glasgow.

At almost the same time that the special grand jury's term was extended, just after the fall election of 2008, then-Governor Rod Blagojevich of Illinois signed "Drew's Law," although Glasgow resolutely refused to call it that—he didn't want anyone, especially some clever defense lawyer like Brodsky, to claim that the legislation permitting hearsay, which he and Wilhemi had promoted, could be characterized as a "bill of attainder"—that is, a law designed to charge only one person. That wouldn't be constitutional. So Glasgow despised the media's fascination with the term "Drew's Law," even if it captured the core of why Glasgow thought the law was necessary.

By the winter of 2008–09, the Peterson case had largely faded from the broadcasts and newspapers. Instead, the man who'd signed "Drew's Law" into force, Blagojevich, was the new man in the news, soon to be charged, by a federal prosecutor, with crimes related to the alleged attempted "sale" of the U.S. Senate seat being vacated by President-elect Barack Obama. "Blago" gave the TV people plenty of fodder, and anyway, as far as the Peterson tale went, it was as if, knowing that the special grand jury was considering charges and squads of investigators were poring over every intimate detail of the Peterson marriages, the news media was content, finally, to allow the law to take its course.

Once the media was off their case, the state investigators had fanned out across the landscape, digging up everyone and anyone who had anything to say about Drew Peterson, Kitty, or Stacy, or, for that matter, Bindy Rock, Gerry O'Neill, or most of the vast cast of characters Peterson had had some involvement with over the previous three decades as both a cop, a saloon keeper, a businessman, and a husband and father. Eventually, they interviewed well over six hundred witnesses and assembled more than forty thousand pages of official police reports. This was a monumental effort, sufficient to drown almost any defense lawyer in a Sargasso Sea of paper and conflicting accounts. For Brodsky, even if he didn't yet know the full dimensions of the task that he would soon face, it was prima facie evidence of Glasgow's intent to use all the powers of his office to make it as difficult as possible for anyone to defend Peterson. The sheer volume of discovery, Brodsky thought, was meant to hamstring any defense. To the ISP and their fellow investigators, it was atonement.

Then, finally, on May 7, 2009, Peterson was arrested and charged with the murder of Kathleen Savio, based on an indictment voted by the special grand jury. No charges were filed in connection with Stacy Peterson's disappearance, the event that had started the ball rolling, amidst the pumpkins and costumes and cobwebs, more than two years before.

"Will County State's Attorney James Glasgow and Illinois State Police Captain Carl Dobrich announce that Drew Walter Peterson was arrested today after a Special Grand Jury issued an indictment for first-degree murder alleging he killed Kathleen Savio five years ago," a press release put out by Glasgow's office declared.

"At the request of State's Attorney Glasgow and Illinois State Police detectives, Circuit Judge Daniel Rozak issued a warrant for Peterson's arrest Thursday afternoon. Judge Rozak set bail for Peterson at $20 million. He must post 10 percent or $2 million to secure his release while awaiting trial." Peterson might have been well-off compared to most retired suburban cops, but not even he could raise $2 million in cash or property to secure bail. So Peterson would have to stay in jail.

"Illinois State Police arrested Peterson without incident late Thursday afternoon during a traffic stop at Weber Road and Lily Cache Lane in Bolingbrook," the press release continued. Peterson was taken into custody only a few blocks from 6 Pheasant Chase Court and 392 Pheasant Chase Drive.

"The two-count Bill of Indictment alleges that Peterson, on or about Feb. 29, 2004, 'without lawful justification and with the intent to kill Kathleen Savio, caused Kathleen Savio to inhale fluid, thereby causing the death of Kathleen Savio.'

"Kathleen Savio, who was Peterson's third wife, was found dead in her bathtub on March 1, 2004. Charges were not filed in the case five years ago by the prior state's attorney, who held office when Kathleen Savio was murdered." In other words, the press release implied, the failure to charge Peterson in 2004 was the fault of Glasgow's rival and predecessor, Tomczak.

"Glasgow reopened the case and convened a Special Grand Jury to investigate her murder in November 2007. The Special Grand Jury also is investigating the disappearance of Drew Peterson's fourth wife, Stacy Peterson.

"Drew Peterson is scheduled to be arraigned at 1:30 p.m. Friday, May 8 in courtroom 405 at the Will County Courthouse, 14 W. Jefferson St., Joliet.

"The Will County State's Attorney's Office reminds the public that an indictment is not evidence of guilt. A defendant is presumed innocent and is entitled to a fair trial at which the government has the burden of proving guilt beyond a reasonable doubt."

Of course, if Glasgow didn't believe Peterson was guilty, he would not have asked the special grand jury for an indictment.

The next day, Peterson appeared in court for his arraignment on the murder charge. Asked how he pled, Peterson was very clear.

"Not guilty," he said.

34.
Defending Drew

Well, Peterson had been expecting this—as a former cop, he surely knew that a prosecutor doesn't spent eighteen months investigating something and then *not* ask for an indictment. But as the special grand jury's term dwindled down to its last weeks, Peterson still harbored a faint hope that the jury would stand up to Glasgow and refuse to indict. After all, from Peterson's point of view—or at least, that of his lawyer, Brodsky—there was no evidence to support a charge of murder. Except, of course, the damning hearsay that Glasgow had convinced the legislature to accept as proof under "Drew's Law."

So Peterson settled into the Will County Adult Correction Center, not happy, but not surprised at this development. The kids were taken in by his brother Paul and his son Steve. Because of his past as a police officer, Peterson was kept in isolation from the other prisoners—as a retired cop and a former narc, he was a prime target for other inmates, either from a quick thrust from a sharpened toothbrush, or from someone desperate to make up a bogus story of a "confession" in order to promote a possible early release on their own charges.

Like any other conscientious defense attorney, Brodsky's initial efforts were devoted to getting Peterson out of the slammer. That meant getting Peterson's bail reduced to a manageable amount from the astronomical $20 million.

On May 22, 2009, Brodsky asked for a substantial reduction in Peterson's bail—to a half million, at most. Glasgow opposed any bail reduction. He had, Glasgow told the court, a witness ready to testify that Peterson had once offered him $25,000 to kill Kitty.

If true, this seemed to be a slam-dunk witness against Peterson. Unlike most hearsay evidence, "statements against penal interest" by the alleged declarant—in this case, Peterson himself, if he'd actually offered someone $25,000 to kill Kitty—were admissible, and no fancy maneuvering in the state legislature was necessary to get *them* admitted. It was the law as it had been for generations.

But were the statements true? Did Glasgow's witness have credibility? Was there any corroboration to support the story? Did the witness have some reason to lie, some sort of bias against the former Bolingbrook cop? Where and when were the supposed statements made by Peterson? If, for instance, the witness claimed that the statements had been made on, say, February 14, and Peterson could prove he was in Florida on the same day, would they be admissible at a trial? Or, if there was evidence that the witness was someplace else when he claimed the statements were made—what then? It's very easy to make assertions—what counts in a criminal case is whether they can stand up after thorough investigation. But for the purpose of maintaining Peterson's bail at $20 million, the mere fact of their existence would be sufficient, unless Brodsky, as Peterson's defense attorney, chose to try to expose them as false. But Brodsky's attempts to cast doubt on the unnamed witnesses' credibility came to naught, and Peterson remained in jail.

Meanwhile, the prosecution filed an affidavit of prejudice against the judge originally assigned to the case. Glasgow and his staff had been unhappy with the judge's ruling in an earlier, unrelated case his office had filed against Peterson, a complaint charging Peterson with illegal weapons possession. The judge had dismissed the charge when the prosecutor refused to provide Brodsky with voluminous discovery, including all the details of the grand jury investigation that had been going on for months.

After a new judge was selected, it was Peterson's turn to object. The defense filed an affidavit of prejudice against the replacement judge, since she had ruled against Peterson in the reopening of Kitty's estate a year earlier.

Finally, a judge satisfactory to both sides was selected. This was Stephen White, a veteran of the Will County bench who was closing in on his retirement. Likely, the Peterson case would be the last big case of Judge White's career.

After this, Brodsky focused his attention on the new hearsay law. He was perfectly happy to see it referred to in the news media as "Drew's Law," even though that description drove Glasgow up the wall. The idea that Glasgow had cajoled the state's lawmakers to make a law that applied only to his client, Brodsky thought, only demonstrated the base political motives of the investigation. By July of 2009, Brodsky's team of lawyers had formulated a constitutional attack on the new statute, claiming it was unconstitutional: It evaded the Sixth Amendment right to confront witnesses against a defendant.

The Sixth Amendment guarantees anyone accused of a crime an inviolable right to cross-examine any witness who testifies against him:

> *"In all criminal prosecutions, the accused shall enjoy the right to . . . be confronted with the witnesses against him . . ."*

In Brodsky's view, "Drew's Law" unconstitutionally allowed third-party testimony, allegedly from both Kitty and Stacy, even though neither could be cross-examined as to their truthfulness. The fact that one was dead and the other missing didn't give their statements to third parties—like Susan Savio or Neil Schori—special validity. Brodsky contended that if his client couldn't confront the original "declarant," i.e., Kitty or Stacy, a court had no business allowing the supposed statements to third parties in as evidence. In his view, it was akin to giving gossip the same status as a recorded statement.

"Allowing the judge to determine what statements are credible ["reliable," as the new law defined it] is 'fundamentally at odds with the right of confrontation.' " Or so Brodsky's side asserted in their effort to wipe out "Drew's Law." Leaving the question of what testimony was "reliable" up to an elected judge without requiring confrontation was contrary to the Supreme Court's 1994 decision in *Crawford*— particularly in situations when a witness was unavailable, as in the cases of Kitty and Stacy, the defense claimed. It was tantamount to "dispensing with jury trial because a defendant is obviously guilty," Brodsky argued. The whole idea behind "Drew's Law" demolished the concept of innocent until proven guilty before a jury of one's peers. Leaving the crucial question of reliability to an elected judge was far too wobbly a standard. "What the court deems reliable in one case, another could deem unreliable. Such an arbitrary and capricious standard clearly strips the defendant of his constitutional right guaranteed by the Sixth Amendment."

Brodsky elaborated:

"The new hearsay law, Drew's Law, as written would allow gossip, innuendo, rumor and back-fence scandal to come into a court of law and masquerade as evidence. As lawyers and judges, we know how people act, and the wild and hurtful things they say and do in divorce cases. Often after the case is over they regret what they say and are ashamed of their behavior. Just because someone dies during the divorce case does not make the things they say any more reliable. The statements are the product of the same emotions, and are just as tainted."

The way Glasgow had drafted it, "Drew's Law" allowed impermissible hearsay, and as approved by the state legislature and signed into law, failed to distinguish between idle talk and "testimonial" speech, such as proffered in a legal proceeding, Brodsky contended. "Therefore, it is unconstitutional as written . . ."

Besides this Sixth Amendment objection to "Drew's Law," Brodsky and his team said the statute was a prime example of "ex post facto"—passing a law after something had happened to make what had already happened illegal. This, too was barred by the Constitution, Brodsky asserted, under Article 1, Section 10:

> No State shall, without the Consent of the Congress . . .
> pass any . . . ex post facto law . . .

Under this clause of the Constitution, a forbidden ex post facto law was one passed by a state to make something illegal that was previously legal under the then-existing law. In essence, it was applying the present to the past, an attempt to make people guilty later for something they had done when it was legal at the time. It would be akin to arresting someone in 1926 for drinking alcohol in 1916, years after Prohibition was passed in 1919.

The new hearsay law, Brodsky contended, had only been sponsored by Glasgow because of all the publicity the Peterson case had generated after Stacy's disappearance.

"When the defendant's fourth wife disappeared in October of 2007, the public and press automatically assumed foul play. The public and press immediately began to scrutinize every part of the defendant's life: his friends, his family, his comings and goings. They camped out at his home, and also began looking into the death of Kathleen Savio."

It was only because of the intense media speculation that Kitty's body was exhumed, Brodsky continued. Then came the two new autopsies, one by Dr. Baden, whom Brodsky characterized as "a paid consultant and talking head for Fox Entertainment Network? [sic]"

When the two new autopsies resulted in a finding of homicide, Glasgow had half of what he needed to prosecute—a crime. But because there was insufficient evidence to charge

Peterson under the existing law, Glasgow decided to change the law. That was out-of-bounds, Brodsky contended. The Illinois State Supreme Court, only two weeks after Peterson's arrest, had ruled in another case that "a law is ex-post facto if it is retroactive and disadvantageous to a defendant. A law is disadvantageous to a defendant if it criminalizes an act innocent when performed, increases the punishment for an offense previously committed, or alters the rules of evidence making a conviction easier." That's exactly what "Drew's Law" did, Brodsky contended—made Peterson's conviction easier to obtain, by altering the rules of evidence.

Brodsky had one more card to play: He wanted the court to move the trial away from Will County because of all the publicity surrounding the case. He performed an Internet search for "Drew Peterson" and discovered that the number of hits involving Peterson outnumbered those for "Rod Blagojevich" by a margin of two-to-one.

Brodsky filed these motions in August 2009. The court had scheduled a status hearing for August 10, and both sides appeared. Peterson was brought in, shackled hand and foot. He sat in the jury box, guarded by a single female deputy sheriff. After a few minor preliminaries, the prosecution and defense lawyers adjourned to the judge's chambers to sort out various issues out of the eyes and ears of the news media, which occupied the last two of the three rows of courtroom seating. Peterson soon struck up a conversation with the reporters. His tone was light, his demeanor wryly insouciant, and, as usual, self-deprecating.

Asked how he was getting along with the experience of being in jail, Peterson said it wasn't so bad. The food wasn't nearly as bad as he'd once been led to believe, he said, but "the isolation is kind of irritating." Because of his past as a police officer, he had to be kept in solitary confinement, away from the other prisoners. Not having anyone to talk to for most of the time, the hours dragged on, day after day. "Sometimes I think I'm losing my mind," he joked. But his friendly tone and frequent smiles hardly made him seem insane.

After about an hour of closed-door discussion, all the

lawyers emerged, and Peterson was escorted from the courtroom by the sheriff's deputy.

Later, outside in front of the courthouse, Brodsky tried to explain to the news media why his motions were important, for everyone, not just Drew Peterson. Any person accused of a crime has always had the right to confront witnesses against him—that's what the hearsay rules were designed to ensure. And using political power to make it easier to convict someone on the basis of evidence that previously was forbidden could set a terrible precedent.

"The rules can't change just because someone is unpopular and disliked," he said.

In early October 2009, Judge White heard arguments on Brodsky's motions. As the moving party, Brodsky went first, claiming that "Drew's Law" violated the Constitution in allowing hearsay in violation of the Sixth Amendment's guarantee of the right of confrontation, as well as the ban on ex post facto. Glasgow himself argued for the state, maintaining that the new law was entirely valid under Justice Scalia's exceptions in *Giles*.

Throughout the arguments, Peterson sat at the defense table, shackled as usual. He seemed to follow the arguments closely. This was a vital hearing for Peterson—if Brodsky could convince Judge White to toss "Drew's Law," the charges against him in all likelihood would have to be dismissed.

After hearing from both sides for a little over an hour, Judge White adjourned the court for lunch. He would, he said, have a decision in the afternoon.

Shortly before 2 p.m., White returned to the bench. Peterson, sitting at the counsel table, looked crestfallen, almost wan. It appeared that Judge White had already told the lawyers of his decision, judging from Peterson's expression.

And so it proved: Judge White found "Drew's Law" not to be a violation of the Sixth Amendment, in that it had always been possible to use hearsay evidence when the testimony involved a witness who was prevented from testifying by force or threat. And since that had always been the case, there was no ex post facto. The judge said he agreed with Glasgow: The new law was simply a "codification" of existing common law.

That meant that, if Judge White found the proposed hearsay to be "reliable," Drew Peterson would have to go on trial for his life. At the very least, it meant many more months in solitary, and if convicted, almost certainly a lifetime of similar loneliness. All in all, it was a dire prospect for someone who had only wanted to be the life of the party.

35.
Reliability

The so-called "reliability" hearings required under "Drew's Law" began on January 19, 2010. In setting the scene, the *Tribune* that morning reported that Glasgow intended to call at least sixty witnesses to validate fifteen hearsay statements supporting the proposition that Peterson had murdered Kitty. Of course, the way the law had been written, the judge had only to find by a preponderance—51 percent—that the hearsay statements had actually been made, and if so, that they were likely true. Or at least, under the way Glasgow and Wilhelmi had written their statute, "reliable," and "in the interest of justice."

The *Tribune*, in setting the stage for these hearings, reported that authorities believed that Peterson had knowledge of things about Kitty's death that "only the killer could have known." This was somewhat astonishing: How did the newspaper's reporters know what Peterson had told the ISP, and whether it included facts "only the killer could have known"? If this was true, why hadn't Peterson been charged with a crime back in 2007, or even 2004?

On balance, it seemed the newspaper's unsourced assertion was probably a leak from the police or the prosecutors, and even at that, not anything Peterson had said directly to the police, but derived from some of the hearsay evidence—such as Schori's assertion of what Stacy had claimed Peterson told her after Kitty's death. This was, in a way, a three-carom shot on the evidentiary pool table, allegedly Peterson to Stacy to Schori. Perhaps significantly, four of the first five readers to comment on this report on the *Tribune* readers' blog site doubted the constitutionality of "Drew's Law" because it deprived Peterson of the right to confront the original witnesses against him—Kitty and Stacy, the dead and the missing. Some of the doubters said that while they thought Peterson was probably guilty, the use of possibly extra-constitutional evidence against him was an even greater sin, and that higher courts were sure to throw a guilty verdict out.

The *Tribune* also reported that the "reliability" hearings were expected to last three weeks, an estimate that Brodsky concurred with. This, too, was somewhat astonishing: Given that only fifteen hearsay statements were at issue—from Schori, or the divorce lawyer Smith, or the Savios, or Cassandra, or Maniaci, or Mims—this suggested that Brodsky et al. had elected to attack the credibility of the witnesses against Peterson even before the actual trial.

It also suggested that the prosecutors wanted to establish the reliability of the critical statements by showing the entire context in which they were made. If, for instance, the prosecutors were able to establish police incompetence in the initial investigation of Kitty's death, that would tend to make her earlier hearsay statements about Drew's supposed threats to kill her more reliable than if the police had left no stone unturned. In a way, it was a form of addition by subtraction.

"This is them [prosecutors] laying out their case," Brodsky told the *Tribune* on the eve of the hearings. "People should not think this is going to be the trial." Still, it was obvious that the cumulative effect of the testimony would be to show why Glasgow's prosecutors believed that Peterson was guilty of murder, but under the legal standard of a "preponderance of the evidence," rather than "beyond a reasonable doubt." It seemed likely that at least some of the 240 potential jurors already sworn in would pay close attention to the media reports of these proceedings, even if they weren't supposed to. It was, in a way, giving Glasgow's prosecutors two bites at the apple, a mulligan before the actual trial, almost like a second grand jury, but in public. Brodsky tried to induce

Judge White to order the hearings closed to the media and the public, but Judge White said no.

Brodksy wanted to use the hearings to show that the hearsay against Peterson was fundamentally unreliable, based on the witnesses' personal dislike of Peterson. "We think that even in this questioning, a lot of beliefs that people have about what was said and who said them are going to be burst, dashed," he told the *Tribune*.

In light of Judge White's earlier decision to rebuff Brodsky's assertion that "Drew's Law" was unconstitutional, and the very light burden of proof, that decision by the defense seemed slightly odd. Wouldn't it have been better to lie in the weeds, not aggressively cross-examine the hearsay witnesses, and save the heavy artillery for the actual trial, on the assumption that the low threshold of admissibility already sanctioned by Judge White was insurmountable? In other words, tactically, might it have been better to save the credibility attacks for the actual triers of fact, the eventual jury, assuming an unbiased one could be seated? With an all-out cross-examination at the "reliability" phase, Brodsky might tip his hand as to how the defense intended to attack the prosecution's case, and thereby give Glasgow's side the opportunity to shore up his own case over the following weeks.

On the other hand, this *was* a media event, and one certain to generate a lot of publicity for everyone. . . .

In any event, the reliability phase of the case of *Illinois vs. Peterson* actually involved seventy witnesses. Perhaps the most shocking evidence that emerged during the hearing was the seeming lack of professionalism exhibited by the state police during their initial investigation of Kitty's death in 2004.

"Prosecutors spent a month tarring Drew Peterson with hours of testimony about how he supposedly killed his last two wives," Hosey wrote for his newspaper, *The Herald-News*, after the hearing was over. "But after all the witnesses and all the arguing, in the end, it was the state police who may have looked the guiltiest of all." Still, the failures of the Illinois State Police in the matter of Kitty's death made Peterson look more culpable than ever. *Cui bono?* Who principally benefited from such lackadaisical work? Peterson, it seemed quite clear.

Among the initial witnesses at the "reliability" hearing was Tom Morphey, Peterson's stepbrother. Strictly speaking, Morphey's hearsay testimony of what Peterson supposedly told him wasn't subject to the reliability test under "Drew's Law." It was already admissible under previous law as a statement against penal interest by Peterson, a long-recognized exception to the rules banning most hearsay testimony. But the prosecution wanted to present it to Judge White in order to establish the context of Stacy's disappearance, which in turn might help establish the reliability of Stacy's own hearsay statements about her fear of her husband to her sister Cassandra, the Reverend Schori, and the divorce lawyer Harry Smith, whose thirdhand statements supported the notion that Peterson had murdered Kitty. If Morphey's testimony helped reinforce the notion that Stacy was dead because of something she knew about Peterson and Kitty, those thirdhand statements from Stacy gained added reliability.

Morphey testified that on the night before Stacy vanished, Peterson told him that Stacy was planning to have him evicted from the 6 Pheasant Chase Court house, file for divorce, and get all the money as well as custody of the children. Morphey said Peterson told him he planned to do something about this. Peterson then asked Morphey how much he loved him, according to Morphey.

"I do," Morphey said he replied.

"Enough to kill for me?" Morphey claimed Peterson then asked him.

"I said, 'I always assumed you killed Kathleen,'" Morphey testified he told Peterson.

"He said, 'I would never have killed Kathleen. She was a good mother.'"

Morphey testified that the following night, Peterson had called him to the 6 Pheasant Chase house to help him remove a barrel from the Peterson bedroom. As had been reported by Geraldo Rivera more than two years before, Morphey claimed the barrel was "warm to the touch." He assumed that it was Stacy's body in the barrel. Morphey said he didn't look inside the barrel, and didn't know what Peterson did with it after they removed it, although Peterson had said something about keeping it in a nearby storage locker for an extended period.

As he'd already suggested he would, Brodsky attacked Morphey's credibility, suggesting that previous mental problems and alcohol use had made his testimony unreliable.

Brodsky hammered Morphey on the obvious question: If he really thought his stepbrother had murdered his fourth wife, why hadn't he called the police?

He was scared, Morphey said. He thought his stepbrother might kill him.

Sharon Bychowski testified in much the same vein as she had previously related to Hosey in *Fatal Vows*, to the effect that Peterson and his young wife frequently squabbled, and as to Peterson's demeanor once she was reported missing. The bad blood between Bychowski and her former neighbor was evident. By this point, Bychowski had talked several times to Will County prosecutors, including to Glasgow personally, and was utterly convinced that Peterson had murdered her friend Stacy. Brodsky attempted to undermine the reliability of her testimony by focusing on her anti-Peterson bias, but Bychowski was adamant: Her former next-door neighbor had done something to his wife, her protégé in responsible motherhood.

Then came the testimony of former ISP investigator Patrick Collins, once the lead investigator in the death of Kitty. Now retired from the ISP, Collins's account of his efforts to find out what had actually happened to Kitty in 2004 suggested at best a slipshod investigation.

Collins admitted that he'd hardly pulled out all the stops

in his investigation of Kitty's death. "If I had to do certain things over again, yes, I would," he said. But from what he'd seen at the scene, he thought from the very beginning that the death was an accident, and once the pathologists determined that to be the situation, the case took on a much lower priority. He'd seen no defensive injuries on Kathy, he said.

He also admitted that he'd granted Peterson special treatment as a fellow police officer during his investigation, including allowing him to sit in on his interview with Stacy. That, of course, was a cardinal error—any thorough investigation demands that critical witnesses be interviewed separately.

Nor, Collins admitted, had he ever interviewed any of the Savios as to their suspicions. That in itself was an astonishing admission, given all the squabbling over Kitty's estate, and Harry Smith's suspicions about Suds Pub.

The Reverend Schori was called, and testified that during a counseling session with Stacy—presumably the same August conversation he'd already told Fox News about—Stacy told him that Drew had told her to lie about his whereabouts on the night Kitty died. Stacy had told him, Schori said, of Drew's odd behavior on the night Kitty drowned—particularly the fact that she couldn't locate him anywhere in the 6 Pheasant Chase Court house that night, or on his cell phone. When Peterson did reappear, he was wearing black and carrying women's clothing, Schori said Stacy told him. Peterson put the clothing into the washing machine.

The Savios, Cassandra, and Sharon Bychowski all testified that both Kitty and Stacy were afraid of Drew, as did Victoria. Drew's son Eric even testified that he'd seen his father physically abuse Kitty in the 1990s. The former assistant state's attorney Fragale testified that she'd never received Kitty's "he will kill me" letter of October 2002.

Devastating testimony was delivered by Kitty's boyfriend, Steve Maniaci. He testified that only two days before Kitty's body was found in the tub, he'd seen no bruises or scratches on her body. Shown photographs of Kitty's body in the tub, Maniaci grew emotional. He said that one of the pictures was all wrong—Kitty habitually put her hair up before taking a bath; in the photo from the scene it was down. He said that in the days before her death, Kitty was increasingly worried that Peterson might try to kill her to get all the marital assets for himself.

On the night Kitty's body was discovered, Maniaci testified, he confronted Peterson at the 392 Pheasant Chase house.

"I sure hope you didn't have anything to do with this," Maniaci said he'd told Peterson. When Peterson denied any involvement, Maniaci said he remarked, "Well, it sure worked out good for you."

Maniaci said he'd voiced his suspicions of Peterson to the Illinois State Police, and was assured that Kitty's death would be investigated as a homicide. But years later, when Glasgow's prosecutors showed him copies of the ISP reports from 2004, none of his suspicions were recorded.

Kitty's divorce lawyer Harry Smith also testified. He said Stacy had talked with him a few days before she vanished, and had told him of her "plan" to divorce Drew, take the kids, and get all the money. The word "extortion" was used in court. Stacy had told him, Smith said, that Drew was angry with her, because he believed that she had told someone that he had killed Kitty. Maybe it was true, maybe it wasn't—how could Smith know for sure how Kitty had died? But even if it wasn't actually true, it certainly gave Drew a motive for murdering Stacy, if that indeed was her "plan," and if her assertions to Reverend Schori were the first phase of her campaign, calculated to later buttress her credibility at crunch time. Based on Smith's testimony, Peterson seemingly might have had to shut the mouth of his fourth wife forever, whether she was telling the truth or not.

The unprecedented hearings ended at the end of February 2010. Judge White said he would seal his rulings on the admissibility of the hearsay statements until the actual trial, which he tentatively set to begin on June 14, 2010. Judge White had already ruled against the defense motion for a change of venue, but said he might change his mind if it was clear that, after questioning the 240 people previously selected in August 2009 for the jury pool, an unbiased panel of twelve and alternates could not be seated. Judge White's decision to seal his rulings on the reliability until a jury was sworn in—one which had just been exposed to vast publicity over the hearsay in question—seemed a bit strange, in a way: If some hearsay statements were going to be either included or excluded, wouldn't it be better to know which, before questioning potential jurors as to their possible bias, and what veracity each juror might place on them? Was this any way to ensure a fair trial?

In effect, the judge's decision to seal his rulings on the controversial hearsay statements until *after* jury selection seemed to telegraph that, under the "preponderance" standard of "Drew's Law," *all* of the statements, at least in Judge White's opinion, should be admissible.

Thus, after more than two years of almost unrelenting publicity, much of which suggested that Drew Peterson was a wife-killing, habitually lying, philandering greedhead, the stage was finally set for justice—or at least what passed for justice in a made-for-cable-television *cause célèbre*.

If all of the hearsay statements were admitted into evidence, and sustained by higher courts, a sharp turn in American jurisprudence would have been made: From now on, it would be what people said others *said* about you, or *heard* about you. And if you were judged guilty in the court of popular opinion (though that opinion was for the purposes of getting money from advertising) before actually appearing at a formal trial, before a jury of your peers, you were likely doomed, under those circumstances.

None of this is to say that Peterson wasn't responsible for the death of Kitty, or the disappearance of Stacy—perhaps only he knows the real truth of what happened. In retrospect, Peterson should have taken the advice of Richard Herman and the other defense-lawyer talking heads on cable television—he should have clammed up, and stayed inside the cake.

ACKNOWLEDGMENTS

The case of Drew Peterson and his wives, which fascinated television viewers for months on both broadcast and cable while also consuming a small forest's worth of newsprint and magazine pages, is one that has been made peculiarly, almost diabolically, complex by the sheer volume of the attention paid to it by the news media. In other words, the more it was reported, the crazier it got.

Ordinarily, similar cases involving missing wives never get the full glare of the news media spotlight. Indeed, in any given year, literally tens of thousands of people go missing, most of them of their own accord, usually without sinister connotations, and almost never with the full-court press treatment that the Peterson saga attracted. But the disappearance of Stacy Ann Cales Peterson, with its back story of a death of a previous wife in a bathtub, and a rather colorful husband/cop, a former undercover police drug agent, generated an outsized amount of attention, and soon became a phenomenon. The whole thing revealed much about American culture in the first decade of the 21st Century: how an attractive young blonde mother of two became, for a time, a subject of national conversation, as the media tried to make an entire country into a small town, for the purpose of making money.

Because of publishing deadlines, it was necessary to finish this book without a final denouement—was Drew Peterson really guilty of murdering his third wife, Kathleen [Kitty] Savio Peterson by drowning her in a bathtub? And if so, how did he do it? What role, if any, did Peterson play in the disappearance of his fourth wife, Stacy Cales Peterson? As of this writing, it will be up to a jury to decide, a jury that will have to rely on ghostly hearsay testimony from the last two wives, one dead and one missing, via second and third parties, to decide if Drew Peterson was as evil as they supposedly claimed he was.

And even with a guilty verdict, there will certainly be appeals. So the final truth—or at least, the *legal* truth—might well take years to uncover.

The intensity of the news media coverage of the Peterson wives' tales made sorting fact from rumor extraordinarily difficult. It was as if 43 cooks (the official police investigators) had crowded into a tiny kitchen to create an omelet (one dead woman, one missing woman), while observed by hundreds of food critics (the news media). The relatively recent phenomenon of the blogosphere (the salivating would-be consumers of the omelet) only added to the kitchen's miasma of aroma and soot. Certainly, there was a lot of shouting all around.

What I've tried to do in this book is narrow things down to actual facts, and put them into some sort of perspective: who did what, when they did it, and what they said about it at the time. That, to me, is the art and the craft of journalism, which should eschew ratings and circulation as dominating factors in the writing/reporting equation.

In trying to do this, there were a number of people who were especially helpful. One of the most helpful was Joseph Hosey, whose coverage of the Peterson saga for his newspaper, and his early book on the case, *Fatal Vows*, were extremely helpful in sorting out who did what to whom, and what they said about it at the time. Peterson's lawyer Joel Brodsky also provided a great deal of assistance, at least in terms of clarification of important facts. Charles Pelkie of the Will County State's Attorney's Office provided vital perspective. The Will County Court staffs, particularly those in charge of the county's archives, were unflaggingly cooperative and polite, despite having been besieged by hordes of reporters between 2007 and 2010. The myrmidons of the courthouse electronic security gate were enormously patient, despite my having metal in my going-to-court dress shoes, which had to be removed to gain admittance, along with my belt and cell phone, which could not itself be admitted because of its built-in photographic function, which I never use.

Most particularly, I would like to express my appreciation to those who facilitate the Internet website of acandy rose.com, who collected a huge amount of material on the Peterson story, much if not most of which would have ordinarily vanished into the ether, in years gone by. Walter Cronkite thanks you, too. It was only through that website's efforts that it was possible to reassemble this confusion into some sort of coherent, chronological order, so that people could have some idea of what the hell actually happened.

Assembling this account took far longer than I initially anticipated, and was much more difficult than it seemed at the start. I owe great debts of gratitude to Yaniv Soha and Charles Spicer of St. Martin's Paperbacks, and Jane Dystel of Dystel and Goderich Literary Management, for their patience and forbearance, especially when I was losing my sanity over the multi-media-made contradictions of late 2007.

Thanks to all,

Carlton Smith
Reno, Nevada
July 1, 2010